*f*P

OTHER BOOKS BY JOHN McNALLY

FICTION

America's Report Card:
A Novel

The Book of Ralph:
A Novel

Troublemakers:
Stories

ANTHOLOGIES

Bottom of the Ninth:
Great Contemporary Baseball Short Stories

Humor Me:
An Anthology of Humor by Writers of Color

The Student Body:
Short Stories About College Students and Professors

High Infidelity:
24 Great Short Stories About Adultery
by Some of Our Best Contemporary Authors

WHEN I WAS
A LOSER

*True Stories
of (Barely) Surviving High School
by Today's Top Writers*

EDITED BY JOHN MCNALLY

FREE PRESS

New York London Toronto Sydney

FREE PRESS

A Division of Simon & Schuster, Inc.
1230 Avenue of the Americas
New York, NY 10020

Page 285 constitutes an extension of this copyright page.

These works are memoirs. They reflect the authors' present recollections of their experiences over a period of years. Certain names and identifying characteristics have been changed and certain individuals are composites. Dialogue and events have been recreated from memory and in some cases have been compressed to convey the substance of what was said or what occurred. Certain episodes are imaginative recreation and are not intended to portray actual events.

First Free Press trade paperback edition 2007

FREE PRESS and colophon are trademarks of Simon & Schuster, Inc.

For information regarding special discounts for bulk purchases,
please contact Simon & Schuster Special Sales at 1-800-456-6798
or business@simonandschuster.com

DESIGNED BY ERICH HOBBING

Manufactured in the United States of America

1   3   5   7   9   10   8   6   4   2

Library of Congress Cataloging-in-Publication Data

ISBN-13: 978-1-4165-3244-6
ISBN-10:   1-4165-3244-7

CONTENTS

WHAT'S UP WITH THAT HAIR?
85

THE OUTSIDERS
107

WHAT I DID OVER
MY SUMMER VACATION
147

ANATOMY OF A LOSER
157

IN GOD WE TRUST
221

MORE LOSERS IN LOVE
251

INTRODUCTION

I knew a kid in high school—let's call him Bill—who couldn't catch a break. At the annual high school theater festival, Bill ran up behind a girl he thought he knew and put his hands over her eyes, only to realize (too late) that she wasn't the girl he thought she was. The girl—this perfect stranger whose eyes he covered—took offense, and so her boyfriend, who'd been standing nearby, decided to do what dumb guys do best: He pummeled Bill.

Another time, while Bill and I trailed behind a cute girl in our high school, Bill decided to imitate the quirky way she walked. What he failed to notice was that she was facing a large plate-glass window that reflected everything happening behind her. She saw Bill, quickly spun around, and flipped him the bird. "Shit head!" she yelled.

Yet another time, Bill sent a cassette tape to my girlfriend, in which he confessed a variety of mushy feelings he had for her. My girlfriend brought it over to my house one night and played it for me. Instead of letting it be—I was the one with the girlfriend, after all—I decided to remix the tape, using my crude stereo equipment, so that Bill would stop speaking in the middle of sentences to repeat the sappy things he'd said, sometimes repeating them three or four times in a row, sometimes even stuttering them (my doing, of course). Oh, yes, I was a hilarious guy all right. My girlfriend did-n't think so, but my friends did.

My point? For starters, "loserdom" is a moveable feast. Bill, who already had a long and glorious history as a loser, appears to be the

obvious loser when he sends the cheesy tape to my girlfriend. But
then my girlfriend exhibits some loser qualities of her own by playing the tape for me. By story's end, however, the biggest loser turns
out to be yours truly. I took this poor kid's heartfelt sentiment and
turned it into a personal (and cruel) joke. As fate would have it,
though, I got my comeuppance. A few months later, after breaking
up with me, my girlfriend attended the next big dance with Bill,
leaving me alone with my cleverly edited cassette tape, a tape that
was curiously no longer all that funny. The joke was on me. And it
was a good joke, too. There's nothing like love's reversal of fortunes
to really drive the stake through one's heart.

My other point? We've *all* been losers. Come on, admit it: You
were a loser. You wouldn't be reading this book if you weren't. But
you also probably know the truth, that *everyone* has been a loser at
one time or another—a loser in love, a loser in fashion, a loser in
social skills.

It's not so bad when you're an adult. You come to accept your
loser qualities, whatever they may be. And the loser moments
aren't quite as horrific as they would have been when you were a
teenager. One of the reasons it's not so bad is because you've found
other losers to commiserate with. The only adults who cling to the
idea that such a thing as *cool* actually exists are those middle-ages
guys with toupees who drive convertibles, and we all know what
those guys really are, right? Losers!

High school, however, is different. Cool isn't an illusion. Cool is
the Holy Grail. Cool is what everyone is trying (but failing) to
attain. And it's inside that bubble of adolescence—where everyone
holds up their magnifying glass to you—that being a loser takes on
a whole new meaning. Every perceived defect, every blemish, every
wrong word . . . it's all being monitored and analyzed by everyone at
all times. Adolescence is the first Homeland Security: Big Brother
(in the form of your classmates and, perhaps, your *actual big brother*)
keeps a never-blinking eye trained on you. In response, you're
always looking at yourself in the mirror; you're always self-
conscious to the point of paranoia. *That's* high school.

The irony is that we love our losers in literature and film. Holden Caulfield? Loser! Napoleon Dynamite? Big Loser! Why do we love them so? Maybe we see bits and pieces of ourselves in them, even if they're more charming, more daring, or funnier than we'll ever be. It's probably for this reason that we love to see celebrities' yearbook photos. We look for their zits, their bad teeth, their terrible hairdos. The photos don't lie: What they reveal is that *famous people are no different than us.* And so these grainy high school mugshots confirm what we have suspected all along, that all the beautiful people were once losers, too! (Or so we'd like to believe, anyway.)

The long and short of it is that loserdom is perfectly fine so long as we're not the brunt of it. If we have some distance, we may even be able to laugh at our own former loser selves. *Maybe.* But we can certainly laugh at, or feel empathy with, or cry for other people who've gone through (and survived) those days. Hence, this book. I gave this sample directive to a handful of writers: Write a personal essay about being a loser in high school. I didn't set any other parameters for the subject. I didn't restrict their definition of "loser." What I got back was a rich selection of essays that stretch across the emotional spectrum. Many are quite funny—a few, in fact, are *howlingly* funny—but some are heartbreaking. You'll read about crushes, cliques, ditching school, bad hair, being an outsider, summer vacations, and religious epiphanies. Will Clarke gives us a peek into his use of subliminal advertising when he ran for student council treasurer. Julianna Baggott suffers the ultimate humiliation in front of her boyfriend at the hands of her sister. Hell, even Zza Zza Gabor makes an appearance, showing up unexpectedly at Tod Goldberg's house. (No, really, she does.)

This book is a testament to our will to survive, to keep on chugging despite having suffered the worst of humiliations, some of which may now seem downright ridiculous, some of which are as serious as they come. And so I dedicate this book to all losers everywhere, past and present. Take comfort, I say. You're not alone!

LOSERS
IN LOVE

My Friend Likes You

Lisa Gabriele

"Jesus Christ, what are you staring at now?" my mother asked. She was dusting the stereo console with one hand, smoking with the other. My face was like a half moon peeking through the side of the window box curtains, my knees pressed to my nonexistent breasts.

"Nothing. I'm just thinking about something," I said too defensively. I must have been sitting there for an hour, trying to act dreamy and unspecific about my motives, trying to look as benign as a cartoon girl on a birthday card, crouched in a window box, serene about her blessings.

"Well, think about something else. He's too old for you," she said, stabbing out her cigarette in the giant crystal ashtray.

Buddy was my first crush. I was nine, maybe ten, when it hit me that I loved him. He was the boy across the street who babysat us when our parents got together and drank too much. He was anywhere from fifteen to eighteen years old, I had no idea. Age was bunched together like that when I was young. I don't know what it was about him that I crushed on, but I believe he must have paid attention to me when I wasn't expecting or needing it, a rarity back then. As a child, I was always expecting and needing attention. Also, I knew my crush on Buddy was inappropriate. Even if I had an inkling about what lovers did, which I did not, I was also aware that he was too old for me, so there was nothing to do about my crush but stew. And I did. For years.

I have an old picture from my tenth birthday party, not "old" like in those "Western" photos from Six Flags, where boys hold guns and girls are dressed like happy whores. Rather, seventies-sepia "old," where colors are both vivid and depressing. In it I'm holding a red lawn dart. I'm wearing a brown, orange, and ochre striped shirt with fat lapels and high-waisted moss-green bell bottoms. My hair is Toni home-permed, about which I am unhappy. I am looking toward Buddy, though smiling at the camera. You can see Buddy's tummy jutting into the frame. A bit of his profile. I used to stare at that photo and will his body fully into the scene. I used to try to remember every detail of that day, when he was a teenage boy hovering around the periphery of the neighbor girl's lame birthday party, helping with the games, eating the potato salad, only because his mother was my mother's best friend and she was there, too. Back then I would have convinced myself that he came because he loved me. He paid extra attention to me not because it was my birthday party and my parents fought all the time (less so when other people were around), but because he wanted to be near me, a little girl, who *for sure* had special powers. They kicked in around that age, when my dad began to arrive home later and later, and my mom's sadness settled around us like permanent dust. Around then I began to believe I had the power to will people to love me, by virtue of my full concentration on the object of my affection, morning, noon and night, and my ability to outwait even the Second Coming. The fact that people often didn't return love was beside the point, because at that age, my parents began to demonstrate that just because someone wasn't telling you and showing you love, didn't mean they didn't feel it. And pay no attention to the broken dishes, the beer cases on the porch, the bills on the kitchen table, the skipping record player that greeted our mornings, our mother sleeping on the couch next to it, the same couch upon which the church counselor would sit every Sunday night looking at her fingernails instead of at the piles of laundry, or the Kraft dinner-encrusted pots, or the flea-bitten cat my brothers and sister and I hungrily gathered to our beds each night. Those things had nothing to do with love. And sometimes, if you waited, love came back. So I learned to wait, to stay silent, to stew. Eventually waiting became something I was very, very good at. After all, a crush is only made up of a little love and a lot of waiting. Problem is, wait too long, and that bit of love grows into an unruly mass of feelings that become utterly disproportionate to the facts. Though try telling a teenaged girl that her feelings aren't facts. As a child that disparity is simply confusing. And I did not know it then, but my crush on Buddy would become the template upon which all my high school crushes would be based; they were silent, painful, and epic. Because when you add booze, divorce, high school, and hormones, that space between who you are and who you love becomes an unfathomable chasm.

*

Crush is such an appropriate word. All mine had weight, mass, and density, and in the throes of a crush, under the spell of one, I felt flattened. When a crush passed me in the hallways in high school, it was as though I was wearing a lead X-ray vest under my clothing: they couldn't see into me, but I could see into them.

By the time I reached high school, home life was intolerable. My parents began their brutal dance; my mom would kick my father out of the house, he would leave for several months, feel remorse, and then return. The only thing that sustained me were my crushes, and the attendant fantasies they created. And because I wasn't popular and pulled-together, I hung around other moony losers.

We traded details like hockey cards.

"Saw Trevor at the Fish & Chip," my friend Sandy would say.

"Oh yeah. Heard he feathered his hair," I'd say.

"Oh my God he did. It looks so good."

"Yeah. He's so cute."

"Have you seen Kirk today?"

"He was on the bus," I'd whisper hoarsely.

She'd nod, maybe squeeze my hand as though sensing I had had my daily fix, had taken my medication that morning. But it was unspoken among us that our crushes were completely unattainable. The people we loved didn't give us the time of day, and that was the point.

"Oh my God," she'd say if she spotted my quarry. "There's Kirk."

We would instinctively move to a location from which to better watch unseen.

*

Kirk was small and freckled, popular and funny. Back then, if a boy had pale skin, light-colored eyes, dark hair, anything Irish or English about him, I was a goner. If he made those in his immediate periphery laugh, I was rapt.

I sat behind Kirk in tenth grade. He'd make me laugh out loud and Mrs. Grenier would whip a white piece of chalk at my chest. When I entertained the improbable, though terrifying, prospect that he liked me, too, I got sloppy. I started to wait for him before going into class. I stared too long at him, to the point of awkward discovery. I tried to cork the crush the best I could by changing my patterns, where I walked, where I ate, how I breathed, but I couldn't. When Jill M. suddenly became his girlfriend, at first I was deflated and angry, but relief quickly replaced the sadness. Being someone else's boyfriend meant I could reinvigorate my crush on Kirk. He was containable, watchable, entirely mine again. In my head, that is. And it was there that I could imagine him fighting with Jill once he discovered that it was *me* he really loved. I could imagine us dating, getting married. I could see us laughing and walking. We'd have two children, and we'd live near his parents, who were nice to me and each other. It wasn't my last, but Kirk was my first high school crush, which meant he enjoyed charter membership. And though the intensity of my feelings for him came and went all through high school, they were reliable. Like radio signals. Like migratory birds.

*

My crush on Mark G. began under the watchful eyes of God. I figured out that the best vantage point from which to watch the back of Mark G.'s head was in church. My crush started on his hair and moved down to his surprisingly manly hands. I would stare at him as though he was a lava lamp and I was a high hippy. I cared more about him than I did my sister, or Olivia Newton John. I started to smoke cigarettes in the mirror, practicing the way I'd look and talk to him if I ever got the chance. I joined the Octagon Club, an organization his dad founded for bored kids from troubled homes. He made his restless sons attend to set examples. At meetings I honed my talent for not looking at the one thing I loved the most: him. Not wanting to be discovered again, I began to excel at pretending to ignore the object of my desire. This crush, too, was long-lasting (two years), potent (it physically sickened me to see him, be near him, talk to him), and utterly futile (he thought I was unattractive, weird, but intermittently funny). Mind-, body-, and spirit-wise, my crush on Mark G. was perfect because it hurt like fuck.

The problem with my teenaged crushes was that I took them as seriously as I did myself. So telling my first (then-closeted) gay friend, Bailey, about my crush on Mark G., signaled the end of one of the best crushes I had had on a guy. I was new to gay boyfriends so failed to realize that Bailey, as did everyone, probably also had a crush on Mark G., one far more fraught than mine. So I was unaware that Bailey's need to tell Mark G. that I was totally in love with him had less to do with hurting me than with Bailey needing to vicariously experience Mark G.'s cruel and swift dismissal. Still, I hated Bailey for sending him a note that said, *My friend Lisa likes you.* I hated him with the kind of weather that pulls down oaks.

Next time Bailey dropped his tray next to mine in the cafeteria I said, "Go sit somewhere else, asshole, I'm fucking killing you with my brain right now."

My friend Sandy said, "Yeah fagboy. Get lost."

It was a small town. We weren't aware that moody, funny, odd girls like us would one day badly need the gays.

*

A crush, once discovered and dismissed, must no longer be maintained, else you become criminally obsessed. I learned that lesson with Frankie. He was a brilliant forward, with a broken nose, and because of his hockey injuries already walked like an old man, which made him seem sexy. He dated my friend's older sister, a mopey, skinny girl who never loved him right. She made fun of him behind his back and talked about his penis. After they'd have sex on his parent's water bed, she said, he'd sometimes spoon her and cry a little over the fact that he was adopted. This creeped her out, but it made my crush take on enormous proportions because I had never heard of a boy being sad and naked at the same time, let alone adopted. I would drive by his house after my shift at the mall. It would be dark when I rounded the corner in the subdivision where rich people lived. I didn't know which bedroom window was his or his parents'. I didn't know what I was looking for, because, fact is, I would have died if he saw me. But being near him that way, in a car that was driving by his house, was oddly comforting, even prayerful. If his Delta 88 was parked in his driveway, it provided a kind of lullaby before I'd head off to my home near the county tavern another fifteen minutes away. Sometimes I'd hear people splashing in the pool behind his house and I'd imagine my thighs wrapped around his waist under the water, weightless and loving. I'd picture his mom handing me an iced tea and asking me to stay for dinner. His dad would regard us fondly. Later in the privacy of their fancy gazebo, he'd advise Frankie that I was the best thing that ever happened to him, *so don't mess this up, buddy.*

When my friend's sister mysteriously broke up with him, I became bereft at how bereft the breakup had made him. While sitting a few feet away, Frankie would confide in my friend the love he had for her sister and his confusion over the breakup. I felt selfish compassion for him because what he was feeling for her, I was feeling for him. I desperately wanted to betray her, to tell him about the cock comment, how she laughed because of his crying, how being adopted was amazing because at least he wasn't aborted. I imagined saying many comforting things to him while we were naked in the dark of his parents' bedroom, the water bed undulating beneath us, postcoitally. Mostly, I envied my friend's sister's talent for casual cruelty, the luxury of the popular.

*

My crush on Frankie disappeared, but what replaced it was pining, the horrible side effect of a crush gone chronic, when it's not allowed to run its feverish course. I was raised Catholic so was keenly aware of the difference between admiring something (crushing) without coveting it (pining). The nuns elaborated that coveting has the potential to turn boys insane and girls into whores. I didn't want that for myself. Pining hurts more, too, because the vigilance, the waiting, is spiked with a kind of hate. All benevolence is removed. The other unruly aspect of pining is that I seemed to require Frankie's acknowledgment, his attention acting like a cold compress to the forehead bringing the pining's fever down. A crush, being wholly selfish and one-sided, demands none of that. Also pining is far more difficult to conceal. But pining did accomplish some good things. My attendance record improved, I dressed better, and took pains with my makeup and hair. Sometimes Frankie would acknowledge me, but it was in the way I now see business rivals behave in financial district watering holes. Men who secretly dread each other will aggressively nod, offer each other too-wide smiles, their eyes and mouth expressing opposite emotions occurring in their brains and hearts.

Also, I was aware I was becoming weird. My mouth hung open while I listened to him speaking. I stared at Frankie's face too much, waiting for it to face me, and I was just too often too coincidentally too much around.

The only cure for pining is geographical, and though I greeted the news that Frankie would be playing hockey and going to high school in a faraway town with desperate grief, part of me was relieved. I could get down to the business of finding another crush. This time no pining. Just the restraint of a crush upon whom I could reinvigorate my talent for necessary fantasy.

*

Jason came soon after, he of the striped socks and the lithe body. He could roller-skate backwards beautifully, while listening to his own music on his enormous earphones. He had confidence. He had the use of a credit card. He had a singular thin braid growing down the back of his neck. He knew about music from England that was not the Beatles. He drove a car that was painted with baby-blue house paint and he was the opposite of being ashamed of it. That's because his parents were rich, so anything that looked poor about him had the glistening patina of unself-conscious irony, a quality urban hipsters today try to emulate.

For no reason except to have something to say, I told Francis, popular and thin, that I had a crush on Jason. I tried to make it sound sophisticated and untrue, though in reality, part of me wanted to try out what our pairing might feel like in the real world. After all, hadn't I caught him looking over at me four times? Probably it was that I was never not looking at him. No matter. Telling Francis was supposed to come off brave-sounding, like its futility was no big whoop, different from the way I told Bailey about Mark G. But mostly I told her because crushes aren't allowed to stay a secret, because crush + secret = pining, which = hell, and I didn't want to go through that again.

Of course, Francis told her sister Susan who told Jason's sister Gina that I had a crush on him. Still, I was baffled when I saw Gina pointing me out to Jason in the cafeteria, and for a moment I imagined Jason had been asking Gina, *Who is that girl and why hadn't I noticed her before? Isn't she friends with Susan's sister Francis? She seems very perfect to me.* So I asked Francis to ask Susan to ask Gina why she had been pointing me out and whispering to Jason. Gina told Susan who told Francis who told me, reluctantly, that Gina had been telling Jason what she had heard from Susan about what I had told Francis about my crush on Jason. Francis winced and I blanched. She was genuinely contrite when she relayed that what Jason had told Gina to tell Susan to tell Francis to tell me was this: though flattered, he thought I was "unremarkable."

I was distraught.

Remarkably so.

*

It was no coincidence that it was around that time that my behavior changed dramatically. The Francises and Sandys were replaced by the burnouts and the stoners. I can't say for certain that I set out to become remarkable, in that I was remarkably drunker than most at parties, remarkably irresponsible with the car, remarkably adept at shoplifting, remarkably sarcastic to parents and teachers, and wore remarkably more makeup and shorter skirts than the others, but I did. And that behavior got me noticed by boys. Not in the way Buddy might have once kindly noticed that I was a sad little girl who could have used a bit of attention now and again. There was nothing benevolent about the boys I messed around with, especially the ones I had had a crush on and eventually "got." (That's how I put it in my diaries: I'm going to "get" him.) When I homed in on them with a beer, or five, in me, all they noticed about me was my willingness to do anything to secure their attention, even for a short time, even for fifteen minutes in the back of someone's dad's Cadillac on the ride home. Sometimes they called, sometimes they didn't. I told myself it didn't matter because after I "got" them, I would no longer have a crush on them. It would mysteriously vanish in a vapor, to be replaced by shame and guilt.

*

Many years later, I realized that feeling unremarkable is a trait common to people who have crushes. How else would a crush exist, let alone flourish to emotionally crippling proportions, if the crush wasn't seemingly superior to its unremarkable admirer? After all, I didn't have crushes on oddball boys, outsiders, artists, or the troubled; that would have meant a certain kind of love of self that was entirely impossible back then. Besides, those were the obtainable boys, ones I could easily "get" (ones I later learned had crushes on me).

No, I crushed on the plainly popular, the obvious targets: the class presidents who wore pastel sweaters tied around their necks, the jock stars who drank too much and joked too loudly, rich, popular boys, the ones who gathered all the light around them for those brief high school years.

Ironically, my crushes mostly grew up to be unremarkable men themselves, men who now live in subdivisions and suburbs, who are fat and drink too much, who rarely finished college, who reluctantly attend couples' counseling, who have children who resent them. I know these things because my sister tells me, she the eye-rolling repository of all my dead crushes.

*

Last month I called my older brother on his cell phone to wish him a happy fortieth birthday. He was drunk and in a loud bar. He said, hey, guess who's here. Kirk! They play hockey together. Kirk asks about me sometimes, my brother says. He tells Kirk I'm great, even when I'm not, for which I love my brother. And though twenty-five years had passed since Mrs. Grenier angrily dotted my sweaters with chalk, when I heard Kirk's name, the dormant part of my heart where old crushes go to retire, banged up against its cage, clutching the bars like an anxious prisoner who hasn't had a visitor in decades.

"Oh yeah? Say hi to him, Dave," I said, sounding remarkably cool. "Yeah. Tell him I said 'hello.' No big deal. How does he look? Is he still married to Jill? Did you tell him I wrote a book? You know what? No, don't mention that. I don't want to brag. Anyway, hey, put him on. I'd love to talk to him."

Dave was quiet for second. I pictured him putting his finger in his free ear.

"You know, Lis, my phone reception's really bad. I can't really hear you. Gotta go, love you."

"Okay. Love you, too. No big deal."

"Okay, bye Lis."

"Bye. No big deal."

Perhaps I am still transparently moony about people. But I don't mind that today because I am back to being unremarkable myself. In retrospect, I'm glad I wasn't a standout, which, in high school, meant to be thin, rich, beautiful, athletic, and from an intact family, because I would not have had my crushes to carry me through those painful teen years. In fact, they wouldn't have been painful to begin with. And I needed those years and all that pain. I especially needed the fantasies, which were as unremarkable as I was, and am striving to be now. Because I dreamed of normalcy, of being picked up by the object of my desire in a clean house, our respectful dates bracketed by the boy's curious parents, who were happy together and busy, probably hosting parties which we'd reluctantly join, a singular grown-up cocktail thrust in our hands.

After years spent spiraling around with so-called remarkable men who couldn't commit, couldn't love, and eventually couldn't hold it together, men who justified their bad behavior as the hallmark of utter uniqueness, as I once did, unremarkable fantasies are my tonic today.

*

It's amazing to watch one of my little nieces get a little crush on one of the many boyfriends I've brought home over the years. They all act the same. They giggle too often, hover too near, stare too much at these oblivious men. I find it endearing and a little flattering. I like that they like what I have, who I am with. But I like to believe that their hearts are too normal, their own intact family lives too healthy, for these crushes to sicken and stall them as mine did me. I pray for that, in fact. And I want to tell them that it's okay to have crushes, necessary in fact, but like anything that can be addictive, that can alter your perception of who you are and what you want. I want to advise them to try to obsess about their crushes responsibly. Don't go overboard, I want to say. Don't grant them too much power. Don't let rejection kill you. And for godsakes don't tell anyone, especially the gays.

*

Today I'm a lot less susceptible to crushes because I've learned a little about love—not, like, how to find and keep it—but at least I know I want the real kind, with a real, and kind, man. Also, I no longer believe that love is something you think about, it's something you do. And I don't choose to cultivate fantasies over trying to deal with realities. For the most part. I mean, you should *see* the guy who goes to the bakery down the street. I swear he looks like Ewan McGregor, if Ewan McGregor was a funny, intellectual, dog-loving happily married father of two, who reads Philip Roth, and plays rugby. So okay, I do have a tiny little crush on him. And, yeah, sometimes I picture us playing with his dog on the beach, no big deal, while his wife (from whom he's divorced, though it's totally mutual, and we totally get along) takes care of the kids (who like me a lot, because they know I'm not trying to replace their mother), but I don't do it often. I mean, it's not like he's the only reason I go to the bakery between 8:30 and 9:00 a.m. most mornings, except Tuesday and Friday, when his kids have swimming. Because they really do make the best coffee, and I need my daily fix.

The B-List Rings Twice

Tod Goldberg

If the truth be known, I would have preferred not meeting Zsa Zsa Gabor at all versus meeting her while covered in the pubic hair of my sixteen-year-old girlfriend. Of course, we can't always predict when washed-up stars will appear on our doorsteps holding thousands of dollars worth of diamonds and even if we could, is there ever a proper outfit for this sort of experience? Retrospect tells me that I probably should have just stayed in the bedroom with my poor, sweet, innocent, incredibly naked girlfriend prostrate on my single bed, Depeche Mode droning on in the background, half-finished Bartles & Jaymes wine coolers littered around us. Retrospect also tells me that I shouldn't have blackmailed a math teacher into giving me a passing grade during my senior year and that I probably shouldn't have stolen all the stereos out of my mom's boyfriends' cars, but then retrospect never knew how to have a good time in the '80s.

I'd like to say that I was surprised by the appearance of Zsa Zsa Gabor, but the fact is that odd celebrities made a habit of showing up at my house during my years in high school. My mother was the society editor for the *Desert Sun*—the local paper of Palm Springs, California—which, in the mid-to-late 1980s, meant that she went to parties for a living, slept with lots of men who owned suit stores or record stores and were chauffeured around in limousines by guys named Three Finger Freddie, and wrote gossipy columns about people who were stars twenty-five years before I was born. There were certain perks for my mother. It afforded her free meals from the finest restaurants, free clothing from the likes of Bob Mackey, and a free form of celebrity not found in most cities: she was recognized wherever she went because she knew famous people, not because she was famous. In another time and place, she might have been Kato Kaelin, but in Palm Springs she was an icon—as much as one can be an icon while earning a small-town journalist's salary.

None of this made me any more interesting or cool. While my mother was going off to fabulous parties with reputed ancillary members of the Bonanno crime family on her arm, I was left to my own devices at home. This wasn't such a bad thing, though there's only so many hours a fourteen-year-old can spend deciphering the odd nipple out of a scrambled Playboy Channel signal before jerking off becomes both pointless and painful. It really wasn't until a few years later (and, frankly, after I stopped dressing like the asexual keyboard player from the Cure) that my mother's absence started to pay dividends, though not always for me; first, my house became the designated fuck pad for the sophomore class of Palm Springs High School.

Not that anyone was having sex with me, of course, but I was happy to serve as host for a modest gratuity. The most frequent visitor was my friend Zach, who liked to bring his girlfriend over for a little afternoon delight. Unfortunately, neither Zach nor I had a car yet and since Zach's girlfriend was actually his mother's best friend, this presented a problem. At first, we'd walk over to the shopping center across the street from the school and Zach's girlfriend—who, it should be noted, was happily married to a cop and was the mother of three small children—would purchase us both an Orange Julius before we all piled into the family sedan for the quick ride over to my house. Eventually, even that got too cumbersome for the lovers, so Zach's girlfriend just started picking us up in front of the school with the Orange Juliuses already waiting.

Sometimes, I'd simply unlock the door and let them in, happy to have my drink on the front patio. Other times, I'd go inside and watch a little 1-800-DIAL MTV in hopes of catching the video for Motley Crüe's "Home Sweet Home" or I'd go out to the pool or I'd just take a brief nap on the sofa. I only really needed to make myself scarce for about twenty minutes at a time; so, if there was nothing compelling to do at the house to take my mind off the fact that my friend Zach was fucking the wife of some cop who, if he was any kind of cop, was already aware of the situation and planning a SWAT offensive, I'd just take a walk around the block. On the final such occasion, I caught Zach and his girlfriend as they scurried out of my house, their faces ashen. Zach's girlfriend got into her car and slammed the door without even offering me her usual tepid thanks.

"What's going on?" I asked.

"Dude," Zach said, "Remington Steele was just here."

"What?"

"Remington Steele, you know? The detective? He was here. He knocked on the door and asked for directions to someone's house. We're getting the fuck out of here."

"You mean Pierce Brosnan?" I said. "The actor?"

"Whatever, dude," Zach said.

"Why did you even answer the door? This isn't your house."

"I was scared," Zach said. "It could have been her husband."

I explained to Zach that plenty of famous people lived in the neighborhood—including, at the time, Herman Wouk, Sonny Bono, and Suzanne Somers—and that Remington Steele probably just went to the wrong house and that everything was fine, they could go back inside. Zach didn't care.

"Dude," he said, "I can't have detectives and shit coming around. Her husband is a cop! Do you know how much trouble I'd be in? Do you know how much trouble you'd be in? Fuck this, man."

I opted not to elucidate to Zach that Remington Steele wasn't a real detective, just like Captain Kirk wasn't a real starship captain. I figured the nuance would be lost on him (and having to further delve into the issue that Remington Steele wasn't even a real detective on the TV show was too much of an existential issue for either of us to comprehend, much less Zach, who, it should be noted, liked to get high by smoking parsley sprigs he stole from the grocery store). Plus, it seemed to me then that our friendship was reaching its natural conclusion—why muddy it with a pesky issue like reality?

"I don't think you should have sex here anymore," I said.

"Don't worry," Zach said. He paused then and leaned in toward me. "She told me if I could give her multiple orgasms, she'd marry me. What do you think of that?"

"I think that's great," I said. "You should totally do that." Zach and his girlfriend drove off that day and while I'm sure I didn't presume it to be true then, I realize it now: there's no fucking way Pierce Brosnan knocked on my front door.

In the intervening years, several stars did arrive, but they always had someone else with them—Artie Shaw had his dog, Paul Newman had his brother, Robert Stack had his wife, Harpo the Clown had his horn—and they generally came with such pomp, circumstance, and advance notice that it was about as exciting as a prostate exam and required nearly as much forethought. How, precisely, do you clean the house in preparation for Artie Shaw's arrival, particularly when he's not even coming inside? I'm still not sure, but the directions were always the same from my mother:

"Clean up all that crap in your room," she'd say, "and that means everything from under your bed, too. And take down all those asinine posters of people in black clothes."

"Do you really think Artie Shaw is going to look under my bed?" I'd ask.

"Listen, mouth," she'd say, "just do it. Maybe Artie will decide he'd like to marry me, be part of a nice Jewish family. Wouldn't you like that?"

"We're not a nice Jewish family," I'd say. "I didn't even have a bar mitzvah."

"Clean your goddamn room!"

Artie Shaw never ended up marrying my mother, but for the next several years her hectic schedule of parties, balls, and dates with men who had scars from bullet wounds kept her out of the house for much of the day and night. After figuring out that frothy orange juice was not equal to the pursuit of my own liberty and sexual adventure, I opted to keep my house to myself, only renting it out briefly to my closest friends, and then only if they swore they wouldn't use my room and wouldn't answer the door.

I should have listened to my own advice.

It was a Friday afternoon and, after much cajoling, I'd convinced my girlfriend Susie that I could, and would, provide her with her very first orgasm. I'm not sure why I had the confidence to make this proclamation, since I'm fairly certain no other woman, girl, or folded pillow had ever received a tremendous amount of pleasure from me, so I decided to take a collegial approach to the situation. I hunkered down in the human sexuality section of the local Crown Books and immersed myself in the fine art of oral sex. I already knew what I needed to know about regular sex, which is to say that my standard twenty-seven seconds of intercourse was not likely to do the trick for Susie, or at least hadn't brought her to the level of exhausted passion I'd read about in Harold Robbins novels, so an oral route needed to be paved. Or, more appropriately, a route toward cunnilingus, which I presumed was something of a higher order of oral sex. I even liked the word. I practiced saying it: *Cunnilingus. We are now going to have cunnilingus, Susie. Did you enjoy the cunnilingus?* I wasn't going to merely perform *cunnilingus*, I was going to hold a symphony! I was to be a master!

I cut fifth period that day and made sure my bedroom was ready: a looped cassette of Depeche Mode singing "Somebody" was cued in the tape deck. Two four-packs of strawberry Bartles & Jaymes were hidden snuggly under my bed in an ice chest. A single red rose was in a vase by the bed. All socks, underwear, and tubes of lotion were discreetly put away. If Artie Shaw could see this now, he'd begin the beguine all over again.

Forty-five minutes into the Symphony of Cunnilingus, the doorbell rang. Things had been going pretty well, apart from the raging case of TMJ syndrome I was experiencing, the way my tongue had lost all feeling, and the upsetting notion that while I'd had an orgasm approximately forty-four minutes prior, Susie seemed no closer and, honestly, had begun to lose faith in my once-vaunted abilities, asking every now and again for me to get more wine coolers from under the bed if we were to keep this up.

"Shit," I said to Susie. "Wait here." I slipped on a pair of cutoff sweats and my favorite Bauhaus T-shirt (a band whose logo I regularly covered myself in but had never actually listened to) and walked out into the entry hall. I peered through the peephole and saw a woman with an enormous shock of hair, huge teeth, and an impossible tan staring back at me. She looked exactly like Zsa Zsa Gabor, but I was fairly certain Zsa Zsa Gabor was dead. Or was that Magda Gabor? Either way, it was a significant moral quandary: Should I pretend not to see Zsa Zsa Gabor and return to Susie and my pursuit of cunnilingus superiority? Should I alert Susie of Zsa Zsa's presence? Should I put on some underwear?

"Darling," the woman said, "I hear you on the other side of the door. Are you going to make me wait here all day?"

I cracked open the door.

"Darling," she said, "I can't see you."

I opened the door wide and there was no mistaking it now: Zsa Zsa Gabor was alive and well and standing on my front porch.

"Is your mother here?" Zsa Zsa asked.

"No," I said. "She's at work."

"At work?"

"Yes," I said. "At the newspaper."

"They make her go in?"

I nodded. There are moments in your life that, as they are happening, seem to already have the quality of memory, so that when you look back on them later on, they feel somewhat like a dream, like you're not sure all the details are accurate because they are covered in a soft focus glow: Your first kiss. Your first dance. The first time you had a conversation with Zsa Zsa Gabor while your face was covered in the reddish—and fragrant—pubic hairs of your girlfriend, while your cutoff sweats were pitching Eagle Scout-worthy tents because your penis had, after forty-four long minutes, finally responded to the repeated stimuli you were providing it, while you tried your best not to shake hands with Ms. Gabor because both of your hands were covered in the sticky fluids of the same girlfriend in question, and perhaps a bit of Emotion Lotion as well, because you sort of lost your *cunnilingus* confidence about nineteen minutes ago and started trying to figure a way out of this unpromisable promise you'd made, but are, as such, determined to get back into that bedroom and prove yourself, Zsa Zsa Gabor be damned!

Zsa Zsa seemed to understand this. She reached into her handbag and pulled out a small black box. "Give this to your mother," she said, all pretense of Darling-this and Darling-that out the door. "She's expecting it."

"Okay," I said. We stood there staring at each other for a moment. In the years since, I've tried to conjure the face of Zsa Zsa Gabor in times when I've needed to take my mind away from certain difficult tasks—like how some men replay Game 6 of the 1986 World Series, or try to imagine their buddy Vitaly's hairy ass—but it never works. Perhaps it's the mixture of honest scorn and, I'd like to believe, abject horror that graced Ms. Gabor's face that day which makes it impossible. Or maybe it's the very real sense that after staring into her eyes for only a brief moment, I knew the odds of me having an erection anytime in the next 24–48 hours were diminishing exponentially with every passing second.

Zsa Zsa still had the box in her hand and I could tell she was assessing the situation as deeply as Zsa Zsa assessed anything, which is to say that she arched her eyebrows, which in most people would cause an appreciable change of expression, but not in the plasticine Ms. Gabor. A few years later, Zsa Zsa was arrested for pimp-slapping a cop and I recall that her mug shot had the same look of benign indecision.

"You'll give this to her, Darling?"

"I said I would," I said. I didn't know what Zsa Zsa's big deal was. In the larger picture of Zsa Zsa's life, it's not like she was the one in the middle of an absurd situation. If, say, Charo happened upon Zsa Zsa's house while she was engaged in a prolonged bout of cunnilingus, well, then I could see where her irritation level might be warranted. But I was the aggrieved party here and did not appreciate her tone. Or her eye makeup. Or the way she actually didn't look so much like Zsa Zsa Gabor as she did a person wearing a Zsa Zsa Gabor Halloween costume.

Zsa Zsa handed me the box and let out a perceptible sigh, as if she knew this was a situation best handled differently, but was resigned to seeing it through to its natural conclusion, whatever the result. "Be sure she gets this," Zsa Zsa said.

"Will do," I said. I watched Zsa Zsa walk back down the driveway where a chauffeured car was idling. When she turned and looked at me, I gave the box a little shake, like a wave. A hand fluttered to Zsa Zsa's chest before she disappeared into the automobile.

I went back inside, set the box down on the entry hall table, and ambled my way back into the bedroom, where I found Susie fully dressed.

"Who was that?" Susie asked.

"Zsa Zsa Gabor," I said.

Susie nodded like that was exactly who she figured was at the door. "I'm feeling kind of sick," she said. "Will you take me home?"

"You don't want to finish up?" I said. I made a flicking motion with my tongue and Susie visibly recoiled.

"No," Susie said.

Several hours later, after I'd dropped Susie back off at home and had concocted several gross fabrications of my sexual prowess in the presence of my friends, I returned home and saw the black velvet box still sitting in the entry hall. My mother was in her room getting dressed for the evening. She was going to a black-tie event that night—a charity, or a ball, or just someone with money spending it—and was wearing one of her free ten-thousand-dollar dresses. I'm not sure who she was dating at the time—either the reputed mobster who owned the men's clothing store or the reputed mobster who owned the record store that burned down every two years or the watch salesman who, after they broke up, came back and demanded that I give him back the gaudy Seiko he'd given me—but the car he'd sent for her was idling in the same spot as Zsa Zsa's earlier in the day.

"Mom?" I called out. "Did you see this box? Zsa Zsa Gabor dropped it off earlier." I tried to sound nonchalant about it all, as if Zsa Zsa always came over when my mom was at work.

"Yes," she said, shouting from her bathroom. "It's way too garish."

"She seemed to think you were expecting it," I said.

"I was going to borrow it but she just wanted to get her name in my column," she said. "Just leave it there on the counter. I'll get it back to her tomorrow." I heard the blow dryer go on, which signaled the momentary end of our conversation. Too garish for my mom? This was a woman who gussied up like Joan Collins on *Dynasty* just to get the mail, who wore gold lamé to bed at night and somehow managed to only buy bedazzled T-shirts. I cracked open the box and saw a necklace rimmed with at least fifteen carats of diamond and banded by gold, platinum, and a bunch of other precious metals I either did not yet know or were too far along the periodic chart for me to memorize. Visions of Hawaii, Paris, and taking Susie on a Wet Seal shopping spree swam through my mind. If I couldn't get Susie off, maybe I could buy her off! Another vision, albeit briefer, of me sharing a cell with an enormous Samoan also flashed by. Opportunity cost was high. My mom walked out then and asked me to zip her up.

"Is Zsa Zsa coming back?" I asked.

"Probably not tonight," she said. "Though her sister Magda may come by later. She's a real doll, so keep your room clean."

The Handgun
of Idle Young Attractiveness:
A Coming-of-Age Essay Complete
with Requisite Humiliation

JULIANNA BAGGOTT

At sixteen, I was unprepared for the public displays of wanting from men—particularly at the university's Olympic-sized pool where it first struck. The moment would imprint so deeply that chlorine fumes would be permanently linked to the nervous specter of desire. I had never been sent to conventions on management and power—which should be prescriptive for young women. I hadn't been assigned texts like Weiss's *The Unofficial Guide to Power Management* or, perhaps vaguely applicable, Whitson's *Chinese Military and Political Leaders and the Distribution of Power in China, 1956–1971*—and, decades later, still haven't. (Who has?) Worse, Monica Lewinsky was still in grade school. It is difficult to imagine the pre-Lewinsky era when no one had yet discussed thongs and power, this new particular brand of ruin via desire. But such a time did exist. Imagine it yawning open at our backs—a thick green field of otherworldliness strewn with grazing cows—or, no, no, even before that, when cows were not yet domesticated and roamed wildly through German forests—while we're at it: before there were such things as German forests or even Germans. Put it this way for the younger set: pre-Hasselhoff.

And you must understand that during my grammar school days, masculinity was so popular that it infused all things defined as good—even my very own mother's sense of palatable décor. For example, my childhood playroom had been carpeted in brown shag, obviously styled off the chest pelt of Burt Reynolds. For those who know Burt Reynolds and his former chest pelt, I apologize for that graphic rendering, but it is necessary if you are to really understand my historical and cultural baggage. For those who were not born early enough to have the pleasure of a pre–*Boogie Nights* Burt Reynolds, he was once the ultra-macho actor who specialized in films about truckers—a fad that wildly infested pop culture, causing all Americans to reidentify themselves (much like the practice of Confirmation for Catholic children) each with their own new name or "handle" à la Honey Bear.

Like all girls—including, one must assume, Lewinsky—I had been given all the wrong information. I'd been told that I was powerless—part of the definition of girlhood at that time–and, on top of that, I was scrawny. I'd been fed *Little House on the Prairie* reruns like free narcotics in hopes of creating dependency. But I had resisted an addiction, perhaps to the credit of Nancy Reagan, who, with her "Just say no" drug manifesto unwittingly affected many areas of the American psyche. (Who couldn't help but internalize the motto coming from Nancy with her alarmingly large head on such a small body? Had her body atrophied while her brain ever-expanded?) Additionally, my love of prairie bonnets had worn thin—there is only a small window in a girl's life when bonnets hold such magnetism.

By the time of the Olympic pool incident, I identified, primarily, as a field hockey player. I wasn't allowed to be a cheerleader. (My mother was a feminist. Ironic, you might say in light of her décor decisions. Please bear in mind that style decisions can be deeply subconscious. How do we explain, for example, my insistence on occasionally wearing ugly brown lace-up shoes other than the fact that they harken back to my years of schooling with nuns in orthopedics who had no need of men. They are my I-hate-men shoes.

Clearly. They parade my inner nun or my inner lesbian or my inner lesbian nun. But I have been oblivious to this subconscious work. Until now, I will've only said of them, Fashion meets comfort.) I soon fell in love with field hockey, the toughness most of all, the way the team would jog off the field, tucking our mouth guards into the tops of our tall green socks. (Another lesbian reference?) My best friend was a twirler, and although I looked down on her for this, I learned all of her routines each summer. Since the field hockey team practiced next to the marching band, I also was an excellent twirler of my field hockey stick, a compromise her coach was willing to put up with: I was second team all-Catholic.

Deep down, I knew that there was no real future in field hockey or in field hockey stick twirling. I had a certain practicality.

Other things about me worth noting: I had an unusual crush on David Mamet, the foul-mouthed playwright. If anyone asked if she had a crush, I would substitute Boris Becker for David Mamet—because this was more socially acceptable. I didn't want to have sex with Mamet. I wanted to be Mamet and therefore cursed profusely whenever I could, which supports the notion that the arts can be a bad influence in the development of character. (Boris Becker was a fine young man.) I also spent a lot of time in the nursing home—the demented second floor where the patients moaned and grabbed at me from their restraints. I was once forked in the arm while trying to move a plate closer to an old man who'd been raised in the Depression. My grandmother was there—mute and memoryless. I thought a lot about memory. I once returned a dead cat to a neighbor—scooping it off the roadside into a box—but was later told that it wasn't the neighbor's cat. I was, in short, thoughtful and morbid and foul-mouthed.

But I shouldn't veer too far from the subject at hand: male-wanting and power.

Let me offer a more pointed documentation of my development. By the day of the pool incident, I had been on my first car date. The date itself is a blur of a remodeled basement and a boy with braces who is now, I believe, a dentist who's listed in the local phone book as Dr. Kaz! (His exclamation mark, not mine.) The date doesn't matter much. It's the predate that counts. A recounting of this event will make readers question whether I'm embellishing for effect—what with the forthcoming amputation, profusion of poodles, and cruelty. Teary-eyed with a sympathetic sting caused by ancient scar, I state sadly: No. No embellishment.

Let's do some role-playing for greater effect: Why don't you be the boy on the stoop?

Okay.

You, boy on the stoop, have just lifted your narrow fist to knock at the door. You hear piano music, something by Burt Bacharach. The house is yellow. You can tell this much even at night. Yellow houses seem born of butter and delight. Plus there's ivy, which gives the house a collegiate feeling, a trustworthiness. Bacharach, a butter house adorned with ivy—who could discount the comfort here?

Inside, what's waiting for you?

My mother is the one at the piano. An anxious woman who always fears poisoning her guests, she's soothed by this playing. And since dinner is over with and the first signs of illness have yet to present themselves, she's playing under the guise of background music, but really she's just killing time to see if someone is going to die.

My grandfather is there. I'm not being gratuitous to shove him up to the front of the description. He's legless. He lost both legs in World War II, and is the first man on record to have survived gaseous gangrene. One of his stumps ends just below the knee, the other just above. He likes to jiggle his stumps, primping them coquettishly while batting his eyes at you. A tough guy in a crew cut, he's funny like this. The definitions of humor are quite elastic in this household.

And my grandmother, usually naked under her muumuu, has collapsed into the overstuffed armchair. A gracious beauty, an ample Southern belle, she's over her addiction to Valium, and the agoraphobia has passed. She once was the type of woman called up onstage to sing with Sinatra in a piano bar—a true story. She's brought her dogs. Five toy poodles: Mimi, Gigi, Angel, Jacques, and Bogie who pad around and occasionally tinkle indoors. Small turds are not unheard of.

And then there's my oldest sister, Kate. I have two other siblings—absent, mercifully, but worth mentioning: a laid-back brother who's away in Europe learning that he doesn't want to be a jazz musician because jazz musicians are, by and large, depressives, and a sister who would have been the youngest had I not been born. This sister, though angelic in many ways, has chased me around the house with a knife, chanting "redrum"—for those who don't catch the reference, *redrum* is *Murder* spelled backward and a favorite chant of the era, made popular by *The Shining*, a book, a movie, a how-to in malicious taunting.

But Kate, the eldest, has just swept in from New York, where she's taken up acting. She moved there with a former manager of George Thorogood and the Delaware Destroyers. (This essay will, for the most part, take place in Delaware, which is unusual in literature and worth noting.) He was an extremely tall white man with an Afro and whose name escapes me. Kate is crucial here. She's wry now, jaded. She's newly convinced that youth is bullshit, that you, boy on the stoop (I haven't forgotten you: poised to knock) are bullshit, too, because you represent youth—at least temporarily to the actress sister Kate as well as for narrative purposes at this point in the essay. (Kate will eventually do quite well in New York—producing a one-act of Mamet's, in fact. But for now she has only been on call-in radio with Howard Stern, a dating show with *penis* in the title. The exact title escapes me at present.)

And me? I'm in my room tending a burn from a curling iron. I regret the Jean Naté after-bath splash. The jingle now plays in my head: *"so fresh so new . . . there's nothing you can't do."* I'm already blessed with a taste for irony and the jingle takes on an ominous quality. It is foreboding.

You, boy on the stoop, knock.

My father, I haven't mentioned him yet, but he's there. He answers the door. I'm his fourth child and so the pretense of meeting a date, shaking hands with a fine young man, has devolved into something else. A chin-uppedness about life's cruelties. A certain self-mockery in the face of uselessness.

Yes. Yes.

He tells you to come in. He introduces you around. The stumps catch your attention. I always forget to warn people about them. Leglessness has an everyday ordinariness for me—and always will.

My mother stops playing the piano. She smiles at you. She is expectant. You don't know what she wants from you. She wants you to tell her that no one is going to die tonight, that she hasn't poisoned anyone. But you don't know this, of course. And so you only smile back.

My grandmother says, "So you're going on a date! Isn't that nice. Now you be good, you hear? You be nice." Did I neglect to mention that my grandmother was raised in a house of prostitution? Is this being nice a veiled reference to money? It's hard to say.

My mother looks at her mother and squints.

And then my sister takes over.

I, upstairs, can hear the raised voice. There's jawing, laughing, a chorus of ha-ha-ha, general yucking it up. I'm not sure what they're saying, but I hurry up now. There's been a change. I can feel it. The quiet timbre of restrained conversation has eroded. They've let themselves loose.

But there's no use hurrying. It's too late now. I'm at the top of the stairs. I can see only you, by the door, and my father's elbow. I start to trot down, to make a mad dash for the door.

My oldest sister is on a roll and she's come to some ending that needs punctuation. She shouts up the stairs. One sentence. Just one. "Hey, Julie, don't forget your diaphragm!"

And even as she says it, I can feel its historic weight. This is the night that my oldest sister said, "Don't forget your diaphragm!" It's a family story. It is immediate lore. It's beautiful in its simplicity. It will be handed down the way other families hand down handmade quilts.

My grandparents roar at this. My grandmother jiggles beneath her muumuu. My grandfather is doubled over his stumps. My father tries to divert attention, asking the boy where he wants to go to college. My mother, too, is trying to cover, asking the boy where he lives.

And, you, boy, suddenly barraged with questions, are that odd kind of boy who digs this kind of thing, who knows a story when you're in one. I look at you. You're smirking. Your expression reads: This is great. This is fantastic. You might come from one of those families that hands down handmade quilts, but always wanted a different kind of family. You look at me, smirking. I'm dying—a little death, a lonesome death where I'll have to be my own pall bearer.

I grab a coat, open the door. You're saying that you'll probably go to the University of Delaware. You're interested in studying art. The word *art* makes you start to laugh suddenly. You can't help it. Art!

I've said, "Goodnight. Goodbye. C'mon."

I shut the door on all of them, another burst of laughter rises up at our backs.

So, that's done now—despite the way the story has lingered for years. Despite the fact that you still see that boy on the stoop from time to time—and he still will ask you about your diaphragm, its whereabouts, your general preparedness for life's surprise moments.

The swimming pool incident might seem minuscule by comparison now. But I assure you, it isn't. You see, the Don't forget your diaphragm night is situated between two very distinct pool incidents really. When I was thirteen, I was still a scrappy, messy tomboy, and I wore a Speedo that my mother bought for me at Gershman's, which was a shop of discount irregulars. Speedos for girls of that age are often symmetrical in nature—meaning the backs and the fronts are just these scooped out things that are hard to differentiate. Hard, especially when your own flat back and front are hard to differentiate. When I was thirteen, I wore my Speedo backward to the pool. Sadly, I didn't notice until I got in the water and paddled around for a bit. There was this puffiness right in the front and a distinct wedgie in back. Worse, of course, was that no one else noticed either.

But the summer after the Don't forget your diaphragm incident, I was wearing a bikini. I got in the water and paddled around, just as I had before. But this time, when I stepped out of the pool, and as I made my way to my towel, I was being watched—ogled, actually—by the college guys all buffed up, by some of the fatherly types, by some of the old professors propped up in their macramé beach chairs.

It was this moment, this stark clear moment, when I suddenly realized that I wasn't powerless. The closest I can come to describing it is that I felt armed. In fact, I don't know that I would have felt more powerful if I'd been carrying a gun. It is the strangest most unexpected twist of events in the course of my life—and I'm not being overly dramatic. I went from being some kid, some snotnose, some pain in the ass, whose sexuality was just a good joke, something to be laughed at—uproariously—to suddenly feeling in command of an audience of men. And I'd done nothing. I'd filled out—minimally. My face had shown up some in a new way. I put on a bikini—a modest one at that. I stepped out of a pool. And suddenly grown men—the ones at the tippy top of the power structure—were suddenly displaced, or so it seemed, by me.

It's gorgeous that the hierarchy can be so easily torqued. It's dangerous, too, because the power is in many ways an illusion. For me, it would eventually become addictive. (But that, my friends, is another essay.)

What I need to say here, I suppose, is that we hand down the wrong messages. We've got to prepare our daughters not only to be wily in a way that the powerless must rely on their wits, but also how to handle power—the handgun of idle young attractiveness.

And now, Lewinsky, Hasselhoff, and Burt Reynolds have become antiquities of bygone eras—and I have, too. Ah, the sadness of the current state of my swimwear, the jokey banter of my sex life. ("Don't forget your diaphragm" still gets the laughs but for different reasons.)

Well, well. Who knew how I'd miss the handgun so very very much? Oh, if I had it back now at that old pool, I'd take sporty aim at a few men, perhaps shoot a few, cursory blows, and then wave it wildly overhead. I'd squeeze off one pop after the next—await the tackle of lifeguards—but I'd go down shooting.

Confessions
of a Cradle-Robber

Maud Newton

The summer between eighth and ninth grade, I finally kissed a boy. Tavi Valbuena and I sat on my couch, plucking at stray strings, tracing the garish flowers and parrots and fruits that covered the cushions, and denouncing the general fucked-upness of the world. At last his lips lurched toward mine. The moment our tongues, nimble and erotic as garden slugs, entwined, my mind wandered to a far more pressing concern: how I'd explain these developments to my friend Allison. She and I had passed the previous two years scheming to make out with boys, but she'd never understand about Tavi.

He was twelve, you see, and I was fourteen. Let me put that a different way: I was heading into my last year of junior high, and he'd just finished elementary school. Even worse, he looked his age. The only secondary sex characteristics Tavi possessed then were a deep, gloomy voice, enormous feet, and a tendency to clamp sofa pillows down on his lap whenever I ate an ice-cream cone in front of him. That first night we kissed, our teeth clashed. Our tongues slid around ineffectually. My glasses battered his cheeks and eyebrows. This was, I realized as the evening wore on, not even proper making out—and so was not worth mentioning to anyone, not even Allison.

The circumstances leading to my and Tavi's liaison were, naturally, complicated. You don't just wind up a cradle-robber overnight. First a pitiful awkwardness must develop. Participation in the school band may occur. Soon a wave of hormones sweeps in. And as these peptides and steroids and various gonadal uppers churn in the blood-stream, they generate a throbbing desperation. Warning signs are var-ious as the stars in the heavens, but here I'll limit myself to those that paved the way for a primary school boy to become my boyfriend.

In the sun my limbs glowed like old-fashioned watch hands. My legs were spindly, yet flaccid. My permed hair and freckles incited com-parisons with the frizz-headed star of *Annie*. My physical being, in short (and it *was* short), telegraphed to the world the truth about the way I'd punt a kickball: that I was more likely to step on it and spring face-first into the dirt than to propel the ball forward. I scratched up several pairs of glasses in the course of perfecting this maneuver.

I entered, and exited, junior high school virtually flat-chested. I say "virtually" because it would be wrong to skip over the two thumbnail-sized nubs that appeared on my upper torso in sixth grade and stayed the same size until my junior year of high school. These starter breasts caused my mother to insist on a training bra— a garment, for the uninitiated, that consists of several elastic bands, two padded triangles, and a hook-and-eye closure that stings like a squadron of wasps when snapped, as it inevitably is, against your most sensitive vertebra. The training bra serves one purpose: to pro-voke adolescent boys into inflicting spinal paralysis on underdevel-oped classmates. The trick is to immobilize the victim just long enough to ask her, "Why wear a bra when you're flat as a table?"

Beyond my appearance, there was the situation at home. Namely, my mother was a preacher. Everyone at school knew she'd founded a church, and that my parents had divorced because of it, but no one discussed the situation in front of me. No one knew how to dis-cuss it. There was no frame of reference for a female pastor, for serv-ices held outside a traditional church building, or for any place of worship where junkies and hippies were welcome, week after week, without regard to drug use or the absence of shoes.

Not long after I entered junior high, Mom's ministry relocated from a warehouse, where it had been safely hidden among wicker wholesalers and auto body shops at the end of a gravel parking lot, into a West Miami shopping center storefront less than a mile from my school. Passersby could peer through the windows into the sanctuary: a yellow room filled with folding chairs and dying ferns, and, depending on the day, possibly with congregants raising their hands to the heavens or passed out on the floor in divine bliss. The adjoining Christian bookstore was lime green and lined with peg-board. There Mom sold Bibles and mugs and crosses and inspirational cards, and books to educate customers on, for instance, *The Healing Power of the Bible* and *Devils, Demons & Deliverance.* Pulling these books off the shelves and flicking through them, I was never sure what to feel. Only one thing was certain: either my mother was crazy, or the rest of the world was.

My school was Evangelical, too, but more conventional. It was affiliated with a squat, tannish nondenominational church that came closest to the Baptist faith in spirit. Stained-glass windows lined the sanctuary. Women taught Sunday school, joined the choir, or just sat in pews, hands folded primly into their husbands'. Somber organ music took the place of tambourines and tongues.

My mother disapproved of the place. "A stinking cesspit of dead religion," she called it. Sending my sister and me to school there was her one act of deference to my father, but it was an uneasy concession. Mom could often be found rising from a chair in the principal's office to nail home some finer point of Scripture. Most memorably, she harangued the administration into convert-ing the annual Halloween celebration into a "Hallelujah party." So, instead of flitting around as ghosts and witches and sexy cats, my classmates joined me in being forced to impersonate biblical figures or pose as creatures from Noah's Ark. One enterprising girl came in a belly dancer costume and called herself Queen Esther. She was sent home for blasphemy, and showing her stomach.

No doubt you can already imagine how popular I was at King's Christian School, but it gets worse: I was pop-culture illiterate. Between my mother's religious leanings, and my father's chronic aversion to pleasure of any kind, I was forbidden to watch television, see most movies, and listen to "rock music," a category encompassing roughly every secular song produced since Buddy Holly's plane went down.

Miraculously, I managed to have a friend. A fellow pale, short girl had passed seventh grade with me in wallflower solidarity. As we moved into our second year of junior high, however, Julie bloomed. Her hair grew out and darkened to a rich shade of honey. Her breasts filled in. New lace-up sandals accentuated her ankles. A few months into eighth grade, she took up with Oscar Acevedo, a seventh-grader who transferred to our school after his last, a Catholic academy, held him back two years in a row.

Oscar pushed the dress and grooming code to its limits and beyond by adopting an asymmetrical, blue-tinged New Wave hairstyle, and an earring he was suspended for wearing on school property. His wardrobe came straight off the cover of a Depeche Mode album: slim-fitting jacket, skinny tie, tight pants. But this was 1984 Miami, where no music other than Top Forty hits and freestyle dance beats ever took hold, where surfer shirts were the height of fashion and oversized Don Johnson jackets were waiting in the wings. So Oscar was ostracized by all but Julie, but I could see why she liked him. He looked good in the pants.

Some days after school I accompanied Julie and Oscar to the park that lay between our school and Belen Jesuit. They sat kissing on the bleachers, his hands up her shirt, hers on his broad neck, while I worked at seeming neither pathetically bored nor pathetically interested. Often I paced, kicking up dirt, around the periphery of the baseball diamond.

If I walked too far, Julie would call to me: "Wait, wait, Maud. Come back. I'm sorry." And she'd give Oscar a look that meant, *She's my best friend, and I don't want her to feel bad, and also I'll be screwed if she's not here when my mom picks me up from "band practice," so talk to her.*

Oscar would valiantly redirect his attention from Julie's breasts to my face, the upper two-thirds of which was concealed by bangs and giant brown plastic glasses with tinted lenses I rarely bothered to wipe clean. "What you need is a streak of pink in your hair," he'd say. "Like Madonna."

"Yeah," I'd say, straightening the collar on my secondhand polo shirt, "maybe that's what I'll do."

The three of us would fall silent. We'd stare off into the distance and try to make conversation about somebody's pregnant sister. Soon Oscar and Julie would be touching again, then kissing. Their discreet pecks accelerated quickly into full-blown feel-up sessions. I hung around nearby, listlessly pulling leaves from the shrubbery, until it was time for Julie and me to shuffle off to her mom's car. We left Oscar on the bleachers with his flushed face and bulging crotch. The pants really were very tight; I'm surprised he was allowed to wear them, but I guess admonishing him would've entailed acknowledging the existence of genitals.

In due course, Julie and Oscar parted ways. And at the promise of a school band trip to Sea World, she dug out her recorder and started going to rehearsals. She begged me to join, too, so we could see Shamu, the killer whale, together. Why she thought this was a good idea, I couldn't understand. Any self-respecting loser knows it's better to slink around in a quiet pair or bland triad than to congregate with a pack of rejects. But I did Julie's bidding, and showed up with a plastic woodwind of my own. The band, including Julie and me, numbered seven.

Someone's father drove all of us upstate in a giant, backseatless van. We sat on crates and sang along to the radio. (At a recent garage sale I'd talked my mom into springing for an FM headset, so I "could listen to the Christian radio station in my room." Since then I'd sat up, night after night, brushing up on Wham! and Madonna and the rest of the Top 40, in preparation for an opportunity just like this one.)

My eye kept returning to Gordon Kidd. At school I knew him as the braying class clown, with food trapped in his braces, hair that showed no sign of familiarity with shampoo, and an unforgivable fondness for fart jokes. But now, passionately crooning Lionel Richie's "Hello," I saw that Gordon's tank top afforded a compelling view of his bicep and the tangle of dark hair under his arm. He wore purple surf shorts that set off the tanned and knotty wonders of his quadriceps. His lips were full and pouty; his lashes were long; and, best of all, as I launched into each new song he squeezed my arm and exclaimed, "How come I never knew you could sing?"

Julie pulled me aside near the women's bathroom sinks at a rest stop. "Watch out," she said. "I think that dork Gordon likes you."

My pulse raced like a runaway metronome. Hope tingled through my chest, down into my fingertips and other parts. But I did my best to conceal my excitement. I rolled my eyes and jabbed at the hand dryer button again. "Oh, God," I said, rubbing my palms together, "you think so?"

She rolled her eyes, too, and smiled. "Duh. Didn't you see how he kept grabbing your arm? He's totally in love."

In love, I repeated in my head. *Inloveinloveinloveinlove!*

We stayed in St. Cloud, a town just outside Orlando, at our band teacher's parents' house—a small, concrete-block affair with green shutters and jalousie windows and a single bathroom. The boys camped out in the Florida room. The girls slept in the guest bedroom, on the other side of the house. And Miss Jan, our director, installed herself between us, in the living room, where she faced the task of confining the sexual tension that radiated from both ends of the place.

The bathroom sat off the hall, beyond the living room. When we tiptoed out to use it, Miss Jan awoke and clicked on the light next to the couch, waiting until we returned to our room to go back to sleep. Over the course of our three-day trip, the circles under Miss Jan's eyes grew darker and deeper, and by the last night even her enormous breasts seemed exhausted. She balanced them on one arm while she sat dozing in the lamplight.

At Sea World, sitting alone among tourists in the killer whale show splash zone, Gordon and I touched hands. He draped an arm over my shoulders. I leaned back against him and felt his muscles tighten. He smelled salty, but familiar, like my towel after a day at the beach.

We held this position for an hour and a half, watching the same show twice more but hardly speaking. At last we wandered over to the souvenir shops, where we picked up keychains and magnets and oddly shaped dolphin squeeze toys and set them down again. We agreed that I would be Gordon's girlfriend.

That night, and all the way back to Miami the day following, a dizzying series of make-out fantasies played through my head: we kissed in my bed, groped atop the vacant stairwell at school, embraced, naked, in the van. In life, though, our lips never met. Back at school, Gordon resumed the position of obnoxious, hee-hawing pariah. He made some hideous bet—he could fart three times in class without the teacher knowing who did it? Whatever it was, he pocketed the money in the locker room afterward. Then he clapped a hand onto my neck, as though to sweep me into the sphere of his flatulence.

Preferring my quiet brand of loserdom to his conspicuous variety, I dumped him. We spent the rest of the year publicly insulting each other.

I'd always longed to be dangerous and wanton, the kind of girl who wore harsh geometric eyeshadow and black nail polish and carried a rubber in her wallet just in case. So my failure to kiss Gordon before the breakup preyed on my mind. I was getting older, after all. I was fourteen now. In the fall I would start public school. If somebody didn't stick his tongue in my mouth before then, it might never happen.

When summer started, I slouched around Mom's bookstore, grudgingly shelving books and stewing over the possibility of eternal chastity. I was trying on crosses one afternoon, wondering if I could talk her into giving me a necklace for my next birthday and then secretly replace the cross with a lightning bolt, when the store bell jangled. Octavio—Tavi—Valbuena and his mom walked in. Three other church women followed, armed with Bibles. They were gathering to cast the demons out of a guy who'd wandered in off the street.

Mom closed the store, and they disappeared into the sanctuary, drawing the blinds used for exorcisms. Tavi and I were left staring at the jewelry.

Tavi was a melancholy soul. He kept his hands shoved down deep in his pockets, and his green eyes fixed off somewhere just above the horizon, even when he was indoors. He was dark—Colombian, with a mix of Indian and Spanish blood—and fine-featured. His diction was impeccable: never pretentious, always precise. Vestiges of my own early Texan accent transfixed and horrified Tavi. He informed me that summer, very gently, that I said "sow," as in the female pig, when I really meant "saw."

He spoke in the deep mournful timbre of an undertaker, and his outlook was equally funereal. The blossoming of gardenias presented him with an opportunity to reflect on the coming nuclear war, which would wipe out every plant and animal on earth. Swimming called to mind the time his dad forced his sister to leap into their pool, even though she had strep throat, and feel around for a retainer she'd lost while swimming laps. Ice cream caused Tavi to contemplate our inability, in South Florida, to experience winter. He and I had known each other for years and often sat together at church, exchanging morose observations to pass the time until the service ended. So his gloominess didn't bother me. On the contrary, I admired Tavi's knack for identifying concrete reasons to dread everything that seemed, to most people, an unambiguous good. I too lived life in anticipation of calamity.

Lightning slashed across the sky. Thunder rumbled in the distance, then boomed just outside. Rain began to pelt the roof; it fell in sheets in the parking lot. A few would-be shoppers tugged at the door, hoping to escape the storm. I pointed to the "closed" sign and turned off the lights.

Tavi and I retreated to the bookstore storage room, which doubled as the children's Sunday school area. Boxes towered behind a divider. A folding conference table sat in front of it, surrounded by the same kind of folding chairs that filled the sanctuary. Slumping into a couple of them, we both sighed. Water began to drip from a discolored spot on the ceiling into a tin pan on the floor. To escape a whiff of mildew, I pivoted in my seat, turning my attention to Tavi. He wore tight little-boy shorts. They were blue, with red piping. Beneath them, his legs were long and nearly hairless—nothing like Gordon's.

"So," I said, "how's your vacation?"

"Depressing." He glanced at me briefly before refocusing on the middle distance. "My dad keeps making me spend Fridays with him."

"That sucks. We should get summer off from our dads."

"I wish." He held out a box of Tic-Tacs, and I took one. "And you?" he asked. "How's everything?"

"Oh, shitty." I said, elaborately casual. I ran my finger back and forth over a scratch on the tabletop. "I had to dump this guy."

Tavi gazed at me again, longer this time. "I didn't know you had a boyfriend," he said. His eyes were wide and dewy, childlike as my little sister's.

Thinking I'd impress the boy with my experience and sophistication, I started to tell him about Gordon, but realized my mistake right away. There was, after all, nothing to tell. Gordon and I sang a few songs, barely touched at a theme park, broke up on Monday, end of story. That's not the way I recounted things to Tavi, though. I stuck to the facts until the part about Sea World, and then veered into fantasyland. "That night we snuck out of the house," I said. "The van was unlocked, so we got in. And then"—here I faltered, not knowing how much needed to happen for Tavi to keep staring at me the way he was: eyebrow raised, a slight flush on his cheeks.

He cleared his throat. "And then what happened?" He was almost whispering.

An electric chill, followed by heat, ran through my body. The ultimate lie sprang from my lips. "We had sex," I said. I shrugged and feathered my hair with my fingers like it was nothing. Then, congratulating myself on this feat of nonchalance, I braced for questions. I tried to conjure up some of the details I'd gleaned from my mom's watered-down *Joy of Sex* knockoff: how to touch a man's body, how to stroke his thing into your mouth, how to move with him inside you.

But Tavi didn't press for details. He didn't even speak until I looked up. When his eyes met mine, they were so grave, I felt like we were on an elevator falling. "That's a terrible sin," he said.

I saw myself through his eyes then: a cheap van-fucker. The sharp mildewed smell seemed to intensify. Even breathing through my mouth, I couldn't escape it; the air tasted like shredded cotton and old lettuce. My stomach rolled with nausea. "I know," I told him. "I'm never doing it again. Not unless I get married."

I was scared. Unless I played things exactly right, Tavi would pass my lie on to his sister, who would confide in their mother, who would tell my mom. And *my* mother would, in concert with my father, shackle me to my bed, take away the phone, and revoke permission to start public school. She'd keep my radio eternally tuned to the lectures of some outraged evangelist.

Still, admitting the truth about Gordon would entail an unthinkable loss of face.

Only one damage-control strategy suggested itself. For Tavi to keep my secret, I needed leverage; I needed to know something equally damning about him. So I set about extracting whatever schoolboy dirt was available. I stretched and sighed like a woman in a bubble bath commercial, closing my eyes as if to seal in the bliss. "It feels good to get that off my chest," I said. "Until now I haven't told anybody—except for God." My voice sounded tinny and ineffectual, falsely enthusiastic even to my own ears, but I patted the back of Tavi's hand, and went on. "You should try it. Tell me your worst secret."

Tavi didn't hesitate. He reached back across the table and took my hand. "I trust you," he said.

Before I could even begin to envision the most basic titillating scenarios—a few guilty wet dreams (I'd read Judy Blume), some furtive whacking off in the shower, an afternoon of strip poker with a neighborhood girl—he tightened his grip on me. I could feel him shaking.

"My dad tried to kill my mother," he whispered.

The story fell from his lips in a rush, but here's what I remember: Divorce papers were served. Tavi's father slammed doors and threw chairs and paced up and down the hall, ranting. "We are Catholic," he kept saying, although Tavi's mom had fled to a divorce-friendly Protestantism a few years before. "The church does not allow this." He careened off in his truck.

The next evening, he returned, seemingly resigned. He parked in his appointed spot, knocked before entering the house, and said he would move out. He just wanted to help Dory, Tavi's mom, have her transmission repaired first. She agreed to follow him to a mechanic he knew. But as they drove further and further out on Tamiami Trail, far into the darkness and away from the lights of civilization, she got an eerie feeling. Another car appeared in her rearview mirror, going too fast.

Dory called out to God. She broke into tongues. Just then a cul-de-sac materialized in the wilderness, and she wheeled into it and sped back the way she'd come. She watched in her rearview mirror as both her husband's car, and the one that had been following her, slammed on brakes and turned to pursue her. When she got home, she didn't say anything, except to instruct Tavi and his sister not to open the door to their father.

Later, after everyone was asleep, Tavi's dad banged on his window. Hoping for a reconciliation, Tavi let him in.

The man pushed past him into the kitchen and made a phone call. He spoke quickly. "It didn't happen," he said. "She got scared." Then he went to the door of the bedroom he and Dory had shared, and rattled the doorknob.

"Get out," Dory yelled, "or I'm calling the police."

He left, but she called the police anyway. And when they arrived, she told them, Tavi, and his sister what had happened earlier that night. Tavi relayed the phone conversation he'd overheard. The next day the court issued a restraining order.

Whether Tavi was telling the truth, I don't know. How accurate my own recollection is now, more than twenty years later, I can't say. And yet the mind plays tricks on you. Descriptions of shocking events like these can etch themselves onto your memory almost as if you'd actually seen them unfolding.

Around the same time Tavi told me his story, my grandmother pulled me aside to warn me I was old enough now to be vigilant about madness: my own, my sister's, and my future children's. She described the descent of her own little sister, Louise, a beautiful girl with hair exactly the same shade of auburn as mine was then, into early dementia.

Louise stepped out of her clothes one hot Texas afternoon, and went dancing down the street, naked, with a scarf. Institutionalized for a time, Louise came home, only to pull a butcher knife from her bathwater and brandish it against her mother. She was returned to the sanitarium, where she died of tuberculosis.

"Always remember," my grandmother said, "insanity skips generations. Although that's debatable in your mother's case."

It was a timely warning. I felt mad that summer—mad with lust, of course, but also with a longing for something I couldn't name.

Although my supposed sex in the van horrified Tavi, his interest in me increased tenfold once the image was planted in his mind.

"I'm in love with you," he announced on my couch a few nights later. Before I could respond—I wasn't sure what to say, but ever since he'd told me about his parents, I'd yearned to kiss him—he pitched toward me and covered my lips with his. They lingered there for a moment. There was another tentative peck or two. And then his tongue slid into my mouth and mine entered his, and the whole enterprise became a disaster. I tried to imagine what Julie would say if she could see this debacle of a make-out session, but the condemnation of the Julie in my head was so complete, I pushed her from my mind.

My tongue continued its stiff, soggy dance with Tavi's. My glasses struck his eyebrow yet again. I took them off and opened my eyes to find him looking at me curiously, that same brow raised, as if to say, *I thought you were experienced. I thought you'd show me what to do.*

His bewilderment continued through the summer. We divided our days between swimming—in the company of my sister, stepsister, and other kids who were unaware of our involvement—and roaming strip malls or a nearby park in search of benches, thatched huts, secluded inlets, rotting picnic tables, and other make-out spots. We wore our clothes over bathing suits, and sometimes we threw off our T-shirts and waded into the Tropical Park lake to make out in the water. I could feel him get hard as he pressed against me.

Nights were even more hormone-crazed. In an unbelievable twist of luck and maternal obliviousness, Tavi was allowed to sleep over a couple of times a week. Consigned to the sofa closest to the kitchen—which teemed with huge flying cockroaches and the occasional rat—he feigned sleep until my mom and stepdad went to bed.

I was impressed by his fortitude; after blundering upon a few giant-fanged, long-tailed rodents on midnight quests for ice water, I'd learned to avoid the entire front section of the house once Mom turned the kitchen light out.

Now all that changed. After midnight I'd sneak out of my room to join him. Somehow, magically, the vermin always seemed to stay just around the corner where the food was—or at least if they entered the living room, Tavi and I didn't notice. We reached up each other's shirts and rubbed our bodies against each other. We kissed until our lips went numb. Sometimes he worked his hands down into the back of my shorts, and slid them beneath my underwear. I let him grope my butt, but when he tried to move to the front, I stopped him. Even I had limits. I wasn't going to lose my virginity to a twelve-year-old.

"Let's not go too far," I said. "I think it's a sin."

And if I didn't say it, Tavi did. He'd grab and pull at me so vigorously, he'd be sweating and panting and crazed, but whenever my hands pushed his away, he'd say, "You're right. God would want us to stop now."

Tavi and I dwelt on many depressing things that summer: his dad, the coming tribulation, the inevitable triumph of the cockroach, the boy at church who'd watched his mother die of an epileptic fit in the bathtub. But it was the constant presence of God (and his counterpart, that tempter Satan) in our world, above all, that infused the relationship with melancholia.

Although I had exactly as much doubt in my mother's teachings as I had faith in them, Tavi was a believer, and as the summer progressed I became infected by his certainty. I envisioned demons hovering over us, laughing, as we touched. I pictured God looking down in judgment. I pulled away from Julie, not only because I shrank from the prospect of introducing her to Tavi, but because she wouldn't comprehend the holy sphere he and I occupied, the line we walked between eternal sanctity and eternal damnation. The van episode with Gordon took on a corporeality in my mind. My guilt was as palpable and sickening as if I'd actually fucked him.

Eventually I confessed. I was sitting on Tavi's lap one night, kissing his ear and blowing lightly into it. The more he writhed, the harder I pressed my ass against him. When he pushed me back against the couch and shoved his hand down the front of my shorts, I let him touch my underwear. But as he worked his way down to the thinnest, flimsiest part of it—the part so wet it kept sticking to my legs—I clamped my hand on top of his. "I never had sex with Gordon," I whispered. "He never even touched me like this."

We lay still, our hands resting on the damp heat of me. Then Tavi pulled back and sat up. He wiped his fingers on the couch. "It's okay," he said. "I mean, Praise the Lord. But you have to promise you'll tell me the truth from now on."

I said I would, but I knew it didn't matter. I knew the relationship would have to end. Our mothers were fighting; the church was dissolving; the holy depressiveness of the summer was fading away.

Tavi and my sisters would soon be off to the Lights for Jesus Summer Youth Camp, where they'd spend a week learning to commune with the Holy Spirit and fend off demons. I'd escaped this joyous retreat by arranging to accompany an old friend on her family vacation. And shortly after my return, my family would be moving out to Kendall, a different Miami neighborhood—for kids like Tavi and me, too young to drive, it might as well have been another city—where I would start public school.

Two days after the new school year started, I broke up with Tavi over the phone.

The following summer, he moved out to my new neighborhood. My mom had shut down her church by then, and our mothers had stopped speaking, but Tavi biked over one summer afternoon. He stood outside my window and talked to me through the screen. When I told him I had a new boyfriend, a Catholic schoolboy I'd met through Julie, Tavi trundled off. He rode down the center of the street, weaving slightly.

I watched him go but didn't feel much.

The focus of my life shifted. At school my friends were secular Jewish kids or nominal Catholics or some other thing they never talked about. No one knew that my mom had been a preacher. I told a handful of people I'd been to religious school, but they misunderstood. In the spring they asked what I was doing for Passover. Christianity, and, by extension, my whole past life, were irrelevant in this new profane world.

Don't get me wrong: I was still a misfit—a drama fag, to be precise. But I had plenty of company. Fifteen hundred kids went to my high school, and among them at any given time were at least fifty freaks prepared to spend every afternoon in rehearsals, to submit to the voluminous and foul-mouthed tirades of our drama teacher, and to dress up as peasants or dancers or greasers in an eventual theatrical production that was almost beside the point.

On weekends my friends and I guzzled Mad Dog 20/20 in

parking lots. We dragged kegs out to Miami Beach, where we played games of truth or dare that tended to involve male frontal nudity. We made bonfires in front of half-dug subdivision lakes.

Things developed swimmingly on the romantic front, too. After a year of feeling each other up on park benches and in the backs of movie theaters, my boyfriend acquired a driver's license and a Toyota pickup, and I forgot about God. Together we mastered some creative gymnastics and lost our virginity in the front seat of his truck. After that we developed a routine. Several nights a week he picked me up from rehearsal and drove out to the warehouse district near Country Walk, where we hid in a shrouded cul-de-sac and had to scramble to put our clothes back on if we thought we heard a cop car. On special occasions we sprang for an hour at Magic Waters, a dubious whirlpool establishment that stank of mold and chlorine but featured a sort of cot in the corner.

I lost touch with Tavi until my senior year, when he enrolled at my school as a sophomore. He walked up to me mournfully the first week. I gave him my phone number.

He called late one afternoon, his voice quavering, his breathing unsteady. He'd dozed off on his couch after school, he said, and awakened to find himself pinned down by a huge red demon with human eyes. It sat on his chest, staring down at him. As he held its gaze, it grinned and flicked its tail. It reached its clawed hand toward Tavi's face. But Tavi cried out to God, and the thing disappeared.

I believed Tavi—and I didn't believe him. One second I thought he was nuts; the next I was convinced he, like my mother, possessed a spiritual sight unknown to the rest of us. I doubted his father's attempt on Dory's life. Then I re-believed in it.

For many years I continued to feel a kinship with Tavi. Our conversations conjured up the same gloomy longings that had once drawn us together—longings connected somehow to a God I didn't exactly believe in, but could never quite seem to extinguish.

SURVIVING
HIGH SCHOOL

Fuck High School

KELLY BRAFFET

High school? Fuck high school. I could do school with my eyes
closed (and due to my developing insomnia and the long hair that
fell down in front of my face, often did). School was no problem;
not in kindergarten, not my senior year, and not at any time in
between. Was I number one in my graduating class? No. Did I fail
math tests on a regular basis? Sure. Was I bugged out about it? Not
really. I wanted to be a writer. Pre-calc didn't figure into my plans.

So, yeah. Fuck school. At least—thought eighteen-year-old
me—fuck *this* school. My high school was the kind of semirural
holding cell where the football team will be funded until doomsday,
but the kids in the marching band played thirty-year-old instru-
ments and only had their uniforms cleaned once a season. The
A-list kids had keggers by the train tracks and the first day of deer
season was an unofficial holiday. By the second semester of my
junior year I'd taken every English elective on offer, including
remedial Speed Reading and Composition Writing courses that I
needed like a hole in the head. In my junior Honors-level English
class, we spent countless hours that I'll never get back taking the
kind of quizzes on *Ethan Frome* where we picked a "symbol" from
the left column and matched it to its "meaning" on the right, i.e.
Cat equals Zenia or *Sled equals freedom*. My senior year I took a
drama class from the same teacher (for the same reason I took pot-
tery: a full schedule earned you an easy extra grade point) and almost
lost my mind when we spent a full two weeks reading *Our Town*
aloud. I reread the play three times before giving up and starting on

a paperback copy of Dostoevsky's *White Nights,* half-wishing that the teacher would confront me so that I could point out to her that I was growing older by the minute, and that my most spongelike learning years were slipping away while my classmates struggled to pronounce "strawberry phosphate."

Yep. Fuck school.

I'll take some of the blame for my high school years being a waste. I was, after all, the kind of kid who carried around Dostoevsky paperbacks, who wore combat boots and fishnets and scowled a lot, who (when forced in the aforementioned Speed Reading class to create a "poem" based on the letters of her name) decided that the E in Kelly stood for "Existentialist." In short, I was a pretentious little shit. I thought high school was a waste of my time, that my teachers had nothing to teach me, and that I'd been born able to experience a depth of thought, emotion and sensitivity that my lesser classmates would never be able to understand. That was why I spent almost every night sitting alone in my bedroom listening to the Cure. That was why, during summer vacations when everyone else in town sunned themselves by the Lynch Field Pool, entire months passed when I didn't speak to a human being outside my family. That was why I spent study halls and classroom lulls writing furiously in an endless series of black-marbled composition books (I think I ended up with about sixteen of them). That was why nobody liked me. That was why I felt so alone.

At least, that's how I remember it. But, to be straight, I had friends. In fact, my sophomore year, I had what might almost have been called a *crowd.* We were what you'd expect: we wore Chuck Taylors and Doc Martens, chained wallets and Jane's Addiction T-shirts. We played in punk bands and rode skateboards, or we hung around watching our boyfriends play in punk bands and ride skateboards. We had shticks, little personality tweaks that made us feel special: signature colors (mine was green), signature totems (mushrooms, frogs, dragonflies), signature Sesame Street characters (mine was Elmo). The rednecks we went to school with made machinegun noises and spit at us when we walked down the hall, and for a while there was even a much-storied "Freak Hit List" in one of the first-floor bathrooms, but most people just ignored us. And let's be honest: we preferred the machine guns.

The Freaks—that was what everyone else called us, and what we called ourselves—had their social echelons just like any other group, and it seemed mostly to have to do with age. I remember being a sophomore, watching the senior girls with their poker-straight hair, dark eye makeup and blood-red lipstick, and thinking that in a few years, maybe it'd be my turn. The ultimate freak achievement was being named "Most Unique" in the school yearbook (although being on the Freak Hit List was pretty good too), and I knew I'd never get that; still, there were only so many of us, so I took it for granted that by the time we were seniors, I'd be almost—if not quite—as cool as Sarah Hlad or Jenn Knesh.

And in the meantime, I had my friends. My friends were brilliant, they were creative, they were weird; they were funny, they were surreal, they were absurd. They did inexplicable things just for the sake of doing them, like painting their heads blue or writing "wheat" on everything they owned. They painted, they drew, they were in hardcore bands and played shows at the smaller and dingier of our two civic centers on the weekends. Let the rednecks of the world make machine-gun noises at them: We were cool. We were *special.* We were better than they were. They'd see.

I loved my friends. And there was a time when, despite the whole alone-in-my-room-listening-to-the-Cure thing, my friends seemed to love me back. On those rare occasions when I turned off the CD player and ventured out into the world, my friend Becca and I would walk to the thrift store in our town's near-dead downtown, stopping to eat fried mushrooms at the greasy spoon that served lunch to the courthouse employees. Or we'd meet up with some of the other girls in our crowd and do silly things, like go to the mall or hold tea parties. These things didn't happen very often; girls intimidated me, and I kept them at arm's length. Even Becca, whose parents lived a block away from mine. She was my nominal best friend for three years, and I think I saw her bedroom twice. As much as I liked her and the other girls I sometimes hung out with, it seemed to me then—and often still does—that they possessed an innate refinement, a delicacy, that I lacked. They had the right clothes, the right shoes, the right hair. Since I didn't, I felt easier around the guys, who seemed to care less, and since I'd spent most of my life around my older brother and his friends, male humans were more familiar to me than the other kind, anyway.

Besides, having male friends was a coup. Having a guy want to date you was nice, but it was like the weather: you had no control over it, and it changed without warning. But being a guy's *friend* was a very different matter. Girls chose each other for friends because somebody was better than somebody else; you absorbed somebody else's cool, or you lorded your own over someone who had less of it. But if a guy wanted to be your friend—well, shit, it probably still meant that he wanted to date you. But if he was too shy to actually ask you out, then you could *pretend* that it meant you were a worthwhile person, no bullshit about who's got the cooler shoes or whose hair makes it to lunchtime without frizzing.

For instance, consider my friend Eric. Eric lived a few streets behind me, and he painted wonderful pictures of flowers, dark colors on dark backgrounds with only the slightest suggestion of petals. For a while, he was in a band with a talented drummer friend of ours, and they did a cover of EMF's "Unbelievable" which rocked much, much harder than the original. He had a quiet voice and a reserved manner that made his occasional bursts of enthusiasm seem almost magical. He would point out stains on my shirts, and then say, gently, "But they're beautiful stains." I remember him standing close behind me in the hallway, putting his chin on the top of my head (he was tall) and telling me that I was the perfect height. He loved me, I think. But, because he was too shy to ask and I was waiting for—I don't know, River Phoenix, I think—nothing ever happened.

There were others. The tall, dark brooder that all of the girls loved and none of us could quite get anywhere with, my punk boyfriend, that talented drummer friend of ours—and what did we do? All of us brilliant, creative kids, each of us troubled in our own way, all trapped inside the merciless bell jar of that holding cell of a high school? Surely we walked the finer edges of sanity: drank too much, slept around too much, did too many drugs. Did we run wild? Did we break curfew? Were we graffiti artists, vandals, shoplifters?

None of those things. We were "straightedge"—which, judging from what happened to some of us after high school, mostly seemed to mean that we didn't know any drug dealers yet. Booze was the province of the redneck dickheads, the jocks, and the cheerleaders who came in on Mondays bragging about keggers down at the train tracks, so that was out, too. And as for sex—dude. Western Pennsylvania isn't Malibu, or at least it wasn't back then. It was conservative; it was Catholic. And freaky we may have been, but back then, we were *not* brave. Keep in mind that during our best year together, we were only sophomores in high school. We couldn't drive yet, and none of us had older friends with cars until later. Our lives were walking-distance-sized, limited to activities we could easily explain to our chauffeuring parents.

So we went to the movies, we went to the mall. One of the girls in the group was the daughter of a Methodist minister, and we spent at least one night hanging out in the basement preschool of her father's church, eating pizza rolls and playing with the toys. My punk boyfriend at the time had parents who were in the midst of a nasty divorce. His mom was living with her new boyfriend, and his dad spent most evenings with the lady next door. Since he was pretty much on his own, we mostly hung out at his house: two teenagers in a house alone. It could have been scandalous if the "hanging out" process had entailed anything other than reading his comic books and playing with Bob, his pet iguana. More than once, while making out with him in his bedroom, kissing in the dutifully impassioned way that teenagers do, I pondered the fact that we *could* have sex, if we wanted to. We never talked about it, but I didn't want to. (He was actually the only person I knew who *did* do drugs, mostly acid, or so he told me. Contrary to the message of every after-school special you've ever seen, he never asked me to trip with him. Not once.)

Later, after my punk boyfriend and I broke up, I remember going to Eric's house after school, listening to My Bloody Valentine and playing with his little sisters before his parents got home, and being aware that there was the potential for something more interesting than that to happen. And I didn't want that, either, because I told myself that I loved Eric with a purer love than that, and I didn't want anything to get in the way of our friendship. I cringe even thinking about it.

Why no sex? Why no drugs? Because I was scared. Fuck high school, you know? My life sure as hell wasn't about my present, so it had to be about my future. And no part of high school—not sex, not drugs, not punk music—was important enough to blow any part of that future on. To be honest, and God forbid I lead any impressionable youngsters down the path of destruction here, but I kind of wish I'd been braver. I like my life; the choices I've made have led me to some pretty good places. But part of me wishes I *had* slept with my punk boyfriend, or Eric, or with anybody. Part of me wishes that I'd skipped school more, that I'd dropped a tab of acid or hit a few of those keggers by the train tracks. That I'd taken a freaking *risk* now and then. Because while my memories of my sophomore year of high school are very sweet and glowing and full of warm feelings and hope, none of it lasted. And I kind of wish I'd walked away with some life experience, something that made the end redemptive instead of just painful.

That end came during my senior year.

When I was twenty-one, during my next-to-last semester of college, the boy I'd loved desperately and hopelessly for the previous two years told me he was seeing his ex-girlfriend: the pre-me girlfriend that I'd always suspected was also the *during*-me girlfriend. I started smoking and playing video games, stopped sleeping and leaving my dorm room and brushing my hair. I told my professors that it wasn't that I didn't *want* to write papers for them, I just *couldn't,* and they accepted this with kind nods and sage advice, because it was that kind of college. And until that time, which was dark and lonely and proof positive that sitting in your room being depressed doesn't do a damn thing to help you get over being depressed—until then, the great heartbreak of my life was my senior year of high school. There I was, finally one of those cool senior girls in combat boots. And everything was wrong. Everything hurt.

Maybe it started the year before. I'd dated an older guy, someone out of school, and so I'd spent more time with him and his friends and less with mine. (Now, him, I slept with. Once. The condom broke and I didn't sleep again until my period started. It was my first major brush with the insomnia that eventually became one of the defining characteristics of my life.) Sometime in the year after we broke up, the punk boyfriend from my sophomore year more or less left school. The rest of us had girlfriends or boyfriends of varying degrees of inter-crowd respectability, and all of the crushes and bonds that had driven and sustained us and kept us together slowly dissolved, one by one. The drummer and another boy had been fighting over Becca since tenth grade; senior year they joined forces and decided that they'd rather hate her, instead. She responded by fleeing to the calmer arms of the honor society crowd, who were real nice and all, but didn't interest me particularly.

Besides, I was having my own problems. The guys had turned on me, too; the drummer even wrote a song about me, called it "The Pigwoman" and performed it at a show where I was not just in attendance, but standing in the front row. (Just in case I missed the connection, everyone else at the show was kind enough to clue me in.) The esteem in which Eric held me withered and died and rotted. There was no more hanging out at his parents' house after school. He pulled back further and further, keeping his increasingly cold distance. Finally, on one awful day that felt then and feels now like the mortal wounding of my high school self, he called me a whore in the newspaper office. We walked home together that day, and I think I yelled at him, and I think he apologized, but I know for a fact that I went home and cried anyway.

I took some pride in being able to make it that long. They'd made Becca cry right there in school.

Those guys: those brilliant, creative guys that I loved so covetously, whose mere friendship had once made me feel the closest to cool I'd ever come. There were a lot of truths that could explain what they did to us. We were going to college, they weren't. We were full of plans for the future, they weren't. In the four years they'd known us, we'd proven that we weren't going to put out; there were underclass girls who would, and did. Although that's unfair, since the truth is that I have no idea if those girls put out or not, and I don't think that was the crux of the issue. Maybe they did, or maybe they had friends who sold weed. Maybe they were just young, and new, and our guys hadn't been trading around crushes on them for the last three years. Those girls, those fifteen- and sixteen-year-olds with their Manic-Panicked hair hanging in front of their thickly lined eyes, their doomed little gazes, and that hip bisexual thing they were all suddenly doing; to those girls, our guys were *their* guys, and our guys were gods. Even the Brooder; even him. (The girl who snagged him shared a name with my college boyfriend's pre-me, during-me, post-me. Cruel, cruel fate.)

Eric calling me a whore was the mortal wound; death took longer. That winter I started dating another guy, who dumped me for no particular reason after only two months. Although I hadn't been aware that I felt any special devotion to him, the breakup destroyed me. The only thread binding me to high school lasted for another year or so, until the summer day after my first year of college when I opened my front door and discovered a letter from Becca inside the screen door on my porch. In twelve pages of increasingly frenetic handwriting, she laid it out: I was a terrible person. I'd always been a terrible person. I would always *be* a terrible person. She had four years of collected proof, times when I'd lost my temper or done something mean or unreasonable. In that letter, I seemed like just another one of the guys, torturing her because it was fun, because I liked to watch her squirm. There was nothing good about the Kelly in that letter, and a terrible person I may have been, but even then, I knew I wasn't *that* bad. And that was it. I was *done.*

Fuck this town.

Fuck these people.

Fuck high school.

I kept the letter for years to remind myself of what I was leaving behind. I kept the letter, but threw my past away. Only one person from my teenaged years remained in my life: a guy outside of our crowd, someone I'd met on the newspaper staff in those bleak days after everything else seemed dead. I was proud of that fact, sort of. "I only stayed in touch with one person from high school," I'd tell people, as if that was somehow a sign that I was a deeply mature, highly evolved person. They'd look at me with an expression that I didn't understand, half bemusement and half pity, and I'd shrug.

I grew up. I was far more of a success as a grown-up than I'd ever been as a teenager. I had friendships, relationships, people who loved me. And the older I got, the more uncomfortable I grew with the teenager I'd once been. Those guys broke my heart, sure, but I wasn't exactly blameless. Yes, Eric called me a whore. At the time, he was dating his first girlfriend; I was jealous and catty, both to her and about her. Most of the things that Becca said to me in her letter turned out, after another five or ten years of reflection, to be true (although I maintain that her delivery method left a little to be desired). As for the Pigwoman thing—well, shit. That I can't explain. Teenagers are just mean, that's all.

When my friends from more sophisticated places talked about their high school friends, I'd blithely toss out that most of my friends had probably OD'd on crystal long ago. Occasionally, I'd hear rumors: one of my friends had been spotted in the mall, wearing white contact lenses and clearly tweaked out of his skull; another was working as a landscaper, and smoking too much pot. A third still lived with his parents. I heard the stories, but told myself I didn't really care. After all, fuck high school.

Eventually, I became a writer. I sold my first book. When I did the obligatory hometown reading, my mother and I drove to the bookstore together. It was raining. I was wearing my New York Writer outfit, tall boots and a skirt with fishnet stockings. Sitting in the parking lot, still in the car, rain bouncing off the pavement around us, I suddenly found myself unable to reach out and open the car door. My stomach was suddenly twisted and sick; my breathing was fast.

I turned to my mother. "What if someone . . . comes?" I asked.

She understood immediately. My mother is cool. "Nobody will come to make trouble," she said. "The kind of people who would make trouble won't bother to show up."

And she was right. The crowd that night was mostly populated by her friends from work, or friends of my brother's. My guidance counselor came, as did my favorite English teacher (no, not the *Ethan Frome* lady), who dropped by, but didn't stay. Nobody else I knew was there. Part of me was elated: I'd left that place, those people, behind, and now I was somebody else, somebody successful. Not the whore; not the Pigwoman. On the other hand, of all the people that I'd known back then and everybody that I'd gone to high school with, not a *single person* bothered to come see me succeed. It was a lonely feeling. For the first time, part of me began to understand those looks my new friends gave me. Eric, Becca, my punk boyfriend, the drummer—they'd all been important to me, once. Now, not a single one of them was still in my life. It was almost as if I'd imagined them.

Except that with each passing year, I knew more and more clearly that those four years in high school, with those people, had gone a long way toward defining who I was. They had defined what I found funny, what I found shocking, what I found desirable and contemptible; they had defined what I valued in the people around me. Those values had been refined since, of course. At sixteen, I'd had no problem dating a guy who claimed he dropped acid the way other people drank coffee; at twenty, I decided not to smoke pot anymore because it made me boring; and at twenty-three I stopped returning phone calls from two people that I otherwise quite liked because I didn't want to deal with their heroin problems. This is what's known in the world as growing up, and the more of it I did, the more I knew I couldn't ignore those four years when I'd started doing it.

Enter the Internet. Enter Google. Enter—and, yes, I'm embarrassed to admit it—MySpace. This is the blessing and the curse of the Internet: nobody is ever lost, and nothing is ever secret.

The drummer was the first I found, on his band's website. He was a full-time musician, touring with a death metal band. He was the one who'd written the Pigwoman song. If I'd found him burning to death the year after we graduated from high school, I would have pulled up a lawn chair and toasted a marshmallow or two. Now, I sent him an email, and received one in return. "Kelly!" it started. "Holy shit." He'd read my book, and liked it; so had a few other people I remembered vaguely from high school. His girlfriend lived in New York, he said, and he was planning to move there himself. We should get together sometime. We should have a beer.

A few months later, I got an email from Becca, who said much the same thing, although instead of a Holy Shit she started her note with, "I understand if you don't want to talk to me, but I want you to know I'm happy for you." It turned out that she, too, was living in New York, working as a crime reporter. We were both dating Red Sox fans; we both had master's degrees from Columbia; we both knit (although she was far, far better at it than I was). Eventually, we had lunch. It was very nice, very civilized. The letter didn't come up.

Then, finally, I got a message from somebody on MySpace who was using a pseudonym (as so many MySpacers do). It took a few rounds of communication for him to tell me his name. "I have a lot of things to apologize for," he wrote in one of the anonymous messages, calling himself "a recovering jackass," but adding that he'd been really impressed with my book. "I'm a one-man KB street team," he wrote. I wrote back that I was happy to have a street team; I also wrote that I thought I knew who he was—after all of those years, Eric still sounded like Eric, even in email—and I hoped he was doing well. I wanted to hear from him.

Hell, it was true. I did want to hear from him. Look: some things, you can't forgive. My college boyfriend lives five blocks from me, which means that there's an entire main drag in Brooklyn that I steer clear of because it's too close to the apartment where he lives with his pre-me during-me post-me, who is now his wife. For two years, I loved him—not crushed on, not lusted after, but *loved*. He took that love as casually as you'd take a religious tract from a crazy person on a long subway trip when your iPod's dead, and he threw it away just as easily. He wasn't a teenager when he did it, either. No excuses there. Sorry, *compadre:* you're not off that hook and you never will be.

But Eric and Becca and the drummer are different. In my head and in my broken heart, they had all been frozen in time, stuck forever in that ugly, miserable hung-up place where we'd all been eighteen and desperate. While I was running from myself, pretending that I'd sprung fully blown and mature from my bachelor's degree at twenty-two, they'd had lives. They'd had tragedies. They'd had experiences. They'd grown up. I was a better person, but so were they.

Eric called me a whore and made me cry. The drummer wrote a song about me and called it "Pigwoman." Becca wrote me a letter telling me I was a horrible person.

But that was ten—wait, eleven—wait, *twelve* years ago.

That was *high school*.

Yeah. Fuck high school.

David Haynes' Day Off

DAVID HAYNES

February: a short but busy month. As the local writer-of-color, you're expected every weekday morning to be up and dressed and on your way to the local school to be part of the Black History Month display in the English department. "Boys and girls, here's Mr. Haynes and he's an actual living writer!" I stand there, posed, pen in hand, a stirring tableau vivant of ethnic literary achievement.

March 1st, I sleep in.

The most troubled schools often request more than posing.

We would really appreciate it if you could say something inspiring to the kids. Give 'em a pep talk; tell them that if they come to school every day and work hard and give it their all, that they, too, can become rich and successful.

In other words, you want me to lie to them, I say, and we all have a good chuckle at that. Them, because they know the long odds on a single one of these kids making it out of the neighborhood intact. Me, at the "coming to school every day" part of the joke. For the most part I didn't. And, it's been my experience that the sort of school folk who invite you to these events tend to start squirming when you brag about having skipped most of your senior year—as I discovered the one time that I, oozing with warm smugness, bragged to a class of high school sophomores.

It's my inability to convincingly lie about what a good student I was that keeps me away from the schools these days—this even more so than the condescendingly shabby way in which the phone rings for only those twenty-eight days in February. I was a terrible student. A genuine slacker if there ever was one. I made an art of malingering, and my mother was my chief accomplice. Or enabler is the better word here—at least she was, until a freakishly late March ice storm put the brakes on our little scheme.

*

In the morning—after I'd finally convinced her how deeply, genuinely and miserably ill I was, I'd go right back to sleep. I've never been a morning person—do most of my best sleeping and dreaming between eight and ten a.m. Unless I was actually genuinely ill— too ill to sit up and take sustenance, which I've only been once in my life—I'd rise in time for the end of *Search for Tomorrow*. Mother was a CBS soap fan—until I got her started on *Days of Our Lives,* which we'd watch after lunch, sitting the afternoon through episodes of *Somerset* and *The Doctors.* Mother did home day care during the seventies, so after the midafternoon naps for all of us little ones, it was time for *Sesame Street* and *Mr. Rogers,* during which the phone calls to me would begin, brimming with reports of what I'd missed that day—which was always absolutely nothing. Not exactly *Ferris Bueller's Day Off,* but, hey, I enjoyed it.

I'm already regretting the parts of the essay that make it sound as if I'm piling on with more bad news about just how awful the American education system is. Trust me: I know how hard teachers work and what a thankless job it is. I put in fifteen years teaching sixth grade at an urban public school. (For the record: fifteen years—never sick, never late.) But let's be honest here: there's a reason that Ferris is America's most beloved character. We've all been to school and we're all in on the joke. I was one of those teachers who, when the parents called and sheepishly announced that the family was off on a road trip through Europe for a month, said, "Have a great time, take lots of pictures, and get in line early for the Mona Lisa." People like you and me and Ferris—people who attended basically decent schools on a semiregular basis—know that (generously) half the time is spent on substance, and most of that can be made up by reading the textbook. (As for the rest, the ones in the not-so-decent schools, well, No Child Left Behind is taking care of them, right?)

So I stayed at home. A lot. And sipped 7-Up and like all good adolescents mostly did not talk to my mother except about how really odd Rachel's hair looked on *Another World* and to puzzle as to why Steve would want to stay married to that insipid Alice anyway.

I was a slug.

*

As did most of you, I hated every day of high school, and most of junior high, too. For all the usual reasons, of course, and a few specific of my own. (Sadistic gym teachers who took the usual glee in tormenting the ungainly fat kid. The obnoxious isolation of being one of a few dozen black kids in among three thousand whites. The unrelenting pointlessness of all of it.) Somewhere around ninth grade I had figured out that whatever the hell the Ritenour School District was about, it had almost nothing to do with the road ahead of me, and besides the regular humiliations of public school life, what I remember most from those days was the constantly present impatience I had to be done with it and get on with the plan. That I wasn't entirely sure at the time what the plan might be is the subject for another essay. But I'd been at least sure of one thing: it didn't involve that place, those people, or anything remotely connected to them.

I *might* have participated more appropriately in the whole high school experience had the gym thing not been so onerous. Like big clumsy kids everywhere, physical education class meant daily humiliation—torturous really, probably criminally so. From this point in my life—as a reasonably healthy and happy middle-aged man—figuring out how not to participate in my daily martyrdom seems both a wise as well as a rational course of action. I got good (really good) at getting out of showing up—and as often as I could.

About seven every morning mother would start with the hectoring to "haul your butt out of that bed and get ready for school"— and she better not have to come in there and ask again. We were a "baths before bedtime" family, and as it is for most of us outside the social mainstream, the morning prep is short and sweet. Find something clean, fluff up the GIGANTIC CURLY AFRO that I wore back then, and start the twenty-minute walk to campus. (Which, while we're on the subject, was another reason to stay home. Who wants to walk twenty minutes on a cold morning in suburban St. Louis?)

"Are you up in there?" she'd yell. I didn't own an alarm clock until I went away to college. They were superfluous, as would have been answering her hector—neither question nor request, rather something more akin to a fire alarm or a threat. On the mornings I'd have planned to stay in for the day I might respond with a barely audible moan, but the key was to lie patiently and wait for the full-throttle assault, which came about 7:15, her vocal fists-of-fury aggravated and intensified by the need to compose the daily tardy note— which she most often would have done the night before anyway.

And, yes, of course, I did plan my days off. Team sports and any days that involved distance running were good days to sleep in— and what can I say that hasn't already been said by Ms. Janis Ian (Patroness of High School Losers) about being chosen last for basketball. I'd have to coordinate all of this with test schedules and be mindful of days when the occasional stimulating thing might actually be going on—an obnoxious but fun project in Spanish class. Oh, and since I was president of the Spanish club (talk about nerdly) I had to show up on Tuesdays. Sometimes (often) since lunch could be a hoot and since gym class was always right before lunch—and also since we never had anything at home for lunch except Campbell's tomato and Ritz crackers—I'd stage a miraculous recovery right around 11:15. You learn a lot about spontaneous remission watching daytime television.

But on most mornings I'd be ready when the bedroom door flew open and she was in full psycho-mom mode. First I'd sigh and then: I'd cough. Just one cough—one of those tragic telltale coughs from movies such as *Camille,* with your dying tuberculosis patients.

Bad acting: the hallmark of malingerers everywhere. A couple of coughs and a phlegmy wheeze and I was golden.

Despite how it sounds, my mother was no pushover. Edna Haynes, a tough New York cookie if there ever was one, had placed herself on a train and moved by herself to Missouri to work for the War Department in the 1940s. She'd raised three kids in fine style on the sometimes meager earnings from my dad's auto body shop, and done it all with an elegance and grace befitting someone who'd come of age during the height of the Harlem Renaissance. You can bet if she'd wanted me up and out of that bed, I'd have been up and out.

It was my good luck that she and my father both had been worn to nubbins by my older brother—a hell-raiser and tomcat who hated school and loved a party and whose location from one night to the next was most often a mystery. My younger sister—no saint either—loved all the drama of public school life, so she'd be long gone before mother and I played our performance. I was the undemanding child. Easygoing for the most part, bright and well behaved. The cause for worry I gave them was my shyness and the fact that I couldn't be bothered with people whom I didn't care for (which unfortunately included many of their closest friends, and a significant number of relatives). They were a social people, the Hayneses, and I, frankly, cramped their style. They had no idea what to do with a child who would just as soon be alone with a good book or his favorite record album.

On the subject of performance art, mother was a drama queen long before the phrase came into common currency, and she'd raised a drama queen in me, and like all our fellow thespians, she knew when she'd met her match. I held the trump, having almost died from an asthma attack when I was eight. Do I feel shame about wheezing away those many mornings and taking advantage of the dear woman's potential guilt over sending an asthmatic child to his almost certain death in the pollen-choked Missouri morning? Maybe. A little. About once every decade, I guess.

What all us bad actors know is you give the people what they want. As do all hypochondriacs, mother loved illness of all kind. Our private family argot was laden with the names of mostly imaginary diseases, such as happy legs and touchy stomach and sticky lungs. (I was booted out of my college health service twice for claiming to be plagued by such nonsense.) While some worship health, my mother's philosophy in life was "Everyone has a little something wrong with them." I live to please and was happy to either invent symptoms of my own or to agree to ones that she prompted me to own. Alas, all good scams run their course, and all of us cons are on the schedule for hoisting, the petards packed with explosives and stowed in our sick bays.

On the late March day in question, it didn't start raining ice until midmorning. It's fascinating the way that many hypochondriacs also get hysterical about the weather. Toward the end of her life, mother would sit in that same bungalow, television tuned to the Tropics Report and eye on any hurricanes which just might have a bead on Missouri or north Texas. Geography never being her strong suit, she'd leave frequent updates on the voice mail and reminding me to fill up the bathtub and buy canned tuna. Ice storms, alas, are the deadbeat parents of the weather world: you never know if they're coming, how nasty or nice they'll be when they show up, and they rarely stick around long enough to make too much of a mess; and this particular event had been insignificant enough that I doubt it's recorded in any meteorological record books. Starting after one rush hour and over before the next, it may in fact have been an entirely local weather phenomena, plaguing a few blocks of northwest St. Louis County before petering out over the golf course. (For the record, I am one of those people subject to otherwise unrecorded natural occurrences—have witnessed clear-sky lightning and am frequented often enough by localized earthquakes, often not sensed by people in the adjacent office. I anticipate a volcano will erupt in my Dallas neighborhood any day now.)

Don't get me wrong: I love weather. In a second, I would take one of those storm chaser field trips, where you speed across Kansas and

Oklahoma on the rumor of thunderheads—particularly if I could do it without actually having to be in Oklahoma or Kansas and without having to be around the sort of people who go on trips like that. And my mother loved weather, too, in her own perverse way. Like a cop loves a car chase—it was all about the adrenaline with her—and it didn't take ten inches of snow or Hurricane Katrina to get her motor running. A glaze of ice, and she's on the phone with the National Guard—or in this case, the Breckenridge Hills Police.

The ice fell steadily during *Love of Life,* and I might have actually wheezed or sneezed a bit that morning, but like a lot of teenagers, I lived like a retired person and one leisurely day ran into another. If I'd ever actually been sick it could have been any one of a dozen mornings. (And the woman smoked like a chimney—and you'd have been wheezing and sneezing in that joint too with the windows closed up all the time.) The storm was over long before *Edge of Night* came on, but, like I said, ice is a tricky devil, and, pale-ontologists be damned, it's not the glaciers that alter life on Earth, it's a thin sheet of glare ice on a suburban cul-de-sac.

Or maybe I had vomited, but I've never been much in the throwing up department. (Trust me: I would have used it.) Or my color changed. Or . . . who knows? It's never made sense to me what happened next.

Sometime on the afternoon of the ice storm—perhaps when I napped before *Another World* came on—my mother went into the linen closet and found an old sheet. With a Magic Marker she made a sign, which she then draped over the storm door (in, might I add, an uncharacteristic feat of dexterity and coordination.) The sign read: SEND HELP. CALL POLICE. SICK CHILD.

Meanwhile, back in sick bay, I felt another spontaneous remission coming on, as it often did when my story was coming on. It was a dog's life, I tell you: up and down all day. Up for my story and down for hers. She knew the drill.

Except, on this particular day, after wrapping myself in a blanket and applying the appropriate amount of contortion to my face, I found my access to the TV blocked.

"You don't look so good," she told me.

"I'm a little better now." [Anemic cough]

"You really need to go back to bed."

[Sigh] "Well, maybe watching my show will make me feel better." [Another anemic cough]

"Go back to bed. I'm probably keeping you home tomorrow, too."

What a deal! A twofer—and I hadn't even had to work at it. So despite my suspicion that, as she sometimes would do, she'd obstructed my own viewing in order to watch *Guiding Light* and *Secret Storm*—which were her stories—I complied.

To my credit, when the paramedics woke me up and asked, "How you doing, big guy?" I had the good sense to wheeze my reply. I'd been being schooled daily by a cadre of television's finest actresses on the art of heroic stoicism. Even as they pressed the tongue depressor into my throat, wan but beautiful Andrea Delaney on *Somerset* was being poisoned with cough syrup by her dotty Aunt Rowena—although the real culprit was her other Aunt, Zoe Cannell, played with relish by Broadway veteran Lois Smith. World-class performers, I'm telling you: and like Andrea I stared nobly at the ceiling and assured them I'd be fine, just let me rest and thank you for coming, you're the real heroes here.

I waited for the truck to pull away before marching into the living room to have it out with her.

"What the hell's the matter with you?"

Granted, an unseemly way to address one's mother, but I could see that she too had been chagrined—at first I thought about my hostile remission, although I quickly discovered that our friends from the rescue squad, whether through eye-rolling or sarcasm or both, had made it clear to her that they knew malingering when they saw it and if he were their son his ass would be out there salting the driveway.

In my defense, the ice had all been melted by then—which I could see when I opened the door to find the sheet still draped over the storm door. (Typical of my mother to leave it up there—a second opinion never hurt, after all.) I might have waved it around and growled and kvetched and ripped it to shreds or I might have dissolved into a snottily viscous mound of mortification. I really don't remember. I do remember knowing that the jig was up and that my days as an aided-and-abetted attendance scofflaw had come to an end. From that day forward, if I wanted to miss school I'd just have to become a garden-variety truant. And, hey, I might be a slacker sometimes, but I'll thank you not to lump me in with your delinquents. They were the people I was staying home to avoid.

We have to forgive these people of course—our parents (as well as the gym teachers and other bullies). It isn't so much that they "knew not what they did" as much as it is that life is too short to haul around buckets of useless old crap. What does it matter?

I know what you're saying: she was just an innocent mother trying to protect her children—and that's a lovely thought. For the record, there was very little innocent about this woman. It took me twenty years to figure out that she almost certainly knew what she was doing all along and had figured that the only way to get me graduated was to get me out of her house. That I might actually have been sick, her own perverse twofer. Imagine: sick and shamed into permanent health. It's like Mother's Day and Christmas rolled into one.

I've neglected to mention the reason that the paramedics came was that two of my best friends from school drove by the house (for some reason I can't recall), saw the sign on the door, and went to a neighbor's to make the call. They hadn't believed it any more than the paramedics had, but—as my mother had counted on—ordinary Americans are always pleased to feed into other people's bullshit. Needless to say my last three months in that hellhole of a high school were worse than ever.

But the world has turned as the world does. The bad thing about reading and writing for a living is that while I'm as prone to self-pity as the next person, I am also forced to regularly consider the evidence. Things could have been worse. A lot worse. I had friends back then whom I cherish to this day, and a mother who was there every day to feed into my bullshit and a father to come home and read us both out for doing so. It was they who taught me what was important in life: that signs in the window get results and that cheesy television is the best television. They made me understand how important it was to know what I wanted in life and think long and hard about how to get it and how not to waste my time with things that didn't help me get there. They made sure I knew that they believed I would be just fine in the long run. Primarily I learned that sometimes you just have to stay home and hang out with the people you love—even if they do get on your nerves and change the channel in the middle of your story. I'm pretty sure they didn't teach any of that up at the local tank, although it might have come up on the days I wasn't there.

Do Not Wear Green
on Wednesdays

Quinn Dalton

This means you're gay. And not just in the '80s "uncool" sense of the word (which is bad enough).

If you are a girl, be beautiful; if you are a boy, be athletic; if you are not beautiful or athletic, be invisible.

Except this is not possible for you. At sixteen, ten years of phys ed have made it empirically clear that you are not athletic, and you have fully convinced yourself that you are not beautiful: there is the problem of the big nose, acne, and a certain attitude—call it melodrama—that pervades your body language and speech. All of this feels well beyond your control. You are so hormonally poisoned that no homework assignment, no bad hair day (and there are many), no offhand comment can be small. At the same time, you love attention. You raise your hand in class whenever you know the answer. You try out for school plays. You join art club and drama club, even though you know that these are uncool (see above). You love to hear yourself talk. You wear green on Wednesdays and let Lissa (who is a year older than you and boasts that she sent her college boyfriend to buy tampons for her) kiss you—even *grope* you once—during play practice. You hope this will make people wonder about you but mostly it just makes them roll their eyes. You try wearing black and slicking red glitter gel in your hair. You scratch "The Violent

Femmes" and "The Dead Milkmen" in black ballpoint on your grocery bag book covers. No one interviews you about any of this.

Years later, while you are still in college, you will run into the boy she dated, now a doctoral student. You will go out for dinner and end up on his living room floor, making out. At the moment he strokes your nipple through your bra, you will fight down the near-hysterical desire to ask him to buy you tampons. You will leave soon after that, and you will never see him again.

If you are lucky enough to have a Boyfriend (or Girlfriend), remember that you are lucky.

In spite of your lack of beauty, your passionate nature, and your inability to redeem yourself through invisibility, you have managed to win the affections of a very nice, good-looking boy. He is a year older than you, a senior. He is an athlete, a track runner. He is not loud or suddenly, inexplicably cruel, like other boys. His friends talked him into trying out for the winter one-act plays, and this is how you met. Fortunately, he was not witness to Lissa's boob grab. Fortunately, he never noticed the red glitter gel in your hair, or if he did, he didn't mind.

You have no idea why he likes you; you ask him constantly to explain—this of course, will be one of many reasons why the relationship is doomed to failure (if you don't count the fact that neither of you have been alive for even two decades yet, and will be better off with other people in the long run).

A typical exchange goes like this: "But why?" you wheedle. Then (giving him something to work with): "We're so different."

"Maybe that's why. Opposites attract."

"But," fishing again here—you can't stop yourself, so hungry are you for protestations of adoration from your Boyfriend—so shocked are you to have one at all: "What *specifically* made you like me?"

"You have a good sense of humor. And," he pauses, bites his sweet, handsome lip. "You aren't scared."

So there you have it. You're a funny girl. You're a brave girl. Someone, this one guy, likes these things about you. Maybe in the future, there will be one other boy, a man, even, who will feel the same. You won't find out for nearly a decade.

Later, your Boyfriend will also tell you that you are beautiful, and you will not believe him, and yet you will squeeze out every ounce of affection he has for you, twisting and demanding more, until, exhausted, he will leave for college and write you a letter to break up.

Do not, when Bart Blotten hoots at you as you walk to your desk in English, appear to care.

This demands delicate maneuvering. Not appearing to care is different from ignoring, in which you appear not to hear. But everyone else hears the hooting, including Mr. Holt, your favorite teacher, who is famous for relating college roofing-job stories to American classics such as *The Scarlet Letter* ("Imagine nailing shingles twelve hours a day in 120-degree heat—now that's penance"). Another note on Mr. Holt—he reportedly sat his daughter down and made her drink beer until she threw up in order to teach her about the dangers of drinking. No one has ever confirmed this story with Mr. Holt or with his daughter, which would be easy enough, because she is in the same grade as you. But should she cheerfully deem this story "a fuckload of bullshit" according to the common parlance of the day, you would simply be ruining a good story. You are very likely not the only one who wishes this story were true. You wish your own father, who also worked his way through college doing roofing, would pound beers with you, too, if only to teach you a lesson. But the similarities between your father and Mr. Holt appear to end with the roofing. The point is that no one wants a good story debunked, and you know it is a sign of corruption in your very being that you would even consider risking such a result.

Mr. Holt, at this moment, is pretending to look over his lesson plan, perhaps hunting roofing allusions in the day's assigned reading, but the rest of the class is looking at you. To ignore the hooting would imply that you are the one person in the room who cannot hear yourself being humiliated. So not only would you be pathetic for being picked on, but you would also be borderline institutional for not hearing said hooting.

On the first day this happens, you look straight at Bart Blotten and try to smile your friendliest cheerleader/booster/homecoming queen smile, which is the kind of stretch that might land you a lead role in the spring musical, since you are none of these things, though you dream of lead roles in school plays. You smile and say hello and Bart Blotten collapses against his seatback laughing at you. You hate that you are blushing so deeply your zits are turning purple under your carefully caked on concealer. You go to your seat and are not, from that day forward, able to remember what Mr. Holt talked about, whether it was Emerson, roofing, or beer bingeing, or some combination of the above.

On Day Two and Three, the same scene is repeated. You do not, and will never, know why you have been singled out for this treatment. You have never had a class with Bart Blotten before. You cannot imagine how you might have offended him in any way, except by your mere existence, which is a thought almost too frightening to contemplate.

But your greatest fear, other than the thought that this torment could go on for the rest of the school year (it is now mid-March), is that it will taint you undeniably, and the jig will be up with your Boyfriend. He won't be able to kid himself any longer that the fact that you're funny and brave (brave? Are you *nuts*?) is enough to balance your obvious unpopularity.

You know these incidents are going to get to him somehow. You decide, with the strategic precision that will serve you well in public relations years later, to break the story before someone else can. Frame the issues. Control the mind-set. You freak.

"I don't know what I've done to him," you say, shaking your head and wringing your hands as your Boyfriend pulls on sweats after a track meet. You have come to cheer him on as he runs in circles, which is so fitting since that's pretty much what high school is, and yet, you won't forget, and will later appreciate, the beauty of young men running—could we call them men yet? Most of them will have to register for selective service in a year; some already have—their flat bellies and slim shoulders, their tipped-back foreheads, their hair lifting off their necks, so fragile and powerful.

"I must have done something to piss him off." You say this knowing Bart Blotten's actions have nothing to do with you, other than perhaps a general understanding on his part that you are a good target. But you would not want to admit this. It would be better if you had in fact offended him, and he were exacting some sort of revenge.

"You shouldn't worry about it," your Boyfriend says, pushing his sweaty hair out of his eyes with the palm of his hand, a gesture so graceful, so inherently devoid of worry, you want to cry. *Opposites attract,* you think. You can't believe you and this boy are the same species.

"But what do I do?" You say this because you wish he would suggest something he could do, like beating this idiot up, but you are not in a '50s sock-hop movie, and this is not the kind of guy you're dating. You know instinctively that Bart Blotten would never mistreat you in front of him, not because he feared the ass-kicking he so richly deserves, but because he likes your Boyfriend. Everyone does. In fact, many people wonder why he is dating you, since you are nowhere near as likable; at least this is what one of his friends said to you recently.

"Just ignore it. Really." He smiles encouragingly. He slings his bag over his shoulder. A free man. He could go anywhere in the world and never meet an enemy.

"Oh, please," you sneer. "Just because no one has ever even looked at you funny doesn't mean you have to give me lame advice."

"You know what?" he says, a wrinkle of irritation in his brow. "Maybe it's your attitude that got him going, and he's just trying to egg you on."

You look at the ground, dizzied by this flash of disapproval. Your stomach is a stone on the points of your hips. "You're probably right," you mumble. Your throat tightens; the goal here is to figure out how to stop yourself from sobbing in the next five seconds. The drama queen in you (she is large; she is demanding) wants you to exploit this welling emotion, but the part of you that is genuine (that feeble glow) wants to crawl underneath something and cry until you're limp. You don't want this boy to know how wounded you are from this; he wouldn't understand, and you know this is just one feature of the canyon between you, the very one that will prove unleapable before long.

You pretend to search for something—house keys, courage—in your purse. You bite the inside of your cheek until you can steady yourself. Your Boyfriend is no dummy; he knows you're upset. "Want to stop by Friendly's?" he asks. And so the two of you will lick cold, soft ice-cream cones, slowly, while gazing at each other, and when he drives you home, you will kiss goodbye with still-cold mouths.

On Day Four, the hooting begins as you enter Mr. Holt's class. You walk over to Bart. He grins up at you. You intend to say something asinine, like "What is your problem?" but instead you lift the front of Bart's desk off the floor and say, "Make another sound and I'll roll you onto your back, you fat pig." You smile the cheerleader/booster/homecoming queen smile again, which you perfected in the bathroom mirror the night before, after crying in your room.

You did not plan to lift the desk and threaten Bart. In any case, you are surprised and quite pleased that you *could* lift it. You are even more surprised that he follows your advice and remains silent as you drop his desk to the floor, only a couple of inches, but with a lovely loud thud.

In fact, the thud is the only sound in the classroom as you return to your seat. You are shaking all over, but still trying to smile. It feels like the smile of a frightened baboon, the way they repeatedly bear their teeth. Your legs almost give out beneath you as you sit.

Mr. Holt, who in general is an easygoing guy, cannot ignore this. "Ms. Dalton," he says apologetically. "Maybe you should go to the office."

So, like a six-year-old who has peed herself, you are walking, mortified, to Mr. Pale's office. Mr. Pale has white-blond hair and light-blue eyes and wears short-sleeved shirts in shades of lemon or beige. His name is actually Mr. Pale. He is a former athlete, football, you assume, with shoulders almost as wide as a doorway and freckled cheeks and forearms. He might be a coach as well as the assistant principal; you don't know. You go to football games to watch the marching band.

Mr. Pale sits behind a thick oak desk planted on carpeting of about the same color. He looks up, raises his eyebrows at you in a what-are-you-doing-here expression.

"I threatened Bart Blotten," you tell him from the doorway. Your knees are still jerking and quivering. Your lips seem to want to pull back from your teeth again. *Don't smile,* you think. You bite your bottom lip.

"What?" Mr. Pale asks. His eyebrows appear to be stuck in the "up" position.

"He was teasing me, and—"

"Shut the door and sit down."

You recount the events of the past few days. Mr. Pale listens with each hand cupping the opposite armpit, the jock arm-fold. He looks down at his ham-thick forearms, frowns. You know that some punishment is forthcoming. Worry flutters in your throat like a swallowed fly. You hate it that you even care.

Mr. Pale glances at the window as if he expects something to sail through it. As if he hopes this will happen. It occurs to you that the whole situation is wigging him out—you in a flowered skirt, explaining how you went all David Banner on some kid—and this helps you relax. Mr. Pale pinches his square chin. "Me, I wouldn't do a thing because it sounds like he deserved it."

Amen.

"But that would set a bad example. So we're going to have to go with detention." He stands now, grabs a pen, shakes out his arms, and snaps his wrists, like he's warming up. He seems to have found some traction again, filling out the detention slip.

There will be three, after school. But, Mr. Pale says, you may choose which days to serve them so as not to conflict with your practice schedule for the spring musical. The fact that he knows you are in the spring musical (though have not yet been assigned a role) makes you blush with pleasure. "You're a good girl," he says. "Don't let this guy get to you."

You leave Mr. Pale's office feeling chosen—you've been censured and yet you've been given consideration because you are among the Good Girls. It does not occur to you then, and will not for years later, that had you been born male and had threatened Bart Blotten with exactly the same on-his-back fate, your favorite teacher Mr. Holt might have said, "All right, guys, knock it off. I should put you up on a roof for a week or so. That would calm you down." The class might have laughed at that. No one would have sat silent in shock. The day would have gone forward, unremembered.

But because you are a girl, and not beautiful, and not invisible, and beyond that because you have threatened a boy, you must be contained. Gently, again because of your girlness. You need to be told you are Good so that you will go back to living up to what Good means for a girl: cowed, compliant, silently enraged.

If you can't do well at cool things, do well at something.

For the last two months of school, Bart Blotten leaves you alone. Among your friends, you are the only one who has ever served a detention, which occurs in a classroom in the Vo-Ed wing at the other end of the school from where the college-prep classes meet. This has brought you an unexpected status that is almost as sweet as scoring the role of your heart's desire in the spring musical, *The Sound of Music*. You are Liesl. You are sixteen going on seventeen in life and on stage. This synergy (a word you haven't heard of yet, but one that will plague many a business meeting in your future) seems a signal that you should pursue your dream of becoming an actress. After all, you go through your days playing a constantly evolving character known as You. How much of a leap could it be to Broadway? Your Rolfe is a lanky boy with mile-long arms and legs and huge feet. In his enthusiasm during dance routines he sometimes forgets his own strength, and you've both very nearly broken bones.

One day, your wonderful drama teacher yells "Stop!" from the front row after witnessing another near-tumble from the stage. She is a petite woman with a loud voice, powered by years of herding hundreds and hundreds of kids from tryout to curtain call, two plays a year for twenty years. "OK, Rolfe, here's what you do. When you take her hand before you turn her, don't yank her around. Just cup her fingertips and hold them gently, you know, like an egg."

Everyone laughs at this, including you. Like an egg? It's not really funny; it's just that everyone's so freaked out all of the time, a bunch of shook-up hormone cocktails, trying to learn pre-calc through a haze of sexual desire, trying to walk down a hallway without making complete asses of themselves. The girls are scared they'll bleed through their gym shorts; the boys are scared their dicks will pop up in homeroom. It's a community of fear, and everyone could use a laugh.

But you think about it later, what your drama teacher said. And you know that this is what you hope for, in the simplest terms. To be held gently.

The stop signs with the white border are, in fact, optional.

You will find this out when you've been on the road for a while. Your driver's ed teacher, Mr. Tweezer (this name is funny enough because of his unibrow, but you and your car mates call him Mr. Tosser anyway), would rage against such blasphemy, but let's live in the real world. The trick is to at least slow down enough to see whether anyone else has opted to stop before you roll on through.

Mr. Tweezer finds your play practice schedule irritating because the only free afternoon you have to get your driving hours in is Friday and he probably would rather be tucking into a six-pack as soon as possible after the 3:25 bell to take the edge off his week. Instead, he's dealing with you, who, of all of his student drivers this semester, is the absolute worst, perhaps the worst in his memory. He's nervous before you get out of the parking lot. A quarter-mile from an intersection, he'll scream, "Two car lengths behind the bumper!" before standing on the safety brake. Yes, you are tailgating a bit, but you're in a hurry to get somewhere, anywhere. "Signal! Signal!" he'll yell. "Slow down before the turn!" Stomp, stomp.

Mr. Tweezer does have a point. You will fail your driver's test twice and squeak by with the lowest possible points on the third try. Of course, in New York, when you're working on Broadway, you won't need a car, right? You are convinced of this. There is so much you don't need to know.

Hold the truth gently, like an egg.

Mr. Pale is not actually your assistant principal's name.

You did not lift Bart Blotten's desk and threaten to roll him on his back, though you wish now that you'd thought to do so. His name isn't Bart, either. What actually happened is that you suffered his hooting campaign for days, maybe weeks. Finally, in tears, you begged your mother for guidance, something you would not have considered doing unless you were at your absolute wit's end.

Your mother suggests giving him a greeting card.

"A *what*?" you ask.

"Write him a nice thank-you note. Tell him how much you have enjoyed his friendship." She raises one eyebrow and purses her lips. "Do it in front of the entire class. That'll fix him."

Your mother is a warrior among women; she can be wickedly astute. Generally this does not work in your favor. And yet she seems to be onto something.

"I can't do it," you say. Your pulse races at the mere thought of it.

"If you can sing a solo in front of the whole school, you can do this."

It occurs to you that your mother is talking about real courage, not the Good Girl stuff where you've already memorized the lyrics and had weeks to get the notes right. And not the courage which boys are assumed, even required, to have, which translates into classroom threats or actual fights, to which they are expected to succumb occasionally, because they are male.

You buy a card at Thompson's Drug. It is pink, with silver glitter. It says "Thank You" in large, looping white script across the front. Inside there is a rhyme about friendship and luck and rarity. To this you will add your own brief remarks: "Bart, it's been so fun getting to know you this year. You are really a great guy. I hope you have an awesome summer—can't believe we'll be seniors next year!!!!"

By racing from your second-floor class and not stopping at your locker, you manage to beat Bart to Mr. Holt's class the next day. You place the card on his desk as your classmates file in. You've already told your friends about the card, and word has quickly spread in American Literature, because everyone is very quiet as Bart walks in. He doesn't even look at you as he walks to his desk; perhaps, like bears, he is only interested in you as a moving target. He sees the card, pauses, picks it up, flips it over. There is no writing on the envelope. He sets his books down and settles into his seat. Thoughtfully you have not sealed the envelope, so the card slips easily out.

Ah, the pleasure in watching him read. The darkening of his cheeks and neck, the moment he glares at you, but has not a word, not even a hoot, to offer in retort. And then the moment when you think to raise your fingertips to your lips and blow him a kiss.

Perfect.

Some days afterward, Bart will confront you after class. "Why did you give me that fucking card?" he demands.

A couple of your girlfriends huddle protectively around you, but you feel bulletproof. "Because I really like you Bart. You act a little funny sometimes, but I think you're sweet."

"Leave me the hell alone," he says before stalking away, and here is where you would like to say that you first knew you wanted to be a writer, not an actress, because you realized the power of words. *The power of the pen,* no less. But this would be too neat, and more than a bit trite. Let's just say that you get the first inkling of how to manage people like Bart, stupid bullies who comprise so much of the world's population. He will party hard in college and get some management job by virtue of his maleness and his whiteness, and he will get married and have a couple of kids and vote Republican and sleep well at night. Bastard.

You will always be a bad sleeper, but this will give you time to think, and after a while you will try to figure out a way to turn those thoughts into something more than a five-paragraph theme. Anyway, this will come later, after you give up on the acting.

Your real Driver's Ed teacher was not named Mr. Tweezer, and was probably not a drinker, as you would be if you had his job. But he did not like you; this is the truth, and the one detention you ever served in your high school career resulted after he tried to find you in Spanish class to reschedule your driving practice, and it so happened that you had flicked that period to take an extended lunch with your Boyfriend. Your assistant principal did let you schedule the day of your detention, however, because of play practice.

You did have a Boyfriend, and he was very sweet. You fell in love with him, and he loved you the way boys love what is in front of them. And then you both went on into the rest of your lives.

Live.

You will, if you are lucky. You won't die, like one of the best male athletes in your class—who oddly, was also very smart and nice to everyone—of cancer. Or like the girl in your neighborhood, one year older than you, also of cancer. Or like an older sister of one of your good friends, who was hit dead-on by a drunk driver. And most likely you won't suffer an accident so bad it takes years for you to remember yourself (sometimes in your worst moments you will wish for this to happen, but again, you will be lucky, and it will not). You will not become an alcoholic; you will not do time, you will not lose everything in a bad business deal. You will marry a man who loves you because you are smart and brave and kind—and beautiful. You will have children. You will live, and you will write about it.

WHAT'S UP
WITH THAT HAIR?

Hair Today . . .

John McNally

My grade school photos tell the story:

In kindergarten, my hair is thick and parted on the side; it has been recently cut by a professional—i.e., the corner barber. My expression, however, is that of someone much older—a man who's been told by his accountant that he just lost everything in the stock market.

In first grade, a lock of hair has twisted onto my forehead like Superman's, but my eyes are bloodshot and my shirt is stained from where I've been weeping. I'm in a new school—an *experimental* school that doesn't have any walls inside—and I have just been reprimanded by every teacher for attending the wrong classes. Thus begins my hatred for authority figures.

In second grade, my hair is crooked, cut that very morning by my mother. I've put on a few pounds since my weeping photo. My vest, which looks like something Frankenstein might have worn in one of the later Universal sequels, is too tight. I'm trying to smile, but I'm clearly disturbed by my new appearance.

In third grade, my hair is slicked to the side and behind my ears—slicked with what, I do not know. I'm wearing wire-framed glasses and look as though I might have been the very accountant who informed my kindergarten self that he had lost all of his money. Furthermore, I look pleased to have delivered the news.

In fourth grade, I've gained a ton of weight, and my long hair curls out in every possible direction. I'm laughing; my eyes are gleaming. If I wasn't nine years old, you'd think I was enjoying the first day of a bender. (Oh yeah. One more thing. I appear to be growing breasts. *That's* how much weight I've gained.)

In fifth grade, I've returned to looking somber, no smile, but it's clear I'm amused by the situation I'm in. This is the fifth school I've attended in five years, and I'm starting to learn irony. My hair, flat once again, has more bulk than ever before.

In sixth grade, I have no control over my hair. It juts out at odd directions, and the beauty school trainee who cut it gave me too-high bangs. I'm laughing—God only knows why.

In seventh grade, I'm fatter than I've ever been. Whatever problems my hair is having is a moot point beside my weight. My future as a security guard is looking frighteningly more promising.

In eighth grade, my hair is a sculpture—thick and wavy—kept in place with a can's worth of Aqua Net. If someone were to come near me with a cigarette, I'd go up in flames. The good news is, I'm starting to slim down, and the blue leisure suit is looking pretty sweet on me.

And so it goes. Fat one year, not quite as fat the next. Hair parted, hair feathered, hair crooked, hair left to its own volition. In grade school, I was like some kind of lycanthrope that could never quite make the final transformation from man to beast. My body would get a stage or two into the metamorphosis and then pause before returning to some previous incarnation, or, rather, some new, mutated version of my original self.

But then came high school. Something profound happened. I became cool—or, perhaps more accurately, the *potential* for cool descended upon me. It didn't happen overnight, but it felt as though it had: one year, I was a 210-pound, five-foot-four seventh-grader; two years later, I was a 125-pound, five-foot-eleven (and still growing) freshman in high school. I was, for all practical purposes, a different person. Girls not only liked me, they pursued me. Not the girls who had known me as a smart-ass fatso; those girls didn't know what the hell to make of me and therefore kept their distance. To them, I was probably a genetic mutant, a freak show act, as appalling as naked conjoined twins doing cartwheels across a splintery stage. But those other girls—girls I would have pined for in grade school, girls who didn't know the fat me—began flirting with me. They sometimes whispered startling things in my ear. It was every fat boy's dream, and I should have wallowed in it. My life, I realize now, could have been a scene right out of Bob Guccione's movie *Caligula*. It was 1979, the tail end of the sexual revolution—before herpes, before AIDS. No one was afraid of sex. Even Jimmy Carter had confessed to *Playboy* that he had lust in his heart. True, I was only thirteen years old, and I would have been happy with a serious make-out session in the back of some older girl's Nova, but my mind often ran rampant with more erotic (and unlikely) scenarios. Sex on a roller coaster. Sex at a Meat Loaf concert. For all practical purposes I should have been cool, but there was a problem: I had been uncool for so long that I had no idea how to handle it. I was like the guy who lives in a school bus until he wins the Lotto. We all know this story. This guy—the Lotto winner—he doesn't know how to handle his newfound wealth, and so he goes a little crazy, indulging every possible vice while annoying everyone who comes into contact with him. I was the fat-to-skinny version of his rags-to-riches. What I know now, that being cool has more to do with attitude than looks, was lost on me at thirteen. In truth, I was cooler as a fat, ironic kid who made snide comments about teachers during class than I was as a skinny kid who wasn't sure how to respond to girls.

It's not easy to admit, but I had all kinds of built-up anger, too, and it came out in fits and starts.

When Juan Gonzalez, a classmate from one of my many former grade schools, came up to me during lunch and said, "You used to be fat, didn't you?" I pulled the straw from my milkshake, pulled it back with my teeth, and then let it go. A glob of shake hit Juan square in the face. He screamed as though I'd flung battery acid at him and then he took off running, never to speak to me again.

One day in the locker room, I made fun of another boy's shoes. "What kind of *guy* wears heels like that? Hey, check out Joey's shoes! He wears *heels*!" And then I saw that only one of his shoes had a heel. The heel was there to compensate for the fact that one of his legs was significantly longer than the other leg. Later, out of earshot, I apologized to him, but he wouldn't even look at me. He, too, never spoke to me again.

In all fairness, I even tortured my friends. Between classes, upon removing my gym bag from my locker, I swung it around a few times, building momentum, until I aimed it at Larry's gut. "Ugh!" he coughed. He bent over and held his stomach. The bottom of the bag had been weighted down with a huge Master lock. "Hey, sorry," I said without the least bit of remorse in my voice. "Let's go." Larry did, in fact, continue to talk to me, but he was less cool than I was, so the hierarchy remained in place.

I'm not proud of any of these moments, but they are what they are: an angry fat kid trapped inside the body of a skinny kid. Eventually, the anger dissipated. What replaced it was a pathological shyness around girls. Certain girls, at least. Girls I wanted to date but couldn't get up the nerve to ask out.

Take Sara. She was in my Dramatic Arts class, and I couldn't help myself: I stared at her. She was big-boned in a way that was not a euphemism for being overweight. At sixteen, she had already bloomed into full womanhood, and she carried herself with confidence: an adult among children. While other girls got perms that didn't complement the size of their heads or that made them look like toy poodles, Sara was living, breathing proof that a perm could not only work but could be sexy as well. She was also one of the very few girls in my school to understand the knee-weakening power of cleavage. I developed a kind of apnea that year, taking quick, unexpected breaths each time I saw her in a low-cut blouse, that spillage of flesh and temptation. Her cleavage spoke to me in a religious way, the way Pentecostals must feel when they begin speaking in tongues. One day in the library, I caught sight of Sara's cleavage. I recognized whose it was and, without looking up take in the whole of her, savored it. Sara was leaning on the counter, waiting for help, and I was around the counter's corner, staring. When I finally did peek up, Sara was already looking into my eyes and smiling. She had been watching me watch her cleavage. I experienced a quick intake of breath, my hormonal apnea, and then I looked away. I pined for Sara. She haunted the rest of my school day, she haunted my after-school activities, but most of all she haunted my nights.

A few weeks later, my cousin Ann, who was one year older, called to tell me that Sara liked me and wanted me to ask her to Homecoming. My cousin never called, and so my mother, who waited downstairs for me, was suspicious. I knew that when the conversation was over, I would have to answer a litany of questions: *What did Ann want? Why was she calling?* My mother liked my cousin, but my mother was also attuned to the nuances of our daily lives. It would be more curiosity than interrogation, but even as I spoke to my cousin, I was trying to come up with answers that would satisfy my mother and keep her from asking more questions. What my cousin wanted to know—her reason for calling—was if I liked Sara.

Well? Do you?

Sure, I said. She's okay. What do you mean by "like"?

You know, she said. Do you *like* her? Do you think she's *cute*?

I guess so, I said. I mean, there are other cute girls, too. She's okay. Sure.

Just okay? She says you're always looking at her.

That's crazy, I said. Looking at her? I laughed.

Well, my cousin said, what do you think? Do you want to ask her to homecoming?

I don't know, I said. Maybe. Let me think about it.

Of course, I never asked Sara to homecoming. In fact, I made sure not to even look at her again, either. I had to push all of her— her wild permed hair, her cleavage—far from my mind. And I could tell that she was angry with me now; she radiated annoyance when I walked into my Dramatic Arts class. I didn't have to look at her; I could *feel* it. I spent homecoming day at Ford City's movie theater. I paid for the first movie, then sneaked into the next two. I went alone, because that's what lonely guys did: they went to movies while everyone else was out having fun.

The good news was, my hair had never looked better. For those first two years of high school, my coif put up no arguments. By and large, I was able to tame it using a hair dryer and without having to resort to various sprays. I kept it not too long and not too short. Mostly, I wore it parted in the middle. These were the good years for me and my hair, the salad days. But then something happened. Between my sophomore and junior year, a latent gene must have awoken. It occurred after a haircut. For some reason, I was unable to part my hair in the middle anymore. It just didn't work. The beautician suggested combing it straight back. It was a new look—and, in all honesty, it didn't look bad (really, it didn't)—so I casually agreed to it. Little did I realize that I would never be able to part my hair down the middle again—ever! My parting days were over. My hair, which had struggled for control throughout all of grammar school, had laid low for the first two years of high school, only to return with a master plan that would finally put an end to this business of trying to be cool.

Concurrent to this, I began wooing the girl who would later be my first real girlfriend. *Beckie.* By the spring of my junior year, we were a couple. I won't go into great detail—there are, after all, few things more embarrassing than high school romance—but I fell into what I was convinced was love. Oh, yes, we had what we called "our song"—the Little River Band's "Take It Easy on Me." And, yes, we had found in each other those physical idiosyncrasies that we liked to wonder over. For me, it was her nose. It was a puggish nose with no discernable cartilage, and so I liked to press it down with my thumb until it was almost flat against her face. "That doesn't hurt?" I'd ask. "Nope," she'd say. For her, it was my, well, it was my hair. "My stud," she would say, rubbing her fingers through it. "Look at your studly *hairdo.*" We were, I thought, a couple for the ages.

One day, while I was sitting at my kitchen table, Beckie walked behind me to mess with my hair. My mother was cooking dinner. The fluorescent lights were bright, unforgiving. I could tell by the way Beckie was touching my hair that it was not out of affection. She had noticed something on my crown.

"How cute," she said.

"What?"

"There's a tiny bald spot here," she said.

"*What?* No there's not."

"Mrs. McNally," she said. "Come here. Look."

My mother walked over, next to Beckie, and parted the hair on my crown. (For the record, my mother was the least sentimental person I have ever known.) "She's right," my mother said. "You've got a bald spot."

I had spent my entire life pushing aside any and all empirical evidence that confronted me. My father was bald; my brother was going bald; a few uncles on my mother's side were bald. I was convinced, however, that I would not go bald. I'd always had hair—lots of it!—and so the idea of *not* having hair seemed preposterous. I'm sure this is how rich people think before losing all their money in a bad investment. *I'll never be poor!* they think, and then, a few years later, they're jumping from the top floor of the tallest building in town.

"Quit touching it," I said, shrugging everyone's fingers away. "You'll only make it worse."

After the bald spot, which was probably no bigger than a dime, had been revealed, there was no going back: it would only get bigger. Beckie and I began to argue, too. We never mentioned the bald spot again, but it had come between us. If Beckie wanted to go one place, I wanted to go another. If I liked a new song, she didn't. One night, while taking a walk, she had mentioned how it might be interesting to date someone of another race.

I was stunned—not that she would be interested in dating someone of another race but that she would be interested in dating someone of *any* race, me being the exception. Had she forgotten that we were still dating? The idea that one day we wouldn't be dating had never crossed my mind. Instead of articulating my fears, I blurted out, "What are you thinking?" to which she replied, "Oh, I see, you're a racist!"

"No, I'm not," I yelled, but she wouldn't listen to what else I had to say.

"I want to go home," she said. "I never would have thought you were a racist."

The end came a few weeks later, in the front seat of my mother's Ford LTD, in the parking lot of R&D's, a grim little ice-cream shop where we often went for milkshakes. I had already bought us the shakes when she finally broached the subject. Even as she gave her reasons for ending it, she absently picked lint off my shirt and straightened it with her palm. I realize now how to interpret these gestures, that I was being cleaned up before being sent out into the world. Many years later, when my first wife began picking lint from my shirt and straightening it with her palm, I knew we didn't have much longer together.

I spent my post-Beckie days in a funk. It was August, before the start of my senior year. A new movie had just come out: *Fast Times at Ridgemont High.* No movie spoke to me more than this one. I would stay in the theater after it had ended and then watch it a second, sometimes a third time. I returned to it, day after day, until I literally ran out of money. One afternoon, I was short a dime and stood outside the movie theater, asking if anyone could spare some change. I was sixteen years old, going bald, and begging for money. Who knew the fall would come this fast, this hard?

On the day of my senior picture, I couldn't get my hair to do what I wanted it to do. It was too poofy, too odd-looking. I wanted to stay home from school, but my mother wouldn't have it. "Not for your hair," she said. I showed up late, miserable. In my photo, I'm trying to smile, but you could see it in my eyes: I'm depressed. My hair, on the other hand, is clearly enjoying this victorious moment. It is a crazy red pompadour, about four inches too high and absurdly wavy, not at all a look I would have consciously given myself. Who, except for a bottom-rung Elvis impersonator, would have?

As I write this, I am forty years old and, by any objective and honest account, bald. I eventually had to admit defeat, as do all bald guys, except for those few who try comb-overs or pay for plugs. I refused to go that route. I wore baseball caps for years—first to hide the baldness, then out of mere habit. Without the cap, I sometimes felt as though I were missing a limb; I would reach up to adjust it only to discover that I was not wearing one. It would never grow back on its own volition, my hair. I can't help imagining an alternative universe, one where Beckie never noticed the dime-sized spot on the crown of my head. Perhaps if the spot had gone unnoticed, it never would have gained the confidence to spread, to eradicate. But sometimes I suspect the baldness didn't start on that seemingly fateful day, that it began years earlier with a flickering premonition. When I look back at my kindergarten photo, that gloomy-faced boy with the big ears, I can't help but wonder if I was having a vision that very morning, a vision not of love lost or of financial ruin, but of hair, *my* hair. Had I already seen its future—or, rather, its grim lack thereof? It's hard to believe that he's not seeing something that will later test his mettle. When I stare into that little boy's eyes, I don't envy him much, certainly not the next several years of his life, but I do envy him his hair—every last shimmering strand.

A Herstory of Hair

AIMEE NEZHUKUMATATHIL

I gasp at all the clear bottles and tubes and bright-colored labels. I think my heart races a bit more. I haven't been in this aisle for years. Certainly not for more than two minutes in passing. My husband and I are in the drugstore, looking for a specific hair gel for my mother, who is visiting from Florida and has forgotten her own. My husband picks a sleek metal tube off the shelf: *Sebastian Potion Nine.* He examines it, scrunches up his nose, and shakes his head. I hold my breath.

"Potion? Sounds like voodoo. What *are* all these bottles? Who needs all this stuff?"

I fiddle with my purse zipper, like I'm distracted and not paying attention, but in truth, this aisle makes me giddy. A little nervous. Oh, I barely put anything in my hair *now*—don't have time to fuss on that anyway—but I spent an embarrassing amount of time in aisles just like this one during my teenage years. When other girls were sneaking around after school with boys or experimenting with cigarettes, I—I was browsing the hair product aisle for gels, mousses, tonics, and yes, even potions. We found the hair gel my mom wanted, and left the store in less than ten minutes, including standing in line at the cashier, which is record timing that I'm pretty proud of, considering I grew up tortured and obsessed over my hair.

Exhibit A: *Bangs Overload*

At one point, I think I had the same amount of hair in the front of my face (which is to say, anything in *front* of my ears) cut into wide, wavy bangs as the entire back of my head (anything behind my ears). I am twelve. The sketchy lady from Fantastic Sam's (who smoked while she cut my hair) divided my hair laterally and made the first half all bangs, the back half, a bizarro she-mullet. This lady teaches me how to use a curling iron. "Yous gotta pouf it, hon. Pouf it!" While she twists and clamps a section of my shelf of slightly damp bangs up off my head a good three inches, she takes a giant can of Aqua Net hairspray and sprays the whole thing—iron and all. My hair steams and sizzles into a tiny cloud over my head and somehow this feels satisfying to me. I watch her very carefully so I can recreate this on Friday nights when I stay home with my family and watch *America's Funniest Home Videos.* Unfortunately, my mother would not let me use any hair product or let me buy hairspray, so I just "poufed" it with a curling iron (the only hair indulgence she let me have that year) and try not to move my head too much so it stays put.

"Geez, whatcha got your hair done up for," my sister asks, snacking on gummy bears beside me on the couch.

"It's Friday! It's just in case." I cross my arms in front of me and sigh as if she should have already known the answer. But we both know there is no "just in case." There's not even a "Maybe, just maybe." There is only the satisfaction of sitting there, my hair *done*—with a full dark pouf high atop my head, trying not to show that I am enjoying watching television with my parents after all, instead of not being allowed to watch a PG-13 movie downtown with the rest of my friends.

Exhibit B: *Asian Shirley Temple*

I am thirteen and toweling off from my shower in my home, a mental institution in western New York. No, I'm not a patient. My mother is a psychiatrist and so for four years—those oh-so-crucial puberty years—we lived in one of the giant Doctor's Quarters—a row of three hefty brick houses atop the hill of the Gowanda Psychiatric Center in this tiny town in western New York. I am in a hurry to meet my friend Mary Esther at the park downtown for ice cream and because of the idea: There Might Be Boys There. Specifically, Jeremy and Billy from seventh-grade home room. I have my hand on the doorknob when I catch a glimpse of myself in the half fogged-up mirror. Huh? I squeak-squeak and rub the mirror in circles for a better view. I remember I audibly gasped. There they were, as if I shampooed them *in* somehow—*pop!*—curls. What once was just silky waves and bounce was now bona fide curl. I'm talking *ringlets*.

I swept my hand over the damp curls in disbelief. All I did was comb out the messy tangle and let it air-dry. I thought of all the commercials for hair product that were so common in the mid-eighties: the fluorescent colors of Dep hair gel; L'Oreal, in their jaunty red, yellow, and blue Mondrianesque color block-designed bottles; and who could forget the purple mystique of the Aussie Hair Care line—from Australia (so *exotic*)—where every gel and spritz spray smelled like grape Kool-Aid.

My mother would *have* to relent now, wouldn't she? Up until that day my curls appeared, I was forbidden to use any sort of hair product. My Filipina mother, perhaps trying to exert some control over her American-born daughter in a teenage world she didn't understand, always had the most ridiculous rules, like, *No reading magazines close to dinnertime! No Spaghettio's or mac 'n' cheese! No phone calls after dinner! No blowing bubble-gum bubbles!* But now I had curls. I needed to *style* the curls. You couldn't just yank up your curls into a giant ponytail. That would never do. Remember, this was the eighties. Curls were all about being *scrunched* in gels, mousse, and styling spray. Some girls from gym class styled their hair in the locker rooms using all three. And no matter what, your bangs *had* to stand taller than your poufiest curl. In short, if you had curls in the eighties, you needed hair product. Period. I changed into clothes as quickly as possible and ran down the stairs to show my hair to my mother, who was cooking breakfast. After my first suggestion of what I wanted to buy at the drugstore, it was clear my mother was not going to budge.

"But *why not*, Mommmm?" I kicked at the legs of the wooden dining table while she chopped tomatoes.

"Hairspray dries your hair too much. In two years, you will have no hair. No more use for hairspray! You too young for hairspray!" Chop-chop. Chop. She slid the diced tomatoes into the omelet that was already sizzling on the stove.

She wasn't changing her mind, so I went to school with a small poodling of hair and returned in the afternoon to brush out the over four-inch-high confection of bangs I secretly constructed before my mother returned home. I would sneak free sprays in the junior high girls' bathrooms from Mary Esther, she of the cute mini-cans of aerosol Aqua Net in her giant purse. Giant purses were something I was also inexplicably banned from using, all the way through high school, actually. *No reason for a big purse. Big purse too dangerous. Too sneaky.* I remember longing to be able one day have a bold, roomy purse to hold—to hold . . . what does a thirteen-year-old need a gee-normous purse for anyway? Contraband bubble gum? Six flavors of lip gloss? No, no, and nope: the answer is simple—more hair products.

Exhibit C: *The Rhythm Nation Years*

In six hundred or so years of Nezhukumatathils, not a one had ever attended a junior high dance, so you can imagine how imperative it was that I choose the correct hairdo and outfit for the occasion. I am fourteen. In eighth grade, this involved fuschia acid-washed jeans and matching jean jacket, turquoise polo shirt with the collar "popped" up, and one pair of fuschia slouch socks worn *over* a pair of turquoise slouch socks, both of which enveloped the hem of my pinned jeans (for the layered look) and then ever-so-artfully, um, slouched and set into pink "LA Gear" high-top shoes. Yes, high-tops. Yes, pink. Hair was set into a supertight French braid, with the end slithering down my back and tied off with a pink bow.

This was the "Summer in Winter" dance, though, according to my friend Candy, "No one but *Seniors* will be wearing bikini tops and grass skirts, so don't worry." Bikini tops? That was a whole other arena of shame and angst—days of sitting on my beloved canopy bed studying the tiny triangle pieces of cloth that passed as my training bra, wondering when I would actually grow into a bona fide cup. Cup, cup—the word still holds so much pride for me since the first time I was ever in a velvety red fitting room at Victoria's Secret in college. A lanky, heavily perfumed and powdered sales associate with a gold tape measure slung around her neck like a circus snake eyed my chest and started guessing actual letters—letters that did not involve the letter *A*—and oh how I showed my appreciation with my checkbook that afternoon and left the store swinging the signature pink shopping bag.

But the dance. And more important: the *hair*! Since this was not a formal dance like Homecoming, no one our age really had official dates and so no one made hair appointments downtown at Positively Mane Street. I didn't have my license yet and most of my spare time (when I wasn't writing reports or finishing up art projects) was spent taping all the Janet Jackson videos off MTV that I could find and trying to re-create her dance moves in the living room while my parents were at work at the hospital. One behind-the-scenes feature of her famous "Rhythm Nation" video-mini-movie depicted the long hours spent rehearsing all the complicated choreography. During practice, Janet wore her hair in a French braid as she popped and locked and jammed for "peace, love, and unity!" No more cutesy, pudgy, "Let's Wait Awhile" Janet Jackson. This whippy braid was the serious, military-style, *I'm going to dance for Freedom*

Miss Jackson. For performances, Janet wore a black baseball hat and a low ponytail. But I preferred her "rehearsal look"—the way the braid whipped my back when I danced to Beastie Boys and Bon Jovi with Mary Esther and my other girlfriends. It was 1988: if Janet Jackson wore it, it was automatically cool. I rocked a tight French braid for all the school dances that year. It was so unyielding, my scalp actually *hurt* when I unwove the braid at night because the strands were pulled so taut from my face. I don't think I need to mention that I danced with exactly *zero* boys that year.

It occurs to me that much of my drastic hairstyle changes during my teen years were a direct result of watching too much MTV. Other hairdos I painfully and painstakingly tried to imitate include Madonna's jaunty cropped hair from the "Papa Don't Preach" video, Very-High-and-Overly-Sprayed Bangs with long crimped, teased hair from the all-girl rock band the Bangles, and a short little pageboy blunt cut like Debbie Gibson. I am amazed that I was able to maintain an A average considering the hours spent watching (and recording and rewinding!) all those music videos.

Exhibit D: *Masquerade*

Why did my art teachers always insist on creating papier-mâché masks in high school? Every year we did this, from ninth to twelfth grade. This process involved smearing Vaseline all over our faces, including our eyebrows, and up into our hairlines to ensure that bits of plaster of Paris did not stick to our faces. Another classmate would then delicately (or not so delicately) lay strips of papier-mâché over our features while we lay across a table like a fresh admittance to the county morgue. We would just wait for the plaster-soaked strips to dry and harden to the contours of our face. The worst part was that we couldn't talk or even laugh. And if our nose itched, we could just forget it.

After the hardened mask was lifted off and set aside to later decorate in sequins and feathers and acrylic paints, there would be the inevitable leftover Vaseline that you could never fully wash (not from the school bathroom sinks and standard issue soap, anyway) out of your hairline—which, by the end of the school day, fully spread like a bad flea/tick treatment to the whole rest of your head. If you had longer than shoulder-length hair (which, of course, I did), all that Vaseline stayed in your hair for a good week.

You could tell when the Unit on Masks took place that semester: all these extra greasy-headed kids with bits of plaster flecked in their eyelashes and eyebrows and on the chins of the guys who, bless them, already sported thick, trappy beards.

The annual school spelling bee for that year also happened to take place during the week of mask making. That week, if I wasn't reading the packet of possible spelling words at the breakfast table, I was making sketches of the mask I had hoped to create—a loud and vivacious flamingo. I was ready—before I knew it, I was a part of the final ten contestants who were ushered in front of a portable bulletin board as a backdrop for the final round since it was being filmed and broadcast on local access television. Soon, it was down to the final three students—one of which was also my younger sister who, on the few times I looked over at her, was smiling and looking straight ahead, her hair pulled into a loose and simple ponytail. You could say I was distracted by her easy smile, or was still thinking about my flamingo design, but the worst part of the whole ordeal was not that I misspelled a word, but my sister's facial expression as she turned to look at me when the announcer solemnly said, "I'm sorry. That is incorrect." My sister's face went from pity, to horror, to being inexplicably amused. I was seething. How could she laugh at my losing? And after we had helped each other study for the bee! Before I left the stage, she whispered, "Aimee, your *hair!*" and pointed to the bulletin board. There, on the wall of bright construction paper, was a giant corolla of a grease stain. During the final rounds, I had unknowingly been leaning the back of my head against the bulletin board and over the course of the competition, the circle of grease was growing and growing into a dark halo around my head. For the entire school to see. And for all the grandparents and parents watching at home on cable access TV. My sister went on to win. And if that wasn't enough injustice, they replayed the spelling bee at various times for the rest of the month. If no one was around, I'd watch in horror the greasy shadow grow around my head. Otherwise, I'd run upstairs to my bedroom and pout and, sometimes, I'd jump in the shower, just to wash my hair for good measure. But every time the spelling bee replayed, my mother would call her friends and tell them to watch, too. She never tired of watching her two daughters duke it out, and her friends indulged her. No one at home mentioned the stain I left on the bulletin board, but I know there were meaningful glances exchanged between my parents. Sometimes I would hear my mom talk in Tagalog to her Filipina friends on the phone and I couldn't understand what she said, but I know it *had* to be about the grease stain. How could they *not* ask her about it? Perhaps even giggles were stifled. I'll never know.

Later that year, The Incident involving homemade mayonnaise and oatmeal scalp masque for deep cleaning and conditioning. We will not, cannot speak of this here. A hamster was involved. There—I've said too much already.

Exhibit E: *In Which the Heroine Travels to a Faraway Land and Eats Ice Cream*

I want to tell you of the years spent blow-drying, ironing, pulling, and tugging my hair to straighten it out. The hours spent examining my hair in the back with a handheld mirror, wondering what color I should dye it to turn lighter than its natural darkest brown. Anything I could do to it to prevent total strangers from asking me, "What *are* you?" Anything to look more like Sara, Americ, Debby, Stephanie, Jennifer—anyone but me. I want to tell you of the first time I visited my grandmother in India during monsoon season and she (fresh from a bath) had joined me on the couch where I was reading and pouting because I was being eaten alive by mosquitoes.

Until then, I had never seen my grandmother wear anything but a solemn long braid down her back or wound into a low knot at the base of her head. But when she sat down next to me, I saw her hair in all its glory for the first time *ever*—long, dark, luxurious curls whipped into neat ringlets. My father had never told me about this, even when he heard my surprise and tirade about hair gel the day my hair suddenly turned curly. This tiny woman that I saw mainly through pictures that were sent to us in mysterious red, white, and blue envelopes—this woman in flesh and bone and soft brown skin—this woman has the *same* hair as me. Until that moment, I had never seen anyone with the same texture of hair as me—no model in a magazine, no one from school, even my father—almost completely bald, and my mother—thick wavy hair to be sure, but no curls. Not even my younger sister (who is sometimes mistaken for my twin) has hair like me. I was speechless. My grandmother must have been uncomfortable with my staring.

"What is wrong? Your mouth is open. Too much mosquito?"

"Too much mosquito?" she repeated.

I closed my mouth and shook my head. "Not too many mosquitoes. Your hair—it's, it's . . . beautiful."

My grandmother smiled, the only time I ever saw her embarrassed, and quickly changed the subject, "But you have hair like this too, no? Let's go get some ice cream. Too hot to be inside today." When she walked away to summon the driver, I saw her smiling as she straightened out her turquoise sari.

I want to tell you that my hair obsession stopped that day, because it did. I now use exactly one hair product to style my hair—a lightweight curl-shaper gel just to keep the frizz in check. I want to tell you that there in India is where I made peace with my hair, but that would be too easy. Of course one could say that as I grew older, my focus turned to other things—a house, a husband, a geriatric dachshund. But I know lots of women my age who still obsess over their hair. I know I could easily be one of them.

Back inside the restaurant, the cool air-conditioning meant relief, even for a few moments. No more slapping my legs for mosquitoes. As long as we were here, I intended on eating my ice cream as slo-o-o-o-wly as possible, since the monsoon had brought a power outage at Grandma's home in the village. No power equals no fan. No fan equals over seventy mosquito bites from head to toe. I wish I were exaggerating. I scanned the dessert menu and ordered one scoop of vanilla, one scoop of mango. Such cold, creamy deliciousness would surely take my mind off the calamine and warm bites on my arms. Across the table, my grandmother didn't even open her menu. Again she smiled, looked at the waiter and simply said, "I'll have the same."

THE
OUTSIDERS

Without a Word

ZELDA LOCKHART

When I have dreams about my siblings, they are as I last remember them—slender teenagers and chubby-cheeked toddlers. When I cover their cryptic eyes in photos, our noses and smiles are the same.

We lived on a West Side city street in St. Louis, Missouri—a middle-class neighborhood in the 1970s. Some houses were wooden; others, like ours, were brick, and held the secrets of arguing parents much tighter than a house of wood. A chain-link fence, and orders to play in the yard unless Mama was home, extended the secrecy perimeter right to the city sidewalk. Through our windows, the glare of our nucleus could be seen from the street—the TV exemplified American families, giving me some faulty comparison for my own life.

A house of eight children, we lived like puppies in a pen, having only each other's company as solace from the things we heard inside our house, but did not speak of. At night, my parents were the nocturnal stimulants for our nightmares—their physical fights, the sound of fist on muscle similar to the sound of punching a pillow. I learned to sleep past my fears, one ear cocked for tragedy.

My mother sometimes slipped into the closet to get away from my father while my sisters and I slept, and I dreamed about her wearing the tights that I lost weeks ago, dreamed about her sitting in the dark and talking to the mouse that I found in my shoe the night before.

I was taught through witnessing events, and watching my parents' reactions to those events, to forget anything that occurred between the space of my waistline and my thighs—to disconnect the responses of my "thing" from my brain. Before adolescence occurred, I had already lost context for my vagina, my period, and physical attraction.

One time when I was nine, my father took my ten-year-old sister and me to visit his relatives in Jackson, Mississippi. To save space, we slept together in one bed, but he slipped his shorts off and made me touch him. The rest is a blur. I remember waking that night and wishing my sister was on the same side of the big brown body as me. The next morning I refused to eat my aunt's grits and sausage, and my father said I was acting ignorant, like I didn't have any home training.

I made a study of my father and my gay brother's cause-and-effect relationship of few words and lots of action.

My brother LaVenson was six years older than me and played every instrument he touched, and sang as if every note were to save his life. He danced, always with a kickball change, shaved his legs, flicked his head and hands, all despite the picture of a man that my father tried to carve on his back with a leather belt.

LaVenson's passion for the flute, a sissy instrument as my father called it, was my mother's favorite of all the sounds on earth. My brother was my mother's secret favorite child, firstborn who remained loyal to her despite all he had seen of her life—eighteen years of whippings that reminded him to keep his mouth shut. Bruised and unprotected, he moved to New York City when he turned nineteen and left the rest of our brood behind. That fall I entered high school, two fortunate bus rides beyond my neighborhood.

Jovan Musk, lotion. It took seven trips to the mall before I figured out Miss H's aphrodisiac scent. She directed the high school gospel choir, a woman who sang with passion, and made me believe whatever she believed about Jesus. All school year I found reasons to pass Miss H's classroom and offer help with setting up chairs and putting away chairs. Over the summer, I bought myself some Jovan Musk Lotion, and when school resumed, I joined the school's gospel choir, just as it was being kicked off campus for becoming a magnet for, as the principal put it, "Funny People."

In the confusion of transitioning to a community choir, some folks slid past auditions, and I was one of them. I remembered my aunt's declaration at church, that I looked like one of the blind mice, and sounded like Little Bo Peep. Flamboyant black men who reminded me of my brother and fag-hag teen girls surrounded me in the gospel choir. I felt like I belonged.

My time in the choir spanned high school, but in teen years, seemed many years long, full of the dark days of my urban adolescence. Miss H's boyfriend, a fellow teacher, was brutally gunned down, Rick James and Teena Marie parted ways, and the owner of Billy's walk-up store caught a bullet in the back and left the first bloodstain and chalk line on our street. Like my peers, I found redemption from it all in love.

I forgot all about Miss H when I met Ciretta. We were both goofy, slightly rejected, background altos. We both had accelerated our academics and only had to check in to homeroom each day before catching a city bus and heading downtown to our jobs on separate floors of Mercantile Bank Tower. Having never been in love before, I didn't know better than to make promises. "We'll always be friends." From that point forward, my life was all Ciretta—the bank, the choir, and the phone.

Every time the phone rang, my mother yelled up the stairs, "It's that damned Ciretta." Her tone accused me of some sin I couldn't identify from watching the Technicolor *Ten Commandments*. Ciretta's voice took me away from the fire-and-brimstone sermons of my pastor, from the memory of my teen cousin in his casket, makeup caked in the bullet hole in his forehead, away from my mother and father's fights, cussing, crying, falling in and out of doors like fighting dogs. Ciretta and I went about the business of intertwining ourselves tightly, leaving no spaces for the world around us to enter.

Senior year we decided we would get Ciretta's grandmother to make us similar dresses—hers blue and mine pink—and that we would attend the prom together. In my head and heart, she was my girlfriend, a truth neither of us spoke, but a truth we had lived for three years. The adult queer men in the choir strongly suggested that two of them come with us as fake dates. Somewhere deep inside of my conscious, in the place where the brain stores all pre-revelatory knowledge, I knew what our friends feared, but Ciretta and I stayed our course without words to acknowledge what we were doing.

My brother came home the weekend before the prom and sang at our church. His mouth hung wide open without shame, and I admired him for his vulnerability. Afterward, he came with my gospel choir group to sing in a church in East St. Louis. I was excited to show him that I could sing out the same way, as long as I was insulated by the other altos, the tenors, and sopranos. That night he disappeared into the East St. Louis night life with the adult men of our choir, and I realized that he lived open and free in a way that I longed to.

The night before the prom, Ciretta and I snuck out of our sleepover and went to a house party that to our surprise was at my uncle's new apartment. Once I realized the unspoken pact that I keep his secret of alcohol, marijuana, and crap games, and he keeps my secret, then I relaxed, got drunk and Ciretta and I laughed our way to her bed at two in the morning.

I didn't remember us getting undressed, but remembered that the flesh of my bare arm across the flesh of her bare chest was a comfort beneath the skin, that took me back before bad memories, before words, and I felt my nerves unclench from where they had learned to hold my muscle and bone like armor to protect me. I slept deep, holding on to her.

Before dawn, I felt her weight shift in revelation, and she pushed me out of the bed. My arms did not know to come under me to keep my face from hitting Ciretta's linoleum floor. She covered herself with the sheet, made squealing sounds at the sober revelation that she and I had been holding each other naked.

"Go home, go home," was all she yelled, but I slept there on the floor until the morning sun, the sound of her grandmother clanking around in the kitchen, and the slap of Ciretta's open hand brought a sober mind. As I was leaving, I tried to bring words up to the surface, but "Please" is all that came out. She sat at the top of the stairs, shaking her head, praying, rebuking me as some demon.

The hurt and confusion were all I felt, unable to process what I'd done right or wrong—feelings with no mental context, no model for the moment I'd just lived, only the raw illiterate emotions of grief. The walk home felt brutal. The sun seemed to pierce through my retina and sear white hot on my brain. I had to keep looking down to see if in fact I was wearing shoes, because I could feel the concrete, the pebbles inside the concrete, through my feet, in my knees, elbows, and teeth.

My sister came to my basement door after hours of listening without shifting her weight on the creaky stairs. I wiped my nose on my bedspread and asked for her to go away. She left saying, "It'll get better," and returned with news that she had called an old boyfriend and asked him to go to the prom with me. I thought I would cry forever; a boy was the most heinous of toxins to pour on my open wound, but I put on my pink dress and told my escort not to think of putting his hands on me. I looked out the passenger window trying not to think about Ciretta; trying not to cry and ruin the mascara lines my mother had so joyfully drawn around my puffy eyes. My chin rested on my corsage all the way downtown. I took the ceremonial prom photo with the boy, evidence for my mother. Then, I ditched him at the photo station, danced all night to sexually suggestive songs like Marvin Gaye's "Sexual Healing," sniffed out the spiked punch, did all versions of the hustle with my choirmates, and came home in a rowdy drunken huddle of my gay male friends. The alcohol numbed the grief of being at the prom without Ciretta, but allowed another wordless emotion, anger. Though it came without images, memories, or reasons, anger came, and gave me fuel to hate my parents—the sound of their voices, the smell of their house.

That summer I took all of my money out of the bank and went to visit my gay brother in New York.

It didn't bother me that it was going to be a twenty-one-hour bus ride. It was my first escape from home. I hoped, without being conscious of it, that my brother would unlock my mysteries, tell me who I was, give me language, category, and culture for what I felt for Ciretta.

The first five hours of the bus ride offered me something I had little of in a house of Lockharts: silence. I craved silence like other teenagers craved sex and pot and money. I knew that I wouldn't completely exhale until the bus got past Chicago, where the other half of my extended family lived—aunts and uncles wove their web of secrets so tight that none of the cousins could escape. Just past Chicago, she got on the bus.

For sixteen more hours I rode with my new crush. We shared stories of our similarly insane relatives; we hugged, curled up, and napped on the bus. She was going to New York to visit her sister; we were the same age, so much in common.

I was taught as a child to only understand white and black, so I did not know her ethnicity beyond the assumption that this Latin girl was Puerto Rican. We exchanged the phone numbers of our New York siblings, and vowed to meet in the city that I did not understand was larger than the Universe. We got off the bus and immediately became camouflaged in the sea of varying shades of brown skin. I took the first deep, intentional breath since birth, and relaxed into the belonging my brother LaVenson offered.

I ingested as much stimuli as a Midwest teen could handle, while my brother carted my bags all over Manhattan. At two in the morning, he insisted that I find a place to store my energy and get on the train back to the Bronx. I imagined his apartment would be like Buffy and Jody's penthouse on *Family Affair,* but began to understand the reality as we exchanged our clean sleek subway train for one painted red, that clattered, smelled like piss, and made the ice cream I was eating seem contaminated.

He was so proud and excited to unlock the door and show off his spacious oasis. "Great space for New York," he exclaimed as he laughed and fidgeted with four locks. "Ta-da." It was more like Horshack's apartment from *Welcome Back Kotter*—dismal, even with Con Edison on in every room. A roach caught my attention as it grazed the tacked-up poster of George Benson. LaVenson went to set my bags down and I yelled, "Uh un! What if a roach gets on my stuff?" which started an hourlong argument that ended in him reverting to his parental role over me, "Shut your ass up and go to bed! Or sleep in the hall." I put my grief and anger into the argument, and mumbled into the night, never thinking for a moment that I had hurt his feelings. The next morning, I was temporarily cured, distracted, because I was excited to see how a gay man lived daily life in New York City.

He promised to take me to his favorite gay club that night. Of course I fantasized all day about seeing that bus girl there. But first, he took me to work with him at Lowe's Theatre, where I endured four showings of *Raiders of the Lost Ark*, all the while annoying the hell out of my brother, the usher. He patiently endured my whispers that came like labor pains, first in ten-minute intervals, then every minute.

Finally, it was time to go, get a hot dog from a street vendor, and buy the Walkman, hot off the streets to fulfill some cliché fantasy I had from watching *Cagney & Lacey*—then to the club.

I was completely overdressed in a tight black T-shirt with glitter letters that announced, "New York," tight black jeans, and of all things, cowboy boots. My hair hung shoulder length, geri curled to perfection. I knew I was cute. While we waited in line, LaVenson chatted and chatted to appear nonchalant as we approached the doorman who put his arm out when I tried to enter. LaVenson, who was known as the Chihuahua of our family, barked, "Hey! What the hell are you doing?" assuming I was being stopped for my baby face, but the bouncer responded. "No bitches, man. Men only." I retorted, queering up my voice and rolling my neck, "Who you call'n a bitch. We got the same thing in our pants. I'm just more beautiful."

All night my brother bragged about my quick wit to his friends while I sat in boredom watching one Village People look-a-like after another. I realized how foolish I was to think that I'd see the Latin girl there. It was the second day of my trip and still no definition of me. But my conscious mind hadn't laid claim to the priority of my visit, so I grew increasingly irritated over the weekend as LaVenson took me to the top of the Twin Towers, across the Hudson River, to lunch in Chinatown, and to every crowded, noisy tourist attraction he thought I'd appreciate.

On my next-to-last day, I was frustrated with the irony that I was homesick for my miserable parents, frustrated that LaVenson had escaped and left me to endure them, that he had not waved some magic wand and rescued me from my own confusion over who or what I was becoming.

After another viewing of *Raiders of the Lost Ark,* I came out to the lobby and yelled at him, "It is lunchtime, and I am starving, and I can't stand to eat another box of popcorn."

To curtail the embarrassment, he gave me five dollars, pointed me in the direction of the Burger King, and told me to make sure I walked the streets of New York as if I knew where I was going, not like some girl from St. Louis who was certain to get mugged. I had never seen a Burger King that wasn't freestanding. This one was in the basement of a building, and I passed it twice, because of the construction out front, all the while I panicked that the sign for Lowe's Theater would be swallowed in the right angles, steam from the sewers, buses, yellow taxis, and faces.

I ordered my burger and sat down to a wrapper so saturated with grease that I could see the burger through the shiny paper. In my Midwest way of polite and nice, I went to the counter, "Miss, this burger is old." She continued to punch the wide color-coded keys on the register and shout orders in Spanish. She was probably exhausted from being on her feet all day, but I was eighteen, queer without a clue of what that meant for a girl. I said louder. "This burger is not good," and put it on the counter. She threw it back at me, "You get what you get," rolling her neck in that way that I assumed only double-dutch-jumping little black girls from the West Side of St. Louis could. She had incited my rage and aggravation with the fact that I would soon return to the trap of my insane parents, without Ciretta to talk to, without the choir, the phone calls. I picked the burger up off the floor, avoiding the walk-worn shoes of others in line, and threw it back, and fixed myself for the fight.

She took off her hat to reveal a head of beautiful loose curls. I thought she was cute, which triggered the frustration of not understanding such feelings, and gave me all the more reason to kick her ass. Four of her counter mates took off their hats too, and they all headed for the swinging door that separated me from the Latino Burger King girls. My dukes were up in an audience of fight-hungry New Yorkers.

My brother came in and arrested the moment in a voice that I thought only my father possessed, "Zelda!" He stood street level at the top of the basement stairs. When he got to where I stood, shaking and angry, he used his body to back me up to a table, and in a negotiating voice that I had never heard, he apologized in Spanish for whatever I had done to provoke the near beating. I sat in the corner on that hard plastic red chair sobbing for being betrayed, though I had never told him or myself what brought about my behavior, never even told him about the girl on the bus.

He ate the greasy burger, sitting with me while I mumbled that I hated him. "Yeah, yeah, whatever, right?" He punctuated every sentence with "Right?" It was so Bronx, so not St. Louis, so, knowing himself.

"I love you. Right? But you really need to go home. Right?" He demanded my attention, "I love this place. I'm home. Right? I'm clear about that. You need to find out your own stuff. Right?" I inhaled the smell of old cooking grease and filth from the bottom of New Yorkers' shoes, dirt that was several generations removed from the cleanliness of actual soil. Occasionally, the subway rattled from even further beneath the earth than the dungeon Burger King. *How can he love this place?* I wondered. My brother stared at me, not offering words.

I didn't know if he wanted me to answer or not, so I just sat with my arms crossed, looking up at the door that I wanted to exit through.

The next summer, I left St. Louis and got on an airplane headed for the southeast Virginia coast. My oldest sister took me to the airport. We stood in the airport silent, until it was time for me to board the airplane. We did not hug, but she asked if I was on my period. When I told her yes, she said, "I can smell your blood," and that stuck with me as a riddle about the line between being alive and being dead.

Salt water, and sand, I had managed my escape to the ocean, and it was two years of first marriage then baby then divorce—working myself in that salty air until I found the word *lesbian*. It was a freely spoken word among my new straight and gay college friends who had been places in the world.

When my brother came out for a visit, I proudly showed him what I had claimed as mine, my small Norfolk apartment, where my son and I each had our own room. During that visit, I knew something was wrong. His skin looked dry, he looked bloated, and he needed to go to the toilet every few minutes.

That night I got a sitter; we went dancing at my neighborhood women's bar, and he never mentioned feeling bad, but danced and laughed until he said his legs ached. The next morning he still did not tell me in the midst of pancakes, playing with my son, and visits from my queer neighbor friends. Before leaving, he went to his bag and handed me the paper from the New York Health Department, which I read several times to understand the medical abbreviations, a column for negative, a column for positive. He did not explain, but left me to ask my neighbor what it meant that across from HIV there was a check under positive.

"Zelda, he has AIDS."

*   *   *

For three years, LaVenson and I visited but did not speak about the growing spots of Kaposi's sarcoma on his arms and legs.

When he was in the last stages of the virus, he talked to me each night to calm the pain in his legs and his fear of death. He said one night, that when he was gone my other siblings would walk away from the cursory relationship that they had with me, said he was the bridge who stood between my emotions and their disdain for something as nasty as a gay woman. I told him he had internalized homophobia, that my efforts with visiting and phone calls is what kept the connection between me and my other siblings. He insisted that, behind my back, he had dealt with any homophobic behavior toward me in the same way that he had dealt with their foolishness toward him. He said he had flown to St. Louis twice to get in their faces about stuff they were saying about me. Speaking through the pain, he was vague, but said he stood in the middle because he didn't want me to deal with that kind of grief. LaVenson told me many other things, mysteries and keys to life, all gifts for the rest of my time here without him, things he understood with the hindsight of a dying man.

At the funeral, my sisters and their husbands insulted each other to the jabs and laughter of our other relatives. They whispered solemnly about my brother's brilliance as a musician, about the antics of his boyhood, and about the cancer that was wrongfully accused of killing him. My white female partner and our son were shuffled off to one corner or another in hopes that no peripheral vision would recognize us.

The program was planned with as much hustle and bustle as I had exerted a week before, the only one of two siblings who came to New York before he died, the only one of eight siblings who stayed to help him cross over, and to comfort my mother while I packed up his Bronx apartment. Sitting on his bed all day, my mother cried quietly looking at his choice of keepsakes, pictures of never-revealed lovers.

"Cancer," they each spoke at his funeral, consoling his first-grade teacher, his high school friends, and looking at me sideways in hope that I'd keep my mouth shut.

*   *   *

In the months that brought my mourning, my siblings each, one by one, refused my phone calls. I couldn't stop questioning if it was the homophobia that LaVenson had warned me of or the fact that a year before his death, I had spoken out about being molested by my father. I wondered if my speaking out was the other "stuff" about me that he had fielded. My oldest sister refused to let me speak with my nephews, and the sounds of their voices disappeared from my mind. My only reference was in my son's tenor giggle and my own voice on the voice mail, which occasionally brought false excitement, then loneliness.

My other siblings and I were in our twenties when my brother died. Eight years after LaVenson's warning, I let go of chasing after their affection. But, just like him, I wanted my mother, and I insisted that I could make her love me. I held firm to that until six years ago, when I decided to expand my own family, and inseminate.

I knew I didn't want to be pregnant with my mother's verbal abuse being blared through the receiver, into my ear, through my veins and into my baby's forming brain. All of my adult life, I had struggled to facilitate my mother's behavior toward me. At one point the rule was, if she felt like she was about to have an attack of name calling or meanness, then I would remind her that I couldn't tolerate that and gently hang up the phone, leaving her free to call some other time when she could treat me at least as civil as a total stranger. Another time, I had the idea that I would apologize to her for whoever hurt her—her father, her grandmother—and that would cure her of the urge to annihilate me. But somehow, those efforts exacerbated the situation.

Finally, I realized that my son had suffered from watching the dynamic between my mother and me, and my future child was bound to suffer the same if I did not relinquish and mourn the hope that my "family" would somehow become like some '70s sit com family. *The Waltons* just didn't have alcoholic parents, a father who molested the children, and John Boy, though I was suspicious, wasn't characterized as gay.

I realized that my insistence on helping my mom be nice to me was my need to be loved by her, and my subconscious belief that I somehow deserved her ill treatment. My lead-up to letting her go consisted of three months of therapy, lots of grief, and time building up my self-love. I started the conversation, when my mother called a week after my birthday, as she often did, to deliver some masochistic message that she had forgotten the day I was born, followed by a hanging up without a belated wish. "Did you have a birthday? I thought maybe." We were silent, and then I told her that I loved her, followed by, "I learned to love myself in a way that I can't permit you to abuse me." I sobbed through asking her not to call me or my son again. But before hanging up I asked her if there was anything that I hadn't understood, or anything that she could say to me to give me some ounce of hope for us. She laughed and said, "Yes. You're crazy."

When I let go of the fear that my mother would never learn to love me the way she did before I was five and had been molested, then all inclinations to pursue relationships where I chased after loves that were not emotionally available vanished. I had cut the main circuit on a misrouted survival impulse.

When I moved to North Carolina, my mother somehow managed to call my unlisted number. I held my breath for several short conversations about gardening. One day I told her that I did not trust, told her that I was waiting for the setup, the emotional manipulation, the thing happening behind my back while she played the old game of distracting me. She said she just wanted to call.

For another year, my mother and I connected over voracious garden-eating deer, and our ability to make each other laugh. When she asked me, "How are you all doing?" I heard her swallow her Adam's apple, and could feel the tension where she was squeezing the phone and the arm of her chair, bracing against the impulse to cuss me out, laugh at me, call me names. I told her the truth of my day, whatever pains, joys, and true relationships existed there. When I was done, she exhaled and said she had to go feed her dog.

She is learning that honesty doesn't equal death. I have learned to anticipate no more from her than who she is, and to be at peace with the fact that in this lifetime, she traversed some emotional waters, and has the courage to be on the phone with me, having true conversations, because I insist on nothing less. Often, though, I feel the eternal low hum of sadness that we still don't have more words that flow beneath the surface current.

Two years ago on Mother's Day, I called her, and in a fit of confession, she said over and over that she didn't know my father had done those things to me. I flashed on all of the times I came to her for comfort and was whipped for saying such a thing. I gently asked her if she could remember any of the abuse she had inflicted. She cried, saying she couldn't remember doing any of those things, and added a twist, "I must have been drunk."

My daughter has never met my mother or any of my siblings, and her tones seem removed from the other Lockhart voices. A few months ago my youngest brother phoned; he had not talked to me since he was thirteen. He updated me on his marriage, child, and his life in general. He seemed chipper, and I felt genuinely happy for someone whom I didn't know. I didn't even recognize his voice. When I began to tell him what I had been doing with my life, he seemed nervous, and said his daughter needed him—an old Lockhart avoidance tactic. A week later, at dinner, my daughter said, "I have a great family," and began to list the three of us, then adding LaVenson, whom she calls her ancestor, then my mother, which she does occasionally, then to my surprise, added my youngest brother. I said to her, "Yes, he is your uncle by blood," but said the names of the family friends who were there since she was born, who come to her birthday parties, know her favorite colors, and said, "That's family."

She is a child who often, and randomly, says, "I love you," who often and less randomly will tell me what I am doing or saying that is unjust. My twenty-year-old son and her have that in common, and friends say, the apples didn't fall far.

Recently my daughter asked me, "Why doesn't your mother visit you, or help you make things, or send you birthday presents?" We sat in the car for a long time before I found what I felt was an honest answer.

I told her that first of all, my mother showed me how to do many things—how to make biscuits, how to rub the top of a cucumber to draw out the bitterness, how to play that game, Old Mister Brown. I took another breath and told her the less comforting truth—that grown-ups sometimes have problems, like not having enough money to pay the bills, like not being loved by other people, and some of them, like my mother and father, didn't ever learn what she is now learning, how to work it out and find what they need without hurting other people. I told her that just like when she used to get mad and yell at her friends because she was hungry or sad or tired, that some people grow up and continue to do that, never learning to deal with pain in ways that are safe for other people.

She asked me if my mother ever hit me. I made myself breathe, and I told her yes. Then she wanted to know if she hit me a lot. I inhaled though my teeth and told her that both of my parents hurt me, but it happened mostly when I was little, and that I got to be a big girl and was able to leave their house so I wouldn't get hurt any more. I told her that because my mother is still learning, but doesn't know any better, that we talk on the phone rather than visit so I can be safe while she learns. My daughter gave me a sense of her own comfort, while simultaneously giving me a huge gift, "I love my home."

I told her my mother is doing much better, and that maybe we could meet her someplace for a quick visit soon. My daughter said she'd like that. That night she wrote my mother a letter to that effect, using the blunt language of a five-year-old: "I love you, and you love me, and one day we will visit," with crayon hearts, butterflies, and birds. On my daughter's birthday, she and I sat one-on-one at Elmo's Diner eating the meal she was allowed to order—french fries, collard greens, chili, and lemonade to wash it all down. My mother called my cell to speak to my daughter.

When we got home, my daughter insisted on ringing my mother again. I had forgotten that my mother could play a harmonica. I had bought my daughter one for her birthday years before, and the two of them played their harmonicas into the phone for a long time that evening.

Mt. Fuji

Erika Krouse

The summer before my senior year, I got a job at a Japanese hospital. We had moved to Tokyo when I was thirteen, and I was now seventeen. I still didn't know if we were leaving, or if I would get to stay in the country and graduate. They never told us much in advance. When people asked if I was a military brat, I said, "No, just a brat," or "Yes. The Corporate Military, IBM." My father had started working for them back when they were a typewriter company, and they had moved us every few years since I was born. It's a tribute to my inner child that I still tell these dumb jokes, and a tribute to my upbringing that there are still boxes I don't bother to unpack, friends I don't bother to make.

The visa for my hospital job had taken four months to get, and the job paid 2,080 yen per day. At exchange rates back then, my salary equaled a whopping $1.62 an hour. I couldn't complain, though—I was paid the same wages as the nurses. The nurses lived there in the hospital, pulling double shifts, eating cafeteria food and then collapsing in tiny cots next to foot lockers. I worked at St. Luke's International Hospital, but back then, I was the only international thing there.

My first day, it was raining. I splashed up to the tan building with silty water dripping from the letters on the front door. It took some time to find my way around the big building to the wing where I would be working. A pretty nurse with bad teeth named Akiko introduced me to all the nurses, doctors, and patients. Nobody spoke any English at all. I bowed up and down about fifty times, like a seesaw. Naturally squeamish, I kept ducking into the bathroom throughout the day to lean my faint head against the cool walls, trying to ignore the smell of rubbing alcohol and imminent demise. In Japan, people go to hospitals to die, and there were patients who lived there for years, but only if they were lucky.

Akiko-san cheerfully taught me how to make beds. This, it seemed, was my purpose. I learned how to peel the sheets off the mattress without touching the stains (blood, urine, diarrhea, occasionally semen), make hospital corners, and then tuck the new sheets in so tightly you could bounce a coin on the surface. Sometimes I did this while the patient was still on the bed, and a nurse rolled them over to the side that was sufficiently tight so I could smooth out the other side. It was important not to have any wrinkles, or I would give the patients bedsores, Akiko warned me. I pulled so hard on the sheets that my hands ached. I had lived in Japan long enough to understand that it is an island far too crowded to allow for mistakes.

Distributing meals was my second duty. Fortunately, each patient's tray was labeled, so I didn't have to memorize allergies or food constraints. Unfortunately, they were labeled in Japanese. Not the easy, phonetic alphabets, either—they were in Kanji, those weird Chinese characters that look like someone dropped a bunch of pickup sticks. I frantically tried to memorize characters, but usually ended up pestering Akiko every mealtime—"Whose?" I asked, and she would tell me, "Ah, Takahashi-san. Inoue-san. Watanabe-san."

My third and last duty was to escort the patients to X-rays, to the bathroom if they were able, or up and down the hallway for walks. This is how I became friends with Sato-san, a sixty-eight-year-old lady with hair always immaculately secured by bobby pins into a high, poufy bun. She clutched my arm hard on strolls down the gray corridor, her fingers like talons, Shiseido makeup flaking from her wrinkles. Sato-san had a son that she wanted me to marry, she said. She showed me a magazine spread of a traditional Tokyo house, impeccably decorated. "*Watashi no uchi desu*," she said—*This is my home*—and she and I were both quiet as we wondered in two languages if she would ever get to live there again.

Suzuki-san was another friend. He was a man in his eighties, and I never understood why he was there in the first place. I never knew any of their ailments. Neither did they—Japanese doctors don't tell you if you're dying, or why. Mr. Suzuki was the healthiest sick person I had ever seen. He bounced in his bed and made sharp gestures with knotted, old arms. He always asked me how I was with a loud, slow *"O Genki Desuka?"* whenever I gave him his breakfast (it seems that the practice of speaking slowly and loudly to foreigners is universal). Suzuki-san had taped a picture of Mt. Fuji next to his bed, and I kept him company while he ate his meal and told me about climbing the mountain eleven times. Relatives snuck him liquor, and when he got drunk, he sang old songs in a loud, quavery voice, waking up the other patients. Sometimes he stuck his face in mine, put his thumbs and forefingers above and below his eyelids, and then pulled his eyes wide open, to mimic my Western eyes. In response, I pulled my eyes into slants in the corners, and he laughed hysterically. He had never seen that before.

There was also Yumiko-chan. It was easy to guess why she was there. Only nineteen, she often wore a pink flowered shower cap over her bald head, while her long, black wig hung from a steel bedpost like a forgotten pet. She giggled and spoke in an infantile voice, even more babyish than other Japanese girls her age. She hadn't left the hospital in years, not for a minute. Yumiko's bed was strewn with about a million stuffed animals, and I had to remove them one by one when I changed the sheets for her.

Yumiko-chan told me that she had a boyfriend. She showed me a framed picture of a gorgeous Japanese teenager, with a sharp chin and lazy, sexy eyes. When I looked closer, I could see that she had torn it out of a teen idol magazine. But I still let her tell me all about him, and how he was going to lift her out of her hospital bed, marry her, and take her away to France. The reason he didn't visit, she said, was that it was too painful for him, seeing her so sick.

I had an imaginary boyfriend, too. His name was Sam—he

went to my school, and I had never spoken to him. Sam wore a leather Members Only jacket and checkered Vans. He drove a motorcycle. He had bad skin and a curly Isro that gave his head a mushroom shape. Sam was the drummer in a bad high school band, and drumsticks usually poked out of the back pocket of his black jeans. He wouldn't even look at me. I could hardly blame him—I was so ugly that the fattest boy in school invited me to the junior prom. When I said no, he said he only asked me because he felt sorry for me.

One of my sacred possessions was a trigonometry test Sam had failed and thrown out. My friend had stolen it for me out of the trash. He had scored an even 50 percent. I studied how he wrote his 7s, his up-and-down handwriting as he wrote "I don't know!" on the blank lines. Sitting on Yumiko-chan's bed, I showed her the math test, and we sighed over it together. He was lost, like me, a stranger. Alone. Neither of us had any idea how to solve for X.

*

Out of every place I ever lived, Japan was my favorite. I fell in love with the sweet-potato trucks and their canned songs blaring out of tinny loudspeakers, the yakitori stands with strips of marinated chicken roasting on sticks, the Siberian winter winds, and the hot, soggy summers that soaked your clothes in sweat the minute you stepped outside. There is no hot like Asian hot. I went dancing in clubs ("discos") that served me free sloe gin fizzes and rum 'n Cokes. I drank pink and purple beer from the vending machines down my street that sold condoms, women's panties (used), or liquor in plastic bottles shaped like robots. The first time I got drunk was on canned piña coladas, and then I threw it all up in the parking lot of my apartment building. I went to Pachinko parlors and American movies with Japanese subtitles. My friends and I used to find our way onto *Roppongi* rooftops and see how far down the block we could run, jumping from roof to roof, way up above the flashing street. Once, we climbed about fifteen floors to the top of a building. Out of breath, we looked up to see a *yakuza* with tattoos and a machine gun lounging against a red door. He silently, lazily pointed the gun at us. We slid and fell back down the fifteen stories, feeling lucky, and unlucky, and somehow left out of something important.

I spent hours every day on Tokyo's clean subways and trains packed with Japanese businessmen stuffed into suits, smelling vaguely of fish and heated milk. There was one point where the train became elevated, and Mt. Fuji popped into view—theoretically, that is. In actuality, it hid. Over four years, I only actually saw Mt. Fuji a few times, even though it was so close. Usually a scrim of clogged air hung before it, in varying stages of opacity. But each time Mt. Fuji showed its pale face behind its wispy fan of clouds and smog, the train passengers murmured, *Fuji-san! Fuji-san!* Everyone crowded to the windows to peer at the volcano, separate from all the other mountains, rising like a ghost in its white dress.

Too ugly to be noticed at home, I was sometimes stared at even in Tokyo, the biggest metropolitan area in the world. A foreigner, I was exotic by association, despite my physical appearance— thick, owly glasses with plastic frames, long monkey arms that poked too far out of the cuffs of my sweaters, my teeth encrusted in thick, gray braces that magically collected food even when I hadn't eaten any. I was so skinny, I bent like a green twig. Back in America, a boy in my homeroom used to ask, "What's the difference between Erika's chest and Kansas?" The punch line was, "Nothing." But in Tokyo, I was an oddity, like a giraffe in Times Square, or a sunset at noon. Or the lone peak of Mt. Fuji. Something strange, and therefore, beautiful.

*

One day, the old lady Sato-san had me paged. When I came to her door, there was a man there. He was sweating in his tight suit—the air-conditioning in the hospital didn't exactly work—and wore dirty glasses, almost as thick as mine. When I entered the room, he stood up. He pushed the hair out of his eyes, and bowed. I bowed back. Sato-san smiled and nodded. "My son," she said, waving a wrinkly hand at him. I bowed again.

Then the man took a deep breath and said, in English, "I am

Sato, and I am Satie." I could tell he had practiced the sentence all the way there.

Satie? That didn't seem like a Japanese name. "Satie?" I asked.

"No. Satie. *Sa-tie.*"

My mouth fell open. Thirty. He was saying, *I am thirty.* I couldn't believe it. *Thirty?* This man was a fossil. An extinct species. His ancient, damp hand was still clutching mine. I wiggled it out of his grasp. Mrs. Sato nodded back and forth between us, as if already planning our wedding. Bowing again, I backed out of the room, then ran and hid at the nurse's station. I couldn't marry a thirty-year-old. I was seventeen. I was in *high school.*

After he left, Sato-san paged me again. "He likes you," she said in a musical voice, and I smiled crookedly. "Next, I must talk to your mother," she told me. I promised to bring her to the hospital so they could meet, because I didn't yet have the language skills to refuse her.

Since nobody at the hospital knew more than a word or two of English, I spoke Japanese for eight hours a day. My Japanese improved dramatically, out of necessity. In a hospital, it's important to understand certain things—"Get ice! Now!" or, "Mr. Kobayashi is allergic to miso." I ate cafeteria lunches with Akiko-san, who practiced her English by sometimes slipping in the three words she knew—"okay," "berry good-o," and "Makudonaludo" (McDonald's).

Within a month, I found myself cracking jokes, telling stories or understanding complicated medical conditions in Japanese, without knowing how I could do these things. It just happened, somewhere between my brain and my tongue. I retroactively tried to trace the linguistic threads on the subway going home, or lying in bed at night. But I never could figure out a grammar scheme or method. I just knew the words, the way a tongue knows a taste. When I went home, my family would suddenly look confused when I spoke at the dinner table, and my sister or brother would say, "Um, Erika, you're speaking in Japanese again." I shut my mouth, dumb. My own language had abandoned me, and I hadn't even noticed.

*

Only Japanese belong in Japan. I had friends who had lived there for most of their lives, but they were still *gaijin*—foreign persons. One of the teachers at my school applied for Japanese citizenship. He had lived there for over twenty years. He was fluent in Japanese—*pera pera*—and frequently slipped into Japanglish in his classes—"*Kono* answer okay, *demo* . . . you can do better, *ne?*" His education was in marine biology, a shared passion of the crown prince of Japan (now the emperor). Every Saturday morning, my teacher went to the crown prince's palace to drink tea with the prince, play chess, and discuss marine biology. But even the future emperor didn't have enough clout to help him. My teacher was denied citizenship. He wasn't Japanese.

If he couldn't immigrate, there was no hope for me, a pimply teenager. I knew I didn't belong there. But I didn't belong in my own country, either. A month and a half before I took my hospital job, Ronald Reagan had ordered the bombing of Tripoli, Libya, to retaliate for an explosion in a German nightclub frequented by U.S. servicemen. Instead of assassinating Khaddafi, the bombs killed his little daughter.

There was an immediate rash of terrorism against all American allies, which included peaceful Japan. A van of explosives was driven onto an American school outside of Tokyo. Just a half block from my house, an annex of the Canadian Embassy was bombed. Helicopters swarmed over my apartment like inquisitive bees. We couldn't go to school for two weeks. We were warned not to go outside. The Soviet Union pointed one of their nuclear warheads at Tokyo. On cable, we cringed as we saw our countrymen cheering, their fists raised, talking about how great it was to blow up Arabs. My native country seemed like a big, cowardly bully, hiding behind its geographic bulk and letting its friends take the fall. When protesters grabbed me and asked me if I was American, I told them I was Canadian.

I promised myself that I would never, ever go back.

*

The summer was waning. Our family still didn't know whether we were staying or going. It wasn't looking good. The eighties boom was over, and the Asian economy was beginning to implode. Most of my friends had been sent back to the States. Nighttimes, I wove my way home between drunk businessmen and grim housewives, wondering if Sam was still in the darkening city. Every time I heard a motorcycle, I inspected the rider's shoes for checkered Vans.

The patients replaced my friends. Suzuki-san told me about his dead wife, and showed me pictures of himself as a younger man on Mt. Fuji with about a thousand other people. Yumiko-chan had gotten a new boyfriend from a different magazine, and was engaged again. Sato-san kept asking to meet my family, and for a copy of my birth certificate.

One day I came to work and the nurses were hysterically running around the hospital in their white Reeboks. They spoke rapidly in high-pitched voices, eyes red and noses running. It all seemed to center around one room, that of a patient named Ito-san, whom I had never seen conscious. The woman had been in a coma since before I arrived. I found Akiko and caught her arm. "What's happening?" I asked, and she looked at me, her lips trembling.

"Ito-san is dead," she said.

She seemed so upset, I patted her arm. "Did you know her very well?"

"No." She wiped her eyes with a little handkerchief. "She in a coma when she came here."

"Then why are you sad?" I asked.

"Because she is dead."

I shook my head. "I don't understand."

"In America, you don't get sad when a person dies?"

"Yes, of course," I said hurriedly, with my last shred of national pride. I remembered that for centuries, Japanese people believed that Westerners ate their children. "We get very sad, just like you. But mostly about people we knew well, people we will miss."

"I will never know Ito-san. She never spoke to me. It's sad to lose what you have," Akiko told me, blowing her nose. "But sometimes it's sadder to lose what you can never have."

*

The news came through one evening. We were being transferred back to America. Even worse—New Jersey. I had never lived there, but I had heard the accent, and that was enough for me. I considered dropping out of high school, taking up a cot in the nurse's room, waiting out my time with Yumiko-chan and her wig. I understood Yumi then, a teenager with wild, romantic blood and nowhere to go.

I waited until the end of my last week to break the news to the patients. I baked cookies for everyone, but ingredients are different in Japan. The cookies didn't seem to cook, only dry out, and by the time I took them out of the oven, they were harder than biscotti. Still, I had to give some kind of *presento,* gifts being the currency of Japan, so I distributed the cookies to patients who couldn't chew them, all of them saying, *"Oishi, Erika-chan, demo katai!"* Delicious, Erika, but hard! They respectfully lay the cookies on their trays until I left shift, and then they threw them into their little wastebaskets.

I procrastinated seeing Sato-san until she had already paged me twice. I walked slowly down the hall and entered her room. Then, sitting next to her bed, I slipped the old lady a desiccated cookie and told her that I was going back to America. "America?" she asked, as if she had never heard of it. "Why?"

"To finish high school."

"But what about the marriage?" she asked.

I didn't know what to say. Sato-san's face hardened. Then she rolled over on her side, away from me. She let the cookie fall out of her hand to the floor.

I never promised to marry your son, I wanted to tell her. *I'm just a kid. I am not thirty.* But she closed her eyes against me.

Suzuki-san wasn't happy with me either, and yanked his arm away as I tried to escort him to the bathroom. "You're going to America, and I'm never leaving this hospital," he grumbled. He wouldn't let me push the trolley for his IV, and when he got to the bathroom door, the wheels caught on the ridge. He pulled at it twice, and it kept bumping backward, the IV swinging on its vine.

Then, suddenly, Suzuki-san swore and yanked his needle right out of his arm. He walked into the bathroom alone, unfettered, like a man.

I went to the nurse's station and reported to Akiko what happened. Akiko shrieked and ran into the bathroom. She pulled him off the toilet and started slapping the inside of his elbow to bring up the vein. Suzuki-san hung his head, his pants pooled around his ankles, his penis drooping. By the time she got the IV back into his arm, his skin was as pale as rice paper. I felt terrible. Akiko-san brought him back to his bed, and he didn't get up again for the rest of my shift.

On my last day, I stopped in to check on Suzuki-san as soon as I came in that morning. The lights were out, and everyone else in the room whispered. Suzuki-san was still lying prone, breathing painfully. He was wearing a catheter and oxygen tubes. *I have killed this man,* I thought. Trying not to cry, I found Akiko, "Did I kill Suzuki-san?" No, no, she told me, but she was busy, and Japanese people are always polite.

The other patients didn't speak to me much that day. It was as if I had already left, were already a ghost. Even Yumiko-chan retreated into politeness, bowing and saying all the proper things, now that I was on the outside.

Before I left the hospital for the last time, Sato-san summoned me to her bedside. She looked at me for a long moment. "I told my son you were leaving Japan," she said. "I called him last night. He was"—then she used a word I had never heard before. I asked what it meant, and she thought for a second.

Then she spoke English to me, for the first time ever. She clasped her worn hands to her chest. "Heart-o," she said. Then she thrust them away, toward the floor by my feet. She looked me in the eye.

"Down," she said.

*

Three days later, I was in America. After we landed, my parents drove a rental car to our new house that night. As we pulled into a dark driveway, I asked, "Is this it? Are we home?"

My family looked at me strangely, and I realized that I was doing it again, speaking in Japanese. Jet-lagged and heartbroken, I stumbled and stuttered, trying to find the words in English. I didn't know how to say it anymore. I didn't even know what language I was speaking, what the right word was for home.

The next day I had to get up for school. It was the first day of my senior year. Walking to the bus stop at the end of my street, I felt exhausted, stewed, like my flesh would drop off my bones.

An American girl was waiting there, my age. She was dressed in a tight black dress, like a hooker. I glanced down at my ballooning blouse and cutoffs and knew I had made a fashion error. She ignored me for a few minutes, kicking stones, so I did the same. Then she said something I didn't hear. "Excuse me?" I asked.

"Are you new?" she asked.

I nodded.

"Where are you from?" She pulled her gum out of her mouth in a long string.

"Tokyo," I told her.

The strand of gum broke and snapped back onto her chin. She peeled it off. Her smooth brows furrowed and she tilted her hair-sprayed head to one side. "Tokyo? As in . . . China?"

"No," I said. "Japan. Tokyo, Japan."

"Oh . . . Japan."

I nodded again.

The girl hesitated. Then she asked, "Like, Japan, the one in China?"

I was still jet-lagged. It was 10:30 at night, back home in Tokyo. The day I had just begun was over, there. Everyone in the hospital would be pulling up their covers and going to sleep. I thought of Yumiko, sleeping with her forlorn wig hanging from the bedpost. Sato-san, staring at the glossy magazine pictures of home before a nurse snapped out her light for her. And old Suzuki, his old finger on the Mt. Fuji calendar next to his bed, tracing the path up the smooth mountain by the reflected light of a streetlamp. The last time I saw him, he was struggling for breath, because of me. I knew he wouldn't make it. Neither he nor I would ever see Fuji-san again. I looked at the wan sun, already risen in this near east, and felt tears starting. I told myself, *This is home now. Here.* But I knew I would never belong here, or anywhere else.

"Yeah," I said, trying to smile at the American girl. "The one in China."

Space Cadet

Sean Doolittle

I was always a bookworm, the kind of kid who stayed indoors on sunny days. By high school, I began to think I wanted to be a writer. Or possibly a concert saxophonist. Then came the movie *Lethal Weapon,* starring Mel Gibson and Danny Glover, and I decided I would become a cop.

Come on. The shootout at the Christmas tree lot? That part where Riggs takes out Endo the torture master? And then he straps on a submachine gun and takes off across the city—on foot!—to finally hand Gary Busey's ass to him in the mud. Right?

Saxophone? I started writing "plainclothes detective" on the vocation questionnaires issued by the guidance counselor. I had an answer to the "What are your plans after High School?" question.

"I'm going to be a cop. Homicide, probably. Maybe narco or vice."

It was 1988. I never chose the badge, the badge chose me. All our lives would change that summer.

*

> *"When I was nineteen, I did a guy in Laos with a rifle shot at a thousand yards out, in high wind. Maybe eight or even ten guys in the world could have made that shot. It's the only thing I was ever good at."*
>
> —Detective Sergeant Martin Riggs

In the only Little League photo I remember, I look like one of the coaches. I literally towered over every other kid on the team. But my growth rate had far outstripped large motor coordination, and so I

137

struggled with advanced athletic concepts, such as throwing. Catching. Hitting.

I clomped through grade school in floodwater pants and orthopedic shoes. I had thin hair, a snaggle-toothed smile. Acne came early, and it came hard. I remember a fifth-grade class exercise that involved joining hands and standing in a circle; by a stroke of dumb luck, I'd ended up next to my crush, the cutest girl in the pod. I still remember the thrill of that small, smooth hand in mine. But even more keenly, I remember the moment she noticed whose hand *she* was holding. She made a noise and jerked away, and then she wiggled all over. She didn't mean to. Her reaction was so involuntary, I couldn't even blame her. The way she shuddered, *I* could feel the cooties.

But this isn't about that. This is an anthology of teenage loser stories, and the truth is, by my teen years, I had more or less grown into myself. Less than some kids, more than others.

Bottom line: it could have been worse.

Here's the important point. My childhood, growing up where I did—in rural southeastern Nebraska, on family farmland my family no longer farmed—set me apart from both the town kids and the farm kids at school (let alone the seething thug factory that was nearby Lincoln).

But it also provided acres of solitude and not too many chores, which suited me more than I probably understood at the time. Such environs may or may not improve eye-hand coordination, but they certainly taught me how to be by myself. And they gave room for a spacious internal life. Add an unpopular streak in the schoolyard, and there I was: physically awkward, pining for adventure, prone to fantasy.

INT. A MIDDLE SCHOOL HALLWAY -- DAY

Two sixth-graders, current best friends, exit the boy's room and head for class. VAN WALLACE is one of the cool kids, a little edgy, a little tough, not the least bit

self-conscious about hanging around with a
dork like ME.

ME has been, of late, in the throes of an
obsession with the book *The Outsiders* by S.E.
Hinton.

>   ME
> Hey, I've been thinking.
>   VAN WALLACE
> Yeah?
>   ME
> Maybe we should start carrying
> blades.
>   VAN WALLACE
>   (incredulous)
> The hell you talking about?
> Why?
>   ME
> You never know. I mean, we
> could get jumped or something.
>   VAN WALLACE
> You're a fucking space cadet.

And so I remained, to varying degrees, as a teenager. I gathered
wool. I heard without listening. I leaped before I looked. I measured
once and cut twice.

I wrecked three different cars before high school graduation, all
because I hadn't been paying attention. My father's insurance agent
actually organized a small-scale intervention in hopes of pulling my
head out of my ass.

Any brutally honest adult might have pointed out that, despite
my well-written essay on why I desired a career in law enforcement,
I was perhaps ill-suited to carry a gun for a living.

They sent me to training academy instead.

*

"Okay, clown, no bullshit!"
—DETECTIVE SERGEANT ROGER MURTAUGH

At some point, somebody brought to my parents' attention a summer program offered by the Nebraska State Patrol. It was called the Junior Law Cadet Academy, or something very close to that. The program was designed for eleventh-graders who thought they might want to be police when they grew up.

To get there, you wrote the aforementioned essay. Somebody somewhere selected a roster of candidates from every district in the state. If you were one of the chosen, you proceeded to a one-day selection process, where you sat before a tribunal of judges and presented your case.

In the hot seat, there came a battery of oral questions. Questions like, "If you were with a group of friends who wanted to do something illegal, how would you react?" Or, "When you see a car pulled over on the Interstate, with two or three cruisers behind it, lights flashing, what do you think about the person driving the car?" Or, "Say a shitbag gets the drop on you, and you forgot your vest back at the hooker's apartment. Your partner is sleeping off a pint of Cuervo in the back of the squad unit. How will he (or she) explain your bullet-riddled corpse to the shift commander?"

I remember a rangy kid with shocking red hair and wild, intense eyes. When it was his turn to respond to the make-or-break question—"Tell us, in your own words, why you want to be a law enforcement officer"—he absolutely shut down the room.

"Crime is a cancer in the body of society," he said. I'm sure he didn't say exactly that, but it was right along those lines. "I want to be one of the surgeons. I want to locate the cancer and isolate it. I want to cut it out before it spreads."

I was sitting with a couple other guys, one of whom happened to be vying for the same position as Crazy Red. "Oh, man," the first guy whispered. "That dude is so in." The kid from Crazy Red's district looked glum and said nothing.

What could I say? Red was killing up there. His neck veins bulged with commitment. Of course he was in.

He wasn't. As it turned out, neither were the two guys I'd been sitting with.

But I was.

*

"Now that's a real badge, I'm a real cop, and this is a real fucking gun!"

—RIGGS

We mustered that June, at the State Patrol's Air Park academy in Lincoln, a motley gang of chuckleheads with little in the way of prior paramilitary training.

Here we'd be given a weeklong taste of life behind the thin blue line. We were assigned to our barracks. We learned how to make our bedsheets tight as a drumhead. At night, there was curfew. In the morning, reveille. If a sergeant said jump, we said, "David Lee Roth– or Chuck Norris–style?"

If we wanted to screw off, hey. We could go home and screw off. Otherwise? For that week, that summer, we were cadets.

The days broke down into four main areas: physical training, class work, field activities, and meals. One day, lunch followed a morning full of crime scene photos.

I remember the photo of the man who'd put a shotgun in his mouth. The one of the elderly woman who'd been stabbed to death in her bed. I remember we had sloppy Joes.

The next day, noon chow followed an hour's worth of highway accident footage. We saw a family mangled up in a wad of steel. An unhelmeted motorcyclist with his brain exposed. Lakes of blood on miles of pavement. *Bon appétit,* Junior Law cadets!

We sat through the class sessions, collectively yearning for the field. One morning, we rode with a trooper who showed us how to locate motorists who used "fuzz busters," those dash-mounted radar detectors designed to alert drivers to speed traps. What you do is, you park on an interstate overpass and trigger the radar gun at random travelers. The ones who slam on their breaks have fuzz busters. We all took turns, cackling among ourselves. The trooper chewed his toothpick and chuckled along, wrist on the wheel, eyes hidden behind mirror shades.

One afternoon, we were taken to the driving course. Here we learned how to navigate high-speed turns. We each had a go at chasing a kamikaze instructor in a fuel-injected Mustang. We howled like banshees, wrangling the wheel, leaving black smears of rubber and clouds of smoke in our trail.

We learned how easy you could get shot if you walked up to the right car the wrong way. We learned how easy you could get shot in a house. How easy you could get shot in a parking garage. We learned how easy you could get shot all kinds of ways.

A guy from the S.W.A.T. unit showed us where to chop a bad guy in the neck with your bare hand if you wanted to make him cry. A guy with a drug-sniffing dog showed us why it's a bad idea to carry pot through an airport in your sock.

It was obscenely, unspeakably awesome. We charged through each new experience, holding back nothing, absorbing all we could. Each day started with a shimmer and left us exhilarated, exhausted, overwhelmed.

Over the course of that week, little by little, I became certain of two things:

1. I was having the time of my life.
2. In no way would I become a cop after all.

*

"I don't make things complicated. They get that way all by themselves."

—RIGGS

Most nights, we fell into a dead sleep. It's hazy now, but I imagine there was exactly the amount of macho bullshitting and ballbreaking you'd expect from a bunch of seventeen-year-old guys strung out on testosterone.

One night, things turned philosophical. I don't remember what kicked off the summit, but for whatever reason, on that particular night we stretched out on our bunks in the dark and talked like the people we actually were: a group of teenagers who didn't have a clue where we were going or how we were getting there.

We covered hopes and dreams. We touched on fears. We reminisced about the events of the week so far. At one point, we began going around the room, each taking a turn voluntarily doing what we'd already done for the selection committee several weeks earlier: we said why we were here.

Most of the guys had cops somewhere in the family. A few had been military kids, were planning to enlist after high school, and saw law enforcement as a reasonable type of job down the road.

What could I say? That I really nailed the written essay? The turn was finally passed to the guy in the bunk next to mine, so it was time to come up with something. Fast.

His name wasn't James, but I'll call him James. I liked him. He was a quiet guy. Not so much the brooding type, just observant and thoughtful, considerate of others, easy to make smile. A nice guy through and through. He didn't say anything for a minute or so, which was good. More time for me to figure out my spiel.

"Well," he finally said, "when I was nine, my mom was bludgeoned to death by my stepfather."

Our barracks grew so quiet that you could hear the locusts in the trees outside. Nobody said a word. For the next while, we kept our traps shut and listened to James tell his story. There was nothing dramatic in his presentation, neither bravado nor tears. He might have been telling us a story about a family vacation.

But he wasn't telling us a story about a family vacation. He was telling us the story of how his mother had been beaten to death by the man she'd married after his real father passed away.

"I'm not really sure if I want to be a police officer," he admitted. "I'm pretty sure I'd like to do something related to the law."

Eventually, we began asking questions. James answered them. Everybody had forgotten about my turn, and so had I.

*

The next day, we went to the gun range. After preliminary training, we fired .38 revolvers at human silhouettes.

The instructor taught us that a trained officer aims for "center mass." In other words, the torso. Particularly the chest. Center mass is the biggest target. It's also where all your internal organs are. "Forget all the crap you see on television," the instructor told us. Center mass is how you stop a bad guy.

It's surprisingly difficult to hold a gun in your hands and make the bullet go where you want it to go. But I turned out to be an okay shot. While James struggled good-naturedly with his aim in the lane beside me, I brought back my paper man with a few misses, a respectable grouping of holes located more or less between the shoulders, and a single, perfect head shot.

"Ahh," the instructor said, grinning. "A show-off. Nice job."

I smiled back, shrugged humbly, accepted the praise. I couldn't bring myself to tell the guy I'd been trying to shoot a smiley face, like Mel Gibson in the movie.

*

The job took its toll. I became preoccupied, distant. My girlfriend left me.

We'd been together almost a year. But in my absence, she'd temporarily succumbed to the American cheese charms of a thirty-year-old fry cook who had a mustache and a sports car. I fantasized about rounding up some of my buddies from the force. We'd pay him a visit. Explain things in a way he could understand. Did this scumbag know who he was dealing with? No, he didn't. He had no idea.

And then, all at once, it was Friday.

It felt disorienting. One day, we were driving cars, climbing walls, shooting guns. Then, just like that, it was over. We graduated, we Junior Law cadets, and returned to our summers, our lives.

I wonder, sometimes, what James is doing now. I kept my silhouette from the firing range on the wall of my room for the next couple years. Then one day I looked at it, felt an odd chill, and took it down.

My girlfriend and I were back together before our senior year started that fall. A handful of years later, we got married. Now we have two kids.

We met at band camp, she and I. Her family had just moved into the school district. She was cute and she was new, which meant she hadn't known me since my cootie days, which meant I had a legitimate shot at her.

I used to joke that it was between me and the trombone player, and he had a cold sore. She's always said that she liked me because I was tall.

WHAT I DID OVER MY SUMMER VACATION

A Nova, an Eyelash, a Snoring Man:

Notes on Adolescent Summers

K. L. COOK

1.

Between my freshman and sophomore years in high school, I moved from Houston to Amarillo, Texas, where I got a job, even though I was only fifteen, at a nonunion movie theater. I was an usher, then a concessionist, marquee changer, preview splicer, and ultimately a projectionist. Two other guys worked there, both a year older than me, named Adam and Matt. Adam was tall and thin, a baby-faced, sweet-tempered guy who was shy with girls. Matt was a flaxen-haired, flabby-bellied boy-man who liked to drink a lot of beer and tell dirty jokes. They took me under their wing, and we spent most of our time together, when we weren't at school or working at the theater, either driving around Amarillo in Adam's black Plymouth Barracuda or drinking beers and margaritas at Matt's house with his identical twin, Mark.

Matt thought of himself as a lucky man. There was evidence for this. The next summer, on two consecutive nights, he found hundred-dollar bills on the floor of the Western Club. Emboldened by this luck, he bought himself a car, his first, a Chevy Nova. Adam and I were there with him and his father the afternoon he bought it. His father co-signed the loan, and that night we celebrated by getting a couple of six-packs and cruising around in the Nova. Matt drove to a medical district on the west side of town—a big place with a winding road and small lake in the middle of it. That was where other kids from the high school often congregated to make out, drink, or fight.

This particular night was hot and breezy. We had the windows down. I rode shotgun. Adam was in the backseat. Matt drove to the top of the Medi-Park road, and then, wanting to see what his new car could do, he gunned it down the hill. He'd had a few too many beers, however, and when he hit a curvy patch of asphalt wet from sprinklers, he touched the brakes, and we started to slide. He panicked and, rather than turn into the slide, stomped on the accelerator, and soon we jumped the embankment. For a magically suspended moment during which the three of us stared ahead with a kind of humorous, open-mouthed awe, we sailed through the air above the little Medi-Park lake.

When we finally hit the water, we floated for a strange second or two. I distinctly remember Adam giggling in the backseat like a little kid. Then the front of the car dipped down and began sinking fast. Water flowed over the rolled-down windows into the seats. Matt tried to open the door, but it wouldn't budge, and he freaked out, shouting, "We're gonna drown, we're gonna drown!" He clambered out of his side window, tipping the car as it was sinking, and then I crawled out my side and fell into the water as the car was almost submerged. I didn't know what had happened to Adam. Had he been able to extricate himself from the backseat? I couldn't see him in the dark water. I struggled in my drenched clothes to find the surface. When I made it, gasping for air, I called out Adam's name but could hear or see nothing. I swam to shore, where Matt sat on the grass, rocking back and forth, as if keening, cursing to himself. Adam was behind him, water dripping from his clothes and hair. The strangest thing, out of all the strange things that happened that night, was that Adam was laughing, dancing back and forth on the balls of his feet. The sight of him there, so incongruous to the whole scene, as if he was still caught in the last stages of his giggling fit, made me laugh as well, even though I didn't want to. Matt's poor car was all but sunk, just the silver ball of the radio antenna glowing above the surface. It was clear that we'd survived something amazing, and the story, no matter how much trouble we got into, would be worth it. Adam just kept dancing and laughing.

Later that summer, I met a girl and during the next year saw less and less of Adam and Matt. At the end of the school year, Adam left for Colorado, either to go to college or to work, I can't remember. Matt had a job at an auto parts store, and I seldom saw him.

Near the end of my senior year, I got a call from Matt. It was one of those calls that you know, before you even pick up the phone, will be bad news. He said that Adam had hanged himself. His mother had contacted Matt and wanted the two of us to be pallbearers. She said that we were his best friends, which made me feel worse because I hadn't been in touch with him in over a year and didn't know what he had been doing in Colorado, what could have made him want to die. His funeral was closed-casket, so I never saw him again. At the time that disappointed me.

At the gravesite, Matt, the other pallbearers, and I held up his coffin and faced Adam's mother. She lifted her veil, and her face seemed literally cracked with grief. I had never seen a face as ravaged by mourning as that woman's face was. She was not old—perhaps late thirties or early forties at most—and I remembered, from my frequent visits to Adam's house, her being a good-looking woman. It shook me profoundly to see her face transformed into a web of wrinkles. I have never forgotten it.

After the funeral, Matt and I went out for a drink, and we resurrected our memories of Adam. The one that made us laugh and then quickly sobered us was the one of that night at Medi-Park, how we might have all drowned together, and how Adam had giggled through the whole disaster, as if privy to a joke we would never quite get.

2.

That summer when we flew into the lake at Medi-Park, between my sophomore and junior years, I lucked into a job as a bar-back at a country-western club on the outskirts of Amarillo. My mother worked as a waitress there. She talked the owner, an obese, red-headed man named Mickey who was in love with her, into hiring me, even though I was only sixteen. I knew if I got caught by the Texas Liquor Commission, the Western Club could have been shut down.

It was a great job, one that inspired awe among my friends, especially Adam and Matt. A bar-back is essentially a bartender's gofer. I washed glasses, refilled the soda gun tanks, kept the beer cases stocked, cleaned the counter, emptied the trash. This was around the time that the John Travolta and Debra Winger movie, *Urban Cowboy,* hit the movie screens. Country-western nightclubs in Texas were hot, especially if they had a mechanical bull, which the Western Club did. It was a huge place, with three separate bars, the bull ring with gymnastic mats all around to cushion the falls of drunken cowboys, a stage for the band, and a sawdust-covered dance floor. I wore a straw cowboy hat, pulled down low over my eyes, to help disguise my youth. During the rushes, I worked at such a frenzied pace that sweat poured from my hair, and my clothes were drenched. The Western Club was hopping every night, crammed so full that several times we were cited for fire code violations by the fire marshal.

I worked with two experienced bartenders, men who relished the kind of money that could be made at a nightclub like this. They shared their tips generously with me, and throughout the night they would pour shots of tequila for my mother, me, themselves, and my mother's younger brother, who also worked there that summer. We were usually pretty drunk by two in the morning, when the club shut down.

One night that summer, after we had closed, my mother offered to lock up so that Mickey, my uncle, and the other waitresses, bouncers, and bartenders could head over to the IHOP for breakfast. After they left, my mother took me to the liquor closet and walk-in. She and I gathered several cases of beer, as well as unopened bottles of bourbon, tequila, and vodka, and carried them out to the trunk of a yellow Trans Am that one of the men in love with my mother that summer had lent us. After we loaded up the trunk with our stash, we had another shot of tequila, and then she tossed me the keys and told me to drive.

We opened the top. I drove the long stretch to I-40 and got on the interstate. Nobody was around. The highway was desolate. My mother urged me to see how fast this puppy could go. I gunned it, past sixty, then seventy, eighty, and then ninety. Nervous, I started to taper off, and she asked me what the hell I was doing.

"Let 'er rip!"

I accelerated again, let the speedometer hover around hundred. The wind whished over our heads, and my mother put her hand on top of her wig to keep it from blowing away. "Faster," she shouted, "faster." We screamed down I-40 into the heart of Amarillo. She reached her leg over and pressed her foot on top of mine so we'd go even faster. She laughed wildly. We edged past 110 mph, zooming down the interstate. I gripped the steering wheel, and then my stomach shot into my throat as we flew past a policeman, who immediately turned on his flashers and sped after us.

I began slowing down, but my mother shouted, "Don't stop!" Seconds later, she said, "Get off here, get off here," and pointed to an exit.

I wheeled the Trans Am off the ramp, still going nearly ninety miles an hour. The stolen beer and the liquor bottles clanked in the back. "Turn here," she said. "Flip off your headlights." She directed me into an alley, where, following her orders, I stopped the car and shut it off. All of this maneuvering could have taken only fifteen or twenty seconds but seems, even now, long and vivid in my memory. We huddled in the seats and listened to the siren as it approached and then roared past the alley where we hid.

My mother and I had our knees on the floorboard, our faces close together on the vinyl seats. Our breaths whistled. Her wig was askew, and one of her false eyelashes was plastered to her cheek like an insect. My body shook, my heart thumping wildly in my neck and temples. She smiled at me, a big enough smile for me to see lipstick smudged on her top two teeth.

"Now that's what I call fun," she said.

3.

The next summer, between my junior and senior year, when I was seventeen, I lived with my father in Las Vegas. I had called him months earlier, desperate to escape Amarillo. He told me to get a lifeguard's certificate and then fly out to Nevada to spend the summer with him. He said he would get me a job as a pool boy at one of the casinos, maybe even Caesar's Palace.

The job never materialized. Instead, I spent the summer floating in his apartment complex pool, walking the suburbs of Las Vegas, reading Ralph Waldo Emerson's essays, and plotting a new and more wholesome future for myself. I rarely spoke to anyone, not even my father, though the silence was not, after a while, awkward. He spent most nights downstairs with his girlfriend, a stewardess-turned-dental hygienist, a thoughtful woman who recommended books to me and read my sad, self-pitying poetry and, in general, gave me the distance I longed for without making me feel unwanted. Those three months were a strange and wonderful time of solitude and reflection, an ironic place for a monkish retreat. It was, I knew then and still believe now, a transformational summer, the turning point in my life. Had my father not granted me that time, had he not encouraged me to loaf and read and dream, I know I would have soon been, like most of my family, married with kids, working some crappy job, forgoing college, and resenting my life.

The first week I spent with my father in Las Vegas, however, was not so benign. I was still secretly taking speed, and I felt betrayed that he had not come through with the glamorous pool boy job.

And perhaps most humiliating to me, his apartment was so small that he and I were forced, until he started sleeping downstairs with his girlfriend, to sleep together in his bed. He had only a loveseat, too small for either of us, in his living room. I had not seen my father in two years, and I felt that he had abandoned my sister and me. He was, in essence, a stranger. I had also just read *Moby-Dick* in school, and I felt like Ishmael bedding down with Queequeg his first night in New Bedford, wondering if the tattooed cannibal might eat him.

My father snored heavily, a habit of his he denied when I was younger until my mother and I recorded him foghorning his way through a nap. That first week, unable to sleep through the noise, I scrutinized him while he slept, something that I'm not proud of when I look back on it. It seems inhospitable, invasive, downright rude. But teenagers are not polite creatures. He was thirty-nine then, tanned, his skin freckled and starting to pucker and sag with sun and age. He'd lost some of the belly he had when he and my mother were married, but he still possessed a good-sized gut that looked ripe enough to thump. The wrinkles etched around his eyes and lips and crosshatched on his forehead disappeared while he slept, except for tiny creases as light as pencil lines. His upper lip vibrated when he snored, his teeth slightly yellowed and rimmed with nicotine stains. Three parallel wrinkles ringed his neck, like garroting marks, and his Adam's apple was not as prominent as in the pictures of him as the skinny kid who married my mother. A few hairs sprouted from his ears. He was handsome enough during the day—or so his girlfriend insisted: "Your father is a *very* handsome man, you know!" But at night that first week in Las Vegas, as I furtively watched him, I felt a little unnerved by what age could do to a man's body.

At seventeen, my body was, except for the excruciating pimples that I monitored with the vigilance of a prison guard, as athletic and smooth and taut as it would ever be. Though tall, I was still a boy in many ways, relatively hairless but muscled and immune to the effects of drugs and junk food. I found myself wondering if my body would grow into my father's. In the pictures of him as a young man, he was skinnier than me, goofy-looking with big ears and freckles. I marveled at the transformation and half-worried that in another twenty years this is what I had to look forward to: my own children examining my ossifying body while I warbled like a whale in my middle-aged sleep.

Soon enough, we worked out our routine for the summer. He moved downstairs, and I had his apartment to myself. I forgot all about those early awkward nights.

At the end of the summer, I returned to Amarillo. Things had changed there as well. Adam had by this time left for Colorado and the fate that waited for him in the mountains. While I was in Las Vegas, my mother had declared herself a new woman and married her sixth husband, a man who made fiberglass port-a-potties. I seldom saw Matt and, in fact, went out of my way to avoid him. I was ready for a new life, a transcendental life promised to me by Emerson.

I saw my father only a few more brief times before he died, four and a half years later, of a massive heart attack. When I flew to Las Vegas for his funeral and viewed his body in the casket, I suddenly recalled those early paranoid evenings in his apartment, scrutinizing his body with that peculiar mixture of adolescent curiosity and contempt. Except for his warbling snore and the rise and fall of his chest, it was like I was just watching him again while he peacefully slept.

I will be, by the time this essay is published, the same age my father was when he died, a fact that both comforts and confounds me. I don't know how a quarter of a century has gone by. More baffling to me is the fact that I have four children, and that my eldest, a boy who looks so much like my younger self that he seems to inhabit my teenage body, will be sixteen.

And I have become that snoring man.

ANATOMY
OF A LOSER

Pound for Pound

James P. Othmer

The easy thing would be to blame the Moon, or the lack of drinking water, which forced us to pour powdered pink lemonade mix directly into the half gallon of Popov vodka, or the fact that I had just chased down 500 times the daily recommended dosage of vitamin E with the very same Popov and powdered lemonade (PPL) concoction. I could blame the energy crisis or Jimmy Carter's sweater or the corrupting influence of the lyrics of Jethro Tull or my parents or the fact that I was a 145-pound sixteen-year-old with some serious confidence issues. But really. Anyone who punches his brother in the face (and larynx, and then runs away) is a loser.

My brother was home from the navy. His ship was in drydock in Philly and for a while he was making his way home almost every weekend. During the previous two years he'd been all over the Mediterranean and Caribbean and he had a sea bag full of stories to tell of foreign women and foreign cities, of bar fights and boxing matches and shipboard lunacy. He had a beard, he had a story to tell, and at over six foot two and 220 pounds, he had muscles. He was everything I wasn't in the summer of 1977, not that I didn't try. Once, when I was holding court by the lake while drinking a quart of Mad Dog 20-20, pretending to be tough and worldly and funny at the same time, one of my friends said I was trying too hard to be like my brother. I stopped talking and walked off with the bottle of cheap overproofed wine. I was furious. But I knew he was right.

Anyway, the day I punched my brother in the face (and larynx, and then ran away) began innocently enough. We left home early in the afternoon with no plan other than to find somewhere to drink outdoors together and get buzzed before heading inside to the bars. We picked up my best friend, Sully, at his house while his mother looked out the window as if I was taking her son on a suicide mission. Sully was a diabetic, had to inject himself several times a day, and often slipped into mild comas while drinking with me, so his mother had a point. For the record, I once told Sully that I didn't care if he drank with me, that I would still love him, and he told me that he didn't care if he lost his arms and legs and eyes to diabetes as long as I promised to prop him up on a barstool and stick a straw in his mouth. Next my brother picked up the half gallon of Popov (P) and we set to mixing it into the water jug with the pink lemonade mix (PL) in the liquor store parking lot. There was a lot of late June light left in the day as we filled our red plastic cups and pulled out, my brother at the wheel of my parent's 1973 Dodge Coronet. We drank and told stories, driving without a set destination over twisting roads wrapped in centuries-old farm walls and the thick trunks of oak and maple trees that seemed to claim a teenaged life every month back then. We stopped by the north side of the lake near an abandoned hotel that had once been a summer resort for Manhattan's elite. My brother told us about drinking a bottle of overproofed rum and jumping ship in Montego Bay. He told us about women with fruit baskets two feet high on their heads. He told us of a bar fight in Genoa in which he grabbed two men around the neck and ran them full speed through a plate-glass window. He told us about being busted in rank and soon promoted again because the captain, despite his wild streak, loved him. He was good for morale and, other than the lapses in shore leave behavior, a damned good sailor. We left the lake and drove to the Top of the World, so named because they were building a cable tower there from which, on clear nights, if you climbed over the fence and shimmied to the top, some said you could see the glow of Manhattan while others, more cynical, insisted it was the nuclear reactor at Indian Point. While we were drinking I told my brother this story:

Late one night a few weeks earlier my friend Lenny and I had picked up a drunken fifty-year-old Norwegian hitchhiker named Bernard but had decided to make a quick stop to climb the tower before dropping him off at the titty bar down the road. When Lenny and I got to the top of the tower and had swung out on one of its arms, our feet dangling a hundred feet over the mortal, sensible world, we could hear the ignition on the Coronet turn over far below and Bernard yelling, "You no take me to titty bar, now I take your car!"

My brother laughed, then reached into a brown paper bag and took out the jar of vitamin E. Sully and I watched transfixed as he opened the top of the brown glass container and held one of the small golden gel caps up to the light. "One of these," he assured us, "will increase your sexual potency . . . tenfold." After he washed it down with Popov and pink lemonade (PPL), I held out my hand. I was as certain as I'd ever been about anything that this was something I absolutely needed, despite the fact that I was sixteen years old, already unspeakably horny, with no girlfriend or sexual opportunities in sight beyond planning my TV schedule around Raquel Welch on the 4:30 movie or Charo on *The Merv Griffin Show* playing classical Spanish guitar in a low-cut dress. I took three Es and chased them with warm PPL. Watch out ladies of the Lake, the Fields, the Top of the World and the Moon! I just increased my raging adolescent sex drive by 300 percent! We drove some more. I remember us picking up a hitchhiker and rolling up the windows and turning the heat on high, despite the fact that it was more than 80 degrees out, and thinking that was funny. I remember stopping at the funeral parlor on Route 6 and my brother talking about his best friend who had died of lung cancer a year earlier and Sully remembering his brother who died of a brain tumor when he was seven. We toasted the dead with vitamin E and a PPL chaser. I remember stopping on lonely Stillwater Road because steam was hissing up out of the radiator. We opened the hood and had a drink while the engine cooled. After a while my brother opened the radiator cap and dropped two vitamin E tabs and a shot of PPL inside. "That should do it," he said. And I remember the town cop who pulled up alongside us while we were still outside with the jug of PPL and the open bottle of vitamin E on the roof of the Coronet. "What the heck are you up to now, Dickie?" he said to my brother.

"Just having some fun, Eddie."

"Well why don't you head home before you hurt someone."

"One more stop, Ed. Then home, okay?"

He didn't say yes or no. And I know that he knew we were on our way to a pretty nice drunk. But my brother had that effect. The cop, he just drove away.

Having already visited the lake and the Top of the World, our choice for outdoor drinking spots was pretty much narrowed down to one. We called it the Moon because it was a barren, rock-strewn, rutted landscape that sat curved on the rise of a hill that was, incidentally, lower than the Top of the World. The developers must have gone broke soon after clearing most of the trees, moving some boulders and doing perc tests because its appearance hadn't changed in years.

A correlation could be made between the moment we ran out of water and started pouring the lemonade powder directly into the neck of the vodka bottle and the moment we started talking about sports and then strength and then fights. My brother was and always will be stronger than me and that bothered me. But I was the better athlete and I claimed, because of my size, the tougher person. Which led to the pound-for-pound conversation. My 145 to his 220. Which led to . . . well I really don't know for sure what else we said in that car from that point on. I know that Sully at first tried to change the subject but he was already slipping, probably into a diabetic coma, but again, I can't be sure. This was one night I wouldn't be able to help him with a Snickers bar, a glass of orange juice. I'm sure I presented my case as best I could, probably some insane formula like push-ups plus pull-ups minus total weight and divided by your time in the forty-yard dash, and he probably laughed at me. The water was long gone. The vodka just about gone. But we did still have plenty of pink lemonade powder. Outside, the real moon began to rise, faintly illuminating the fake moon, and other cars had begun to arrive. But as they got out and began to drink and talk we were still inside our car, half a gallon of vodka ahead of them, operating in our own space and time. As some point, probably when the last of the PLP was gone, we got out and mingled. But whenever my brother and I were in the same group he would bring up the pound-for-pound debate. "Tell you what," he said more than once, sticking out his neck, pointing to his jaw. "If you're so tough you give me your best shot, then we'll see what happens."

I told him to go away. He was my brother. I wasn't going to punch him in the jaw. Besides I'd recently seen him take two horrendous head shots in a bar fight with an offensive lineman from Boston College before regrouping and knocking the college boy completely off his feet. So no. Absolutely not. He was my brother and besides that, unless I knocked him out, which was highly improbable, I'd be a dead man. Then he tapped me on the face once, and again. "Come on."

"Fuck you."

Another tap, light smack. Whatever. His face sticking out, his finger pointing to the base of his jaw. "Come on."

"No. You're my brother." What did I mean by that? That I couldn't punch my brother? Or that he shouldn't be pushing me like this, embarrassing us both in front of all these people? I still have no idea, but I said it several times. Then he slapped me again, fairly softly as far as slaps from a giant go, but enough to send my drunken brain over the edge. I punched him with a roundhouse right on the exact part of his jaw he'd just been pointing to, and as his head snapped back I followed it with relatively straight left to, that's right, his larynx. As he staggered back further, but not far enough, he wheezed or gasped. You pick. But when he stopped staggering he shook his head and the wheeze/gasp became a pants-soiling inducing roar followed by a bull rush toward me. Someone must have gotten in his way long enough for me to realize that the free roundhouse punching part of the program was over for the night, so I ran. I ran across the surface of the Moon faster than my brother, faster than Armstrong or Aldrin or any Apollo astronaut ever could have dreamed. I hurdled gullies and moon rocks, finally coming to rest behind a rock pile in my version of the Sea of Tranquility. I listened to his roars and then the voices of the others, not so much subduing him but reasoning with him, calming him down. Calling me an ass-hole. He left first. Through a gap between two boulders I watched our car pull away, hopefully driven by someone else, preferably not Sully.

Later, I was dumped on my parents' lawn like a freed hostage by friends so afraid of my father that their car barely stopped. It was still early. Probably not much after nine o'clock but to me it seemed like four a.m. Sometime after the glow from the TV and their bedroom lights went out I went inside. In my room, which was next to my brother's, I slid the dresser in front of the door in case he came home drunk enough to still want to finish me off in front of my parents.

But he didn't. At some point when I was asleep he must have slipped into the house and gone to bed. The next morning, afraid of seeing my brother, afraid of letting my father see me so hungover, I opened my bedroom window to take a piss. Halfway through, I heard my brother's window open. Then my brother's head burst through the thick plastic covering that my father had put over our windows that winter to save energy. As he vomited I flinched and recoiled away from the window before he could notice me. But then slowly I leaned my head back outside and watched the last of the pink lemonade–tinged puke fall onto the lawn. When my brother was finished he turned to me as if he knew I'd been there the whole time (or perhaps my pissing had woken him up?). He raised his left hand to his jaw, rubbed it, and then he smiled. "You loos-ened my fucking tooth," he said, finally. All I could say was, "Sorry," and for the time being, that seemed to be enough.

Since then we've grown up, married, and had kids. My brother became a New York City fireman and I went to college and got a college boy job and finally became a writer. We never hit each other again but we have learned to hurt each other in other ways.

We seem to disagree over everything now from Supreme Court justice nominations to the status of post 9-11 Muslims to the attention bestowed upon us by our mother. Some nights we are the best of friends and I hang on his every word and want to believe it all. Others I don't. Sometimes I push back where others would never dare with him. Sometimes I probably invite the verbal smacks, others I think he can't help himself. What's your problem? he asked me, time and again late at night the last time we spoke. Tell me what your problem is with me. Once again I tried to resist. Twenty-eight years later we are still standing toe to toe, ready to put the pound-for-pound formula to a new test. Our wives and children had gone home and he was asking me to hit him once again, this time with my opinion, and once again I couldn't stop myself from obliging.

This time he didn't poke his head through the plastic the next morning and smile. This time we couldn't blame it on Popov and pink lemonade or vitamin E or the fact that we were teenagers. This time it hurt more than ever.

It's four months later and we're still not talking. Twenty-eight years and four months later me and my big brother are still on the Moon, loving each other and doing everything we can to destroy it.

Scoliosis and
an Ogilvie Home Perm

Timothy Schaffert

I'm up on the counter in the kitchen of my grandma's trailer house, permanent solution dripping off the curlers in my hair, seeping out from beneath the thin pink plastic cap, and stinging the skin of my forehead

It's the tail end of my junior year. Next week I'll sit for my senior pictures, so my fake curls need a quick chemical zap. Afros are out at this point in the history of hairdos, but boys still get "body" perms, enough curl and lift to allow for Farrah Fawcett–esque feathered bangs that I can fluff with a neon-green pick I keep in my back pocket. It's all a little too 1970s for this late in the 1980s, but it generally takes about ten years for everything good from every-place else to reach the middle of Nebraska.

There are two brands carried by the local drugstore where I work part-time as a cashier and stock boy; I wanted the Rave home perm—it somehow seems more sexy, with its disco-fat lettering across a box colored in ungirly earth tones—but Grandma prefers Ogilvie's application tools. The Ogilvie, violet-colored and curly-cuey, is fruitier than a box of tampons.

A few of the girls I work with at the drugstore offered to Rave my hair, which I would've preferred. They've graduated from high school, and though they aren't yet quite twenty-one, the drinking age has only just changed and so they're grandfathered into adult-hood, still able to buy booze. We could've sat around on a Saturday

afternoon drinking Riunite peach wine as they acted blasé about their overactive sex lives. Whenever I hang out with the girls at the drugstore, I feel dirty and adult—they're ladies of the '80s, with careers as pharmacy techs and subscriptions to *Playgirl*.

But my grandma's heart would break if I let someone else administer my senior-picture perm. And any guilt I ever feel punches me hard in the gut—at fifteen, I was diagnosed with stomach ulcers. I had to guzzle practically a gallon of a chalky malt, while lying on my side in a hospital gown, for them to X-ray the slimy trail of my anxiety, and when I think of the taste of it a few decades later, I recall the Pepsi and chocolate-covered long john I got afterward at the donut shop where my mom took me to cheer me up, the acid mix of the soda and frosting sizzling in my throat.

Truth, though, I'm thankful for Grandma's expertise with the Ogilvie, because it means I don't have to sit and stew for an hour in a salon. I did that once, as a sophomore. Stuck in the corner with a years-old copy of *Rona Barrett's Hollywood,* waiting for my perm to set, two of the high school's jocks swaggered in for haircuts. They were both seniors, and didn't know me, but I felt like a sad, little boy-princess as they flirted with Joanne, the hairdresser, and as Joanne flirted back. I hated and feared those boys, but I also wanted to *be* them, which was the reason I was sitting there in curlers and a floral smock to begin with. When I was a senior, I vowed, my beauty would be threatening; I'd look like the men who modeled skimpy briefs in the Spiegel catalog. I'd have natural curls and I would dare to wear paisley.

My grandma times my perm with a plastic egg timer that she's had for years, has moved from house to house, despite the fact that one whole side of it's melted from having sat too many times too close to a stove's burner, and that it loudly click-click-clicks the minutes away, then gives you a heart attack when it finally starts beating its bell. Grandma occasionally comes over and wipes the dripping perm solution from my forehead with a dishrag, concerned about my skin. In addition to my ulcers, I've been diagnosed with chronic acne and my mom drives me twenty miles every few weeks to visit a dermatologist's office where I get shots stuck right smackdab into the sore, infected parts of my face.

As a man, when I think about the boy I was, I'll see myself as a constant patient, sitting atop the examining table, the paper crinkling beneath me with every movement, my mother on the wheeled stool in the corner, her purse in her lap, the air in the room needle-sharp with an antiseptic stink. My doctor always looks askance at my mother as she describes my symptoms for me, as if he suspects she's slowly poisoning me to feed her own need for attention. For every woman in my family, going to a doctor's appointment is like going to church, requires she bleach the hair above her lip the night before, sleep in curlers, put on lipstick and a smart pantsuit in the morning.

I've seen this same doctor several times throughout my teens, endured his bafflement over my various conditions and the fact that he never remembers me from visit to visit. A few years after I graduate, I hear rumors that he checked himself into a rehab clinic. I did sense some confusion when I was alone with him in his office as he spoke into a tape recorder. He'd just examined my X-rays to determine if I had scoliosis, and had revealed that not only was my spine crooked, but much of the rest of me was, as well. "Which side of your hipbone did I say sat too high?" he asked me. I couldn't remember, but I was anxious to please him, so I told him it was the left side, feigning certainty, like I knew anything at all about my own ineptly connected skeleton.

Fortunately the scoliosis doesn't require a brace, though at times I wish that it did. A brace would prevent me from pursuing sports for which I have no talent. I choose to run cross-country because it doesn't require teamwork—in such a sport, I reason, I won't be beaten for dropping the ball, or failing to catch the ball, or throwing the ball like a pansy.

And I thought in cross-country I wouldn't get hurt, but I did, regardless. The meets are always held on golf courses, which sometimes means leaping up and over things. During one of my first competitions when I was a freshman, I miscalculated a narrow creek; while the other boys gracefully sprung forward in a mini-jeté, barely kicking up dirt, I landed in the middle of the muddy waters, spraining my ankle. The next year, after being trained in how to use the stride of my long legs to pick up speed on the downside of a hill, I over-strode, tearing cartilage in my knee.

So, though it's tempting to blame my frequent trips to the doctor on the toxins that protect and fertilize the farm I grow up on, on the thousands of nights spent breathing in chemicals as I sleep beneath an open window, or my habit of sunning myself on the lawn in the summertime in cut-off Sergio Valentes, listening to "Shock the Monkey" over and over on my cassette player, watching the crop dusters swoop down and up in a kind of air show as they spray the soil, the wind carrying their plague deep into my lungs, I'm also, admittedly, dangerously uncoordinated. I even broke my arm once in a field-day running-backward race, tripping over my own feet. ("Six more weeks," my addled doc informed me, rapping his knuckles against my cast, when I went in after six weeks to have the cast removed. "But it's *been* six weeks," I told him. "Oh!" he said. "Well then let's get that thing off ya!")

I've gotten speedier in cross-country, but it wasn't rare my freshman year to come strolling in dead last, even the elastic of my tube socks abandoning hope and unraveling, dropping the tops of my socks down to my ankles. But even being the champion loser of every race wasn't as humiliating as showering with the football team after practice. Gangly, long-limbed, stick-thin, my skin barely concealing my skeleton in all its glorious scoliosis, my face puffy and swollen and blossoming with a mutilating acne, normally invisible-me tends to attract attention when completely nude. In addition to my curved spine and crooked hipbone, one side of my chest protrudes due to excess cartilage pushing out the bone; my doctor always told me it would even out as the muscles of my chest developed as a young man, but my chest never develops, and young manhood seems unachievable.

Once, when I was a freshman, one handsome senior football player smiled at me in the locker room, and I smiled back, thinking perhaps he was about to be friendly. But he nudged the guy next to him, nodded in the direction of me in my towel, and said, "P. T. Barnum's human oddity." *P. T. Barnum and His Human Oddities* was the title of a popular HBO documentary, about legendary freaks like the Elephant Man.

Rendering me even more freakish was the fact that I couldn't take my eyes off the guys who were so mean to me. I marveled at the perfect engineering of their bodies as the water rolled along their freckled skin in the showers, their bones in perfect order, the leg bones connected to the knee bones, the knee bones connected to the thigh bones, everything exactly where it needed to be.

*

Toward the end of my senior year, I get more responsibility at the drugstore. Sometimes the druggist now allows me to work back in the pharmacy, where I count out pills and type labels on the IBM Selectric.

When I was a little kid, I yearned for the day I'd be old enough to pop tranquilizers. Whenever the characters in movies got jittery in the '70s, they took a Valium, and just the act of it—pouring a glass of water, rattling out a pill into the palm of your hand, slapping the Valium back and taking a long gulp—looked to be a restorative ritual. To me, back then, being an adult meant listening to Redd Foxx records, pouring booze from a cut-glass decanter in the middle of the day like Sue Ellen Ewing, and taking a Valium to tame the butterflies in your gut. My mom even had to replace the baby aspirin in the bottle in the medicine cabinet with a look-alike candy because, at nine years old, I had decided I needed to take an orange-flavored St. Joseph's to get to sleep at night. She worried the aspirin would give me a syndrome.

"These are the only condoms I'll use," the pharmacist tells me, holding up a reflective black box of lambskin prophylactics. He always insists on stocking the condoms himself, which are kept high on the shelves next to the L'eggs pantyhose display. Then, just a few months before I graduate, he asks me to join him in replenishing the selection of Trojans and Sheiks. The druggist is pudgy and effeminate and flirts with the old ladies by calling them "young lady" in a way that I always find condescending and charmless. He often cries when he has arguments with the store's accountant, a tall woman with an intimidating, bright-red beehive, whose husband owns the liquor store. But the man is nonetheless married, and the father of a new baby.

As the druggist discusses the superiority of his preferred brand of condom, defining its silky elegance in chaste terms, I decide I'll adopt the brand as my own. I have no use for condoms, but I want to educate myself on their proper installation, and to keep one always at the ready in my wallet—teenage boys have a genuine, pre-occupying fear of being caught without a rubber when the opportunity for sex inexplicably presents itself.

I look forward to someday impressing a girl with the extravagance of my lambskin condom. Plus I think it would be kinky to jerk off into one (which I do do eventually, after stealing a box of four; it turns out to be a letdown, and afterward I become terrified that my mother will find the spent rubber no matter how I dispose of it. I end up burying it in the yard in the middle of the night).

*

We begin to stock and inventory the condoms together on a regular basis. In a stern professional tone, he informs me of the mutual benefits of ribbed condoms, and how one must pinch the reservoir tip after rolling one on in order to prevent air from filling it and risking breakage. I learn that one must hold the condom firm at the base of the penis when pulling out, to avoid the condom slipping off to get lost within the dark, murky realm of the vagina.

Then one day he asks if I've ever had occasion to use a condom. I don't ask him to specify whether he means alone or with someone, so I simply say no. "Well," he says, nudging me with his elbow, "there's a group of girls who come in here giggling whenever you're at the cash register. I think they have a crush."

I know the girls he means. They're fourteen, maybe younger; one girl with dirty hair, who wears flip-flops even in the winter, comes in regularly with a note from her mother instructing me to sell her daughter a pack of cigarettes; the mother's always too sick to come in on her own.

The druggist's rubber instruction neither embarrasses nor arouses me, unlike when I actually sell the condoms to boys I know. There are two other drugstores in town, but word got out that I offer a discount whenever I man the cash register. I secretly sell the boys the rubbers at cost when they stop in after school. Handling the boxes, ringing them up at a bargain price, slipping them into paper bags imprinted with the Hallmark Cards insignia, feels illicit, and makes my hands shake and my heart beat fast and makes my already snug corduroys get a little tighter at the crotch. Someday, I reason, my insights into the sex lives of these high school boys, and my almost clinical understanding of the fits and foibles of various brands of condoms, will be the key to my success as a desirable lover for the right girl for me.

*

The girls I most want to take to the prom are the lovelies of the God Squad, a group of virginal evangelicals who are allowed to opt out of reading *The Catcher in the Rye* in College Prep English because of the book's language. Instead they read *Tess of the D'Urbervilles*. While the rest of us wonder what's so corrupting about Holden Caulfield, we see the God Squad poring over their paperback Tesses, with the movie tie-in cover of Natassja Kinski (a girl we all knew had been deflowered by Roman Polanski and posed naked with a python up her leg), and we come to think of them as the true libertines of senior class. Those churchy farm girls, with hair so white-blond it seems almost see-through, always without permission slips for anything worth doing, blossom into sultry Europeans right before our eyes, each one a mini-Kinski seemingly on the very verge of a self-governed defilement.

In my effort to seem not gay, I've let my hair go permless for months, the last little curl finally giving out and straightening up just days before prom, and I've cultivated a mullet which stretches long down the back of my neck. I've grown some fashionable half-shaven stubble on my chin, too, and I've bought a white suit and a pastel-blue T-shirt like Don Johnson wears on *Miami Vice*. I no longer look much like my senior pictures.

As part of the photography studio's senior-picture package, I got one close-up pose airbrushed, my acne smoothed from my cheeks, the severity of my Adam's apple lessened, the harsh, burnt-out curls of my home perm given a soft-focus halo. In all the un-airbrushed pictures I wasn't quite the Elephant Man, but I was definitely no one better than myself; but I swooned when I first saw that pretty, blurry boy. Someone even tells me, as he holds the picture, squinting at it, studying it, that I almost look like Danny Romalotti, the rock star on *The Young and the Restless*.

*

Dateless, I decide to skip the prom, but a friend fixes me up on a blind date with a girl named Ginny from a few towns over, who wants to be an airline stewardess. She looks like a stewardess already, with the bland beauty of a flat-chested plastic doll, her face ghost-white but for some pink lipstick and thin lines of blue eye shadow. I can't believe my good fortune, and I fall instantly in love, beaming with pride when other boys ask her to dance and she refuses with the tiniest no's that lift from her puckered geisha-girl lips. I act all night like the date wasn't blind at all, and that Ginny, eyes wide open, chose me.

After the prom, many of us head over to a party in a barn, and Ginny becomes uncomfortable when a group of boys, after sniffing around the crowd for drugs of any kind, decide to go out into the field to huff some Raid. Ginny knows the date of a girl I know, and the four of us go up the highway to an all-night diner, where we have breakfast at two a.m. The other boy, who drives us in his Dodge Royal Monaco Brougham, speaks all night in a phony, failing English accent.

As we head back to town, the mock-English boy falls asleep, sending the car off the highway and into the ditch. Ginny and I, in the backseat, grab each other's hands and grip tight, but there's no collision; the boy wakes and steers the car right back up out of the ditch, onto the pavement. All of us laugh nervously, make a few jokes, but mostly fall silent, having private moments with our own mortality.

Ginny's hand is still in mine, and I hold perfectly still, fearful she's not aware of it, that if I move an inch, she'll wake from her reverie and snap her hand back. Eventually, she does take back her hand, but sweetly, giving my skin an affectionate goodbye rub with her thumb then gently untwining her fingers from mine, forever. For days after, I stop at moments to close my eyes, not to think of Ginny, but to concentrate on the feel of the press of her skin, and the weight of her hand in mine, which wasn't much. Her hand, even when she was struck with fear, was as light as pure air.

White Anklets
and Blue Anything

ELIZABETH CRANE

Dear Ben,

Now that we've been together for a while, and I feel pretty sure it's going to stick (what with those crazy marriage vows we took a while back), I think the time has come for me to let you in on a secret I've been keeping.

I was not always cool.

It's true.

You can stop laughing now.

No, really. You can stop laughing now. I know the Rick Springfield record probably clued you in a while ago.

Anyway, let's assume I'm using the word *cool* as a relative term. As something not ordained by a group of thirteen-year-olds, but as in the eye of the beholder. Back in the seventies, for most of the seventies, I'm fairly sure the only reason I didn't suffer more abuse at the hands of the class brat was because I had very unintentionally aligned myself with Nina, who, as you know, is still my best friend. Nina, whose coolness level was initially on par with mine, which is to say that coolness was equally absent on both our parts, had been considered by many to be the cutest girl in the sixth grade. But due to a bad haircut and a new set of braces in seventh, Nina was noticeably more awkward the following year, and therefore I was newly qualified to hang out with her.

We became friends in seventh-grade French class, at a small

private school on the Upper West Side of Manhattan. Bad haircut or not, I would not have chosen her as my best friend. I had some extremely complex judgments about her that I'd formulated the previous year. She'd been absent for what seemed like half the year, and in my mind, I was certain it was because people like Nina (i.e., people with more money than us, whatever that meant to eleven-year-old me) could just wake up in the morning and tell their parents they didn't feel like going to school and their parents would say la la whatever you want. I'd had perfect attendance records since first grade, not because I didn't get the occasional malady, but because of a sort of "buck up" mentality in our household. As long as I wasn't suffering from an open head wound, I was sent to school, sick or not, bad weather or good, I'm sure, because I was undead. (By third grade, I was already aware that the "mod" girls did not come to school in a downpour dressed like the Gorton's fisherman, as I was. Lesson # 1: Umbrellas and heavy raingear = uncool. Soaking wet from top to bottom but wearing hot pants = groovy.) I was convinced that the Ninas of the world got to do as they pleased. In any case, at the time, I was doing better in French than Nina, and our teacher suggested I tutor her after school. Somehow, in spite of my (entirely erroneous, it would turn out) judgments, we quickly bonded on a variety of subjects. We were both aspiring writers, both came from academic/classical-music-making families, both liked *The Partridge Family,* though I was alone in my feelings for Danny. I have to give the credit to Nina for us being friends at all—I wouldn't have been friends with me if I were her, but Nina is, simply put, a very nice person. I'm somewhat nice, but I was less nice then. Nina had and still has a quality whereby she's friendly and willing to overlook a lot of flaws if she sees some little seed of good in someone. Whereas I enjoy holding not just my own but other people's resentments long after they've let them go.

There isn't much to report in the way of dramatic incidents, episodes, or occasions. I may not have been the biggest geek of all time, but at no time during the years between 1970 and 1977 was I ever mistaken for cool. I was teased about a few things, but there were others who suffered more than I did. I tended to fly, for the most part, under the radar. In retrospect, I have no idea how I managed this, because I believe the following will justly invite some retroactive abuse, and that former classmates of mine will hunt me down and say *Ha ha* like that bully on *The Simpsons*.

What I do I have is much in the way of evidence. Witness:

1) In seventh grade, I was quite enamored of Fred Astaire, and signed up for tap-dancing lessons. (Nina was a Gene Kelly fan, another bonding point being our love of old movie musicals.) Compare and contrast: other kids in our class were going to see *Tommy*.

2) Also in seventh grade, I signed up for Barbizon's School of Modeling. It should be noted, since you didn't grow up anywhere near the New York tri-state area in the seventies, that the Barbizon School was one of those heavily advertised academies that cost my parents five hundred begged-for 1972 dollars and should have been required to have quotation marks around the word "Modeling." It turns out that modeling isn't something you have to go to school for, but even if you did, probably there ought to be some requirements for admittance, which at Barbizon, there were not. Nevertheless, I had my reasons for wanting to go, one being that I perceived myself to be quite beautiful in spite of the fact that this was recognized by exactly no one else at the time besides my mom. I genuinely believed that the boys at our school were just idiots not to see it. Photographic evidence in the way of my 2 x 3 feet graduation photo from BSM, dressed in a printed polyester leisure suit, handmade by my grandmother to my specifications, proves I may have been the idiot.

3) My wardrobe. At the time I was into blue anything. So I'd get the cool shoes, Wallabees one year, Kork-Ease wedgies another, but I'd get them in blue. Which. Was not cool. It did not occur to me that colors were in style and out as much as anything else. (See also: anklets, white; shirt, maternity; leisure suit, polyester; anything, blue)

4) My taste in music. (See also: Tennille, The Captain and; Archies, The)

5) My taste in literature. With one or two slightly more intellectual exceptions, my preferences at this time ran to *Archie Comics, Mad, Barbie Talk* magazine, and my mother's *Cosmo,* with the occasional true crime story or V. C. Andrews novel thrown in.

6) My taste in movies. (See also: *Boy in the Plastic Bubble, The; Amityville Horror, The; Boogie, Roller*)

7) My taste for Broadway musicals. (All-inclusive, except for *Cats.* Even I was cooler than that.)

8) My words. Witness these random snippets from when I was *fifteen and sixteen years old*:

August 1, 1976. "Nina has a new boyfriend named Tracy. (!?) Doesn't she have all the luck." Further down on the same subject, "Chee!"

October 3, 1976. On attending a pot party where I certainly did not partake. "What is this world coming to? I'm afraid to try cigarettes, let alone blow my mind on acid."

July 24, 1977. "Nina is considering sex with her boyfriend. God. What is this world coming to?"

July 27, 1977. After the deed. "I still like her just as much as before though. She sounds exactly the same and I'm glad I didn't reject her for what she did."

In and of itself, I think you'll agree that my use of the phrase *What is this world coming to?* speaks volumes on the topic at hand.

For several years, a typical afternoon for Nina and me would be spent at one of our apartments, eating toaster pigs in the blanket and watching *James at 15* while my best friend from previous years was over at her older boyfriend's head shop doing, um, it. Nina and I often enjoyed a game of "Who Can Drop a Pin Down the Staircase and Find It First?" At school I would continue to be teased on a semiregular basis. One of my favorite outfits was a smock that yes, as one of the boys liked to point out, did probably look like a maternity dress, and also I was still wearing lacy white cuffed anklets in a school full of rainbow-striped knee socks, which was apparently very third-grade. My memory holds that Nina may still have had a smidge of immunity from the previous year, but she reminds me that this same anklet adjudicator once said to the entire class, in her short-haircut era, "Who's that boy sitting in Nina's chair?" to much laughter. Also, Nina didn't hang with "The Group" as we called them, three or four popular girls and their boyfriends, and she didn't seem to care any more than I did.

The change came sort of suddenly. Nina got her hair cut into wings, and perfect wings they were, always. Any attempt I made at feathered hair failed miserably. She got a pair of adorable bell-bottoms with heart-shaped pockets and the boys sat up and took note. I picked out a few things that were slightly more acceptable than in previous years, but the best I could do was go unnoticed. I still had a few twenty extra pounds of "baby fat." I suppose unnoticed was a step up from noticed and openly mocked, but when your best friend turns into a hottie overnight and you gain a new identity as "Nina's friend," it's in some ways a more painful reminder that you yourself are not considered by anyone other than yourself to be a hottie. That you are not considered anything, really. Witness this more depressing diary entry from December 1, 1976: "I hate being a teenager. I wish I was 18. I get lousy grades. No one wants to date me. I don't do what the other kids do (smoke, etc.). Life so far is not too good." Nina's internal life had its own involved system of insecurities, but from my vantage point it only mattered that she was cute, thin, wealthy, and had a constant string of boyfriends and suitors from that time on. One way we both handled our individual issues was by getting in on the ground floor of what would later become known as codependency. Nina had an inexplicable interest in us dressing identically. We did have one or two of the same garments, and I found this idea to be positively insane, preferring to wear them on separate occasions. Once in a while I let my guard down and mentioned what I'd be wearing to school the next day; there Nina would be in a close approximation of the same thing, the result for me, besides extreme embarrassment, always being the mis-conception around school that the idea to dress alike was mine. (Overall equation: Dressing like twins at age sixteen = unfortunate at best.) I made sure that we had the exact same class schedule for several years. I don't know what I thought would happen if I'd had to endure a class without her in the room, but I did my best not to find out. We were on the phone before school, after school, wrote bundles of letters when we were away, and Nina incurred more than a bit of punishment for calling me long distance at a time when charges were considerably more expensive. If we did not know of, or for some reason were not included in, the other's plans (okay, this was pretty much just me, like at times when Nina maybe, I dunno, wanted to go on a date by herself), then hurt feelings, misunder-standings, and meltdowns always ensued.

But for the most part, where Nina went, I went. More and more there were parties and "discoing" and weekends at Nina's house on Fire Island, where there was a whole other circle of cute boys inter-ested in Nina, although, once in a while, boys noticed me too. These boys, in my opinion, were always uncool. Boys who expressed interest in me were described as "duds" or "yucks." Is it surprising at all that only duds and yucks were interested in the girl who used the words *duds* and *yucks?* I developed my sense of humor, which some-times resulted in people remembering my name.

It's possible that I was left alone as much as I was because, while I was deeply and visibly uncool, I feigned a cool attitude. I did not let it be known that I didn't know anything that one was supposed to know, I did not let it be known that I was capable of being hurt by anyone, and I certainly knew better than to announce that Nina and I spent many a teenage night watching *The Love Boat* or *Donny and Marie.* Although both of us have since had a lot of ther-apy, I'm grateful she's still willing to be my friend. We can actually get through almost a week without a phone call now, and we've lived in different cities for ten years—and I was the one who moved away.

Things started looking up senior year and improved significantly in college. I frequently describe myself as a late bloomer, and since then, although my tastes in many of the aforementioned areas are negligibly more sophisticated, thanks in no small part to your arty presence in my life, if I have any level of coolness, it's only in the way that a forty-five year old can be, which is that I'm happy with my life now. Soon we'll have kids and I'll become hopelessly uncool all over again.

Of course, I feel obliged to mention that as I write this, my skin is broken out, I have my hair in a ponytail with some random bobby pins unsuccessfully holding back the parts that refuse to stay in, something flew into my left eye that feels like a twig, rendering it closed, and I have just pointed out to you the irony of my supposing to write a piece about how I was a geek in school but those days are gone. And you said, "You're married to me. That makes you de facto cool." And coming from the boy who had once a Flock of Seagulls haircut, I know it must be true.

Sports

Owen King

The nagging suspicion that I was a shithead followed me through most of my high school years. My self-image was not unlike one of those photographs of the Loch Ness Monster. There was always something slightly off, but I could never figure out what, exactly. I'd seen the artist's renderings of the beast, the huge, bulbous body, the flippers, the majestic neck, and the wise little head, and didn't the shadowy shape emerging from the Scottish depths look eerily like the real thing? I had to admit that it did—and yet, the doubt remained. It was like the guys who claimed to have girlfriends in other towns, or to have gotten laid over the summer. While you couldn't disprove what they said, it strained credibility. Why were girls in other towns fucking everybody? What was wrong with the girls in my town? Why was there still a dinosaur in this particular lake? Why Scotland?

Of course, when it came to being cool, I didn't have to depend upon unverified photographs or artist's renderings. I had a very concrete idea of how a cool guy looked and acted. To whit:

A cool guy dressed in Gap jeans with a woven leather belt.

A cool guy arranged said Gap jeans and woven leather belt so that the colorful top band of his striped/polka-dotted/moose-festooned boxer shorts showed.

A cool guy carried his stuff in an L.L. Bean backpack, using only one back strap, while keeping his free hand in his pocket as he cruised the halls.

A cool guy wore loafers with no socks when it was warm and hiking boots when it was cold.

If a cool guy was capable of growing facial hair, he would grow a goatee.

Now, I know what you're thinking: this teenage ideal sounds, well, sort of gay. Nor am I so sure that this supposition is entirely unfounded. The rituals of young manhood run rich with homoeroticism. Still, allow me to point you to the most crucial element of being cool:

A cool guy always—*always*—played sports.

And what could be less gay than sports?

*

I played basketball and baseball for all four years of high school, becoming a letterman in the latter as a junior, and ascending to the varsity in the former as a senior.

In basketball at least, I wasn't terrible. I was 6'3"—a size that in Maine automatically makes you a center—and while I was slow, graceless, and jumped as though some demented surgeon had implanted bricks in my ass, I made up for it somewhat by being wide-bodied and long-armed. I wasn't much of a shooter, either, but I had some cunning as a post-up player, a knack for drawing fouls even if I couldn't finish, and I made most of my free throws.

However, I attended the largest public school in the state, Bangor High School,* which meant that unless you were some kind of basketball savant, your only hope was to make steady progress from the freshman team to the junior varsity, and hopefully, as a junior or a senior, to the varsity.

So as a fourteen-year-old I played for the freshman squad under the leadership of Coach Stennett. Coach Stennett, besides holding the record for the most concussions in the history of University of Maine football, had supposedly gone bareheaded into the helmet-

*The Home of the Rams
Call: "What are we?"
Response: *"Rams!"*
Call: "What are we going to do?"
Response: *"Ram you!"*
See? Nothing at all gay about that.

butting circle before the Bangor football team's playoff game that
fall, finally emerging from the mosh pit with a gashed forehead and
a blood-streaked face, like some Down East Conan.

We were all understandably terrified, and in our first practice, he
lived up to expectations.

After lining us up behind the baseline, Coach Stennett
announced, "Boys, I am only going to warn you once. This line"—
he pointed to the baseline—"belongs to me. It is my line. And I do
not want you to stand on my line. Is that clear?"

We nodded.

"Good. Now that we've got that straight, I want to tell you, boys,
we are here because—"

Coach Stennett stopped. He was a trim, fit-looking man, but
behind his square, Poindexter glasses, Coach Stennett's eyes were
small and weird. There was something of the mad scientist about
him. You could imagine him in a butcher's coat, handling organs,
turning them over, making appreciative noises. When he looked at
my teammate Charlie Hankins, a few players down the line, they
seemed to sparkle with creepy glee.

"Charlie," crowed Coach Stennett. "Charlie, what did I tell
you about my line, Charlie?"

Charlie glanced down. The toes of his high-tops were on the
baseline. He quickly jumped back, as if the line were electrified.

But it was too late.

"We're gonna run, fellas," said Coach Stennett, not quite accurately—he wasn't going to run, the bastard.

In the course of the two hours that followed we must have run
something like two-dozen suicides. The exhaustion this caused
was self-perpetuating. Gasping, in a stupor, guys kept staggering forward and trespassing on Coach Stennett's line.

"Fellas," he'd say. "What'd I tell you about my line, fellas?"

For those of you unfamiliar with the terminology, a *suicide* is that
most wicked variation of the basketball sprint, where you run the
first quarter of the court, slap the floor and run back to the baseline,
slap the floor and run to the middle of the court, slap the floor and

run again to the baseline, slap the floor and run three-quarters up the court, slap the floor and again back to the baseline, slap the floor and run all the way up the court, slap the floor and run all the way back to the baseline, rushing through the curtain of black spots now falling across your field of vision.

It's okay to cry; I certainly did.

After the first few suicides, guys started asking to go to the locker room and puke. When one guy shuffled out of the locker room, another guy would lurch in for his turn to retch, and as the two passed each other they would—bizarrely—high-five.

I remember standing in front of the school that night after practice, waiting for my mother to come pick me up. It was late November and dark at five-thirty, and as I stared at our red-walled high school—which with its cylinder-shaped auditorium and long, meandering central building connected by ramps, looked like nothing so much as an ancient spaceship half-buried in the ground—I had the impression that one or the other of us was about to float away into the night. I sat on the frozen grass and monitored the spasms of my leg muscles.

I considered my accomplishments: I had made my first team, survived my first practice, vomited in the company of my teammates. Everything I could have hoped for.

*

And if I ever doubted my sacrifice, the team managers served as constant living reminders of the cold, friendless, and perpetually virginal existence that one risked by not playing sports. Either very fat, or very skinny—but always bespectacled—the team managers were typically the kind of boys who actually paid attention to what was happening on the field during football games while everyone else was flirting. They actually cared whether the high school's sports teams won. They were geeks.

The team managers were also, I see now, poor kids. In my memory they are just a lineup of nervously grinning, acne-afflicted boys with smudged glasses and uncombed hair, all dressed in stonewashed jeans. The team managers didn't have any of the same upper-level classes as my friends and I. Managers were the kind of guys who took machine shop and planned to go to technical college after graduation. Some of them were in the ROTC. I never saw a manager at the movie theater or at Friendly's or, God forbid, at a party. They attended our sports camps in the summer, but not to play. They came to work, to run the clock and pick up the basketballs and fetch things for the coaches, just as they did during the year, except in the summer they received a wage for their service. The managers didn't wear leather weave belts from the Gap, and if by the time we were seniors they were driving cars, the cars were not shiny gifts from their parents, but battered old Hondas that they bought themselves and which were in constant danger of crapping out forever in the subzero winters.*

Irony—the linguistic key of the young and well-to-do, then and now—never seemed to cross their lips, while they could be counted on to laugh loyally on cue at our every razor-sharp jape about fags, hos, tards, and other objects of disdain.

And Ronald Petrie was the king of the managers.

Rotund, and prone to wearing plaid shirts tucked into his unbelted jeans, Ronald was heavy, chubby-cheeked, and—according to the secret code of high school sports managers everywhere—bespectacled. His most trenchant feature, however, was a little black mustache, which clung to his protruding upper lip like some sort of ill moss.

A senior when I was a freshman, Ronald was so dedicated to Bangor High sports that he remained a team manager even *after* he graduated. He just kept right on coming to practices and games, volunteering to lug the bags of equipment and chart statistics, still laughing uproariously when Nick Dunbar minced around the locker room with his dick tucked between his legs and pre-

---

*In Maine you can accurately track the course of winter by the growing number of abandoned cars in high school parking lots. By early April, when the snow melted, in my high school parking lot there were usually about a dozen of them, strange and rusted blooms.

tended to be female, or when Frank Geoghan exhibited his never-washed practice jersey, which each night froze stiff on its hook, so that it could be taken out of a locker and carefully set down on the floor to stand upright, like some awful little teepee.

Our sports teams were Ronald's life, and he must have loved to be around the players, to feel like he was a part of something. Naturally, we loathed him. He was never—and could never be—a part of the team. He was manager for life, and therefore a loser for life. In his own way, Ronald was as distant from our rarified social circles as Scotty, the ravaged veteran who lived in the Bangor Efficiency Apartments and bought us beer for quarters on the dollar, or Twinkie, the forty-year-old, mentally handicapped, Twinkie-enthusiast who hung around the baseball park, and whose real name, to my lasting shame, I never bothered to learn.

Ronald was not just among the pantheon of losers, he was the Zeus of losers. This was because, unlike Scotty or Twinkie, he actually believed that he belonged. Ronald had pride.

He ordered around the other, younger managers, and around try-out time, made vague insinuations of influence with the coaching staff. "They like your attitude, King," he said to me once, at the same time running a contemplative thumb over his mustache, and sounding as if he himself could still go either way on the matter. Ronald was also a sycophant, completely beholden to the stars of the teams—particularly to Peter Lynch and Bert Korsh, our team's foremost cavemen, the kind of guys who considered it the height of wit to take a piss on your ass while you were in the shower. While Ronald would gladly fetch things for the likes of them, with a borderline performer like me, he tended to treat any request as though he were the maître d' of the Bangor branch of Jean-George.

I personally found him irritating, not to mention slightly icky.

The longest conversation I can remember having with him occurred either my sophomore or junior year, as I was attempting to get dressed, and went something like this:

Ronald: "Hey, King. I saw the *Shawshank Redemption** last night."

Me: "Yeah? Good for you."

Ronald: "It was a lot better than *Lawnmower Man. Lawnmower Man* was gay."

Me: "That's interesting, Ronald. I have to go take a shit now."

Ronald (with a nod of understanding): "Do it."

Although I can't recall ever going out of my way to treat him poorly, if I was kind to him it was out of habit. Nor do I mean to make any sort of excuse, when I point out that no one else cared for him much, either. Lynch and Korsh certainly didn't.

They once handcuffed Ronald to a locker, and left him there for an hour or so, until he was crying and howling and hurling himself against the wall. On another occasion, as our bus rumbled home through some frozen night in December, returning from an away game—probably the interminable trip back from Presque Isle—I witnessed as Lynch interrogated Ronald about his sexual exploits.

Perhaps as many as ten of us listened, hunched over in the aisle or draped over the backs of the seats, straining to hear, while Ronald recounted how he had done it for the first time in the parking lot behind the school. The deed had been done in the backseat of his car, he said. It had taken about an hour, he said. She loved it, he said.

"Wow. You fucked her pretty good, did you?" asked Lynch with a little wink.

Peter Lynch was the antithesis of Ronald. Lynch was a three-sport athlete, had girlfriends, had sex, and instead of a pubic mustache, had grown a full goatee. When Lynch walked from class to class he did so in a slightly bow-legged fashion, in order, I supposed, to keep his giant, steel balls from chapping his thighs.

"Yeah, I did," said Ronald. You could see his blush in the dark. "Oh, yeah."

*My father is the author, Stephen King.

"Was she hot?" someone asked, and Ronald said, "Oh, yeah," but then quickly added that we wouldn't know her. She was from another town and she had only been around for the summer.

*

This was my first concrete inkling that not everything I had been led to believe was true. If Ronald was lying about screwing a girl from another town—and it was inconceivable that Ronald, with his mustache and his big, square glasses, was not lying—then wasn't it possible that everyone with a similar story was also making it up? Hadn't I myself spent some time jotting down notes for an utterly fictional anecdote of my own, concerning a girl I met while I was with my family in New Hampshire?*

But things seemed to be going okay: my freshman basketball team went undefeated, and then as a sophomore, my junior varsity team went undefeated, too. I started at center both years, and while I was no star, I was a solid contributor. In my best game ever, one glorious night in Old Town, I went for eighteen points in front of the sold-out crowd waiting to see a showdown between the varsity squads.

As I made one shot after another, a close observer might have seen a slight swelling of my head even as the game progressed. After I hit my first three or four shots, I quietly informed the kid who was guarding me that he had no friends.

"No one likes you," I whispered in his ear while we stood side by side during a foul shot. "You're stupid."

This boy was scrawny, lighter than me by fifty pounds or more, and giving away three or so inches. When he looked at me his lower lip trembled.

Trash talking was common, but this kind of mental warfare, an attack not on his basketball abilities, or his sexuality, or even on the

---

*For some reason, I had it in my head that the location of this fantasy tryst had been the mall. I was going to say that we had done it after hours on a water bed in a furniture store. Sounds like a *Penthouse* letter, doesn't it? Imitation is, I'm afraid, the first stage in the maturation of a young writer.

purity of his female relatives, but on his intelligence, was clearly something new.

"I'm not stupid," said the kid from Old Town.

"Yes, you are. And that's why you have no friends. You're just too stupid to realize it." The man at foul line was going through his free-throw routine, *dribble, dribble,* lift the ball, and shoot. I added, "You can't even read, can you?"

"I can read," he said, tears in the back of his throat, as the ball went up, and clanged off the rim and bounced high. I did a pivot around the Old Town kid, shoved him out of the way with my superior bulk, grabbed the rebound, and scored again.

"Don't lie to me," I said to the kid while we were running back up the court. "Admit that you are illiterate."

But he wouldn't admit it, and the next time I scored, I ran back to defense with my arms outspread, as if I were pretending to be a bird—a big, freaky bird soaring up the court. I continued to do this whenever I scored for the rest of the game. It was a gesture that was meant to say, *Can you believe how easy this is? Can you believe how awesome I am?* In fact, the gesture said, *I have never been this good before and I will never be this good again, so let me freeze it in my mind for all time with an image of myself looking like a perfect jack-ass.*

*

My comeuppance for this behavior came the next year, when to my surprise I did not make the varsity team, and I was instead sentenced to another season with the junior varsity.

After the lists were posted, I was grief-stricken, and approached the varsity coach, Coach Murton, to ask why I had come up short.

"Well," said Coach Murton, and chuckled, "Well." He paused to sip his coffee. He chuckled again.

I really didn't understand. Except for me, all the other starters from the previous year's junior varsity team had made it. Nor had I slacked off. I had dutifully attended Coach Murton's basketball camp, Camp of Champs, over the summer. The basketball pedigree of this Camp of Champs was dubious. It was conducted by the head coach of Liberty University, an institution of higher education, that besides being founded by Jerry Falwell, a gentleman not beloved by my parents, did not exactly qualify as an NCAA powerhouse. I went without a word of complaint. I even purchased a Camp of Champs T-shirt, smartly illustrated with an arcing basketball, and in the background a cross.* Not only that, but I frequently wore this T-shirt. I had run and lifted weights and shot free throws. I had done everything I was told I needed to do. And here was this holy roller looking at me with a laugh on his lips, and an idea in his head that God had literally created the world in seven days, knocked it out like a patio set from Home Depot.

I could have fed him his comb-over.

"We liked your attitude," said Coach Murton, "but we just couldn't find a place for you this year."

They liked my attitude. Hadn't Ronald Petrie told me as much?

I said thanks, and without another word, slipped out the door into the parking lot.

I reasoned with myself that it didn't matter. It wasn't like I needed a scholarship and it wasn't like I was going to play in college. I was going to go to a liberal arts college and study English. I was going to be a writer. Girls were going to like me then, and want to have sex with me. I thought these things, and then when I made it to my car and I was safely along, I sat there and wept.

*

I acquired my first girlfriend and dated through much of this time, and while actual intercourse was too frightening a concept for either one of us, we stayed fully occupied in packing fifteen years of dysfunctional marriage into eighteen months. There were the late-night phone calls, the crying, the "I-love-you-mores," and the typical teenage conviction that the world, perhaps multiple worlds in multiple dimensions, hung in the balance. We were both in the bas-

---

*It's hard not to ponder what exactly Jerry Falwell spent my ten dollars on. Pork rinds? A sliver of the True Cross? For all I know, he never spent it at all. For all I know, Jerry Falwell keeps all the T-shirt money in a big wad of bills tucked up between his ass cheeks in case of emergencies. What an awful thought. I hope he spent it.

ketball program, but it wasn't like we shot hoops together. All we ever did was watch movies and play board games. We shot pool. We played marathon sessions of Uno, Jenga, and other games that are only fun when you're drunk. At some point I realized that I was not just not attracted to this person, but that there was no reason for us to be friends. She didn't care about Bob Dylan, or movies about fighting zombies, or *The Sandman*—all the things I cared about most. And I hated all the shit she liked, too.

If the essence of coolness is a person's relative comfort with themselves—with their desires and beliefs—then I was never less cool, or more of a loser, than I was at this time. We stayed together because we didn't want to hurt each other. We hurt each other by staying together. Our only shared interests were basketball and making each other feel horrible.

We were still dating when I lost my starting spot on the junior varsity—the same one I'd had a lock on for my entire sophomore season—after just a couple of games. My minutes decreased and I drifted farther and farther down the bench.

When I did play, I pressed and missed shots and threw balls away. I felt cursed. To try and reverse my downward slide, I let my hair grow shaggy and adopted a white headband in emulation of my favorite player, Duke great Christian Laettner, then of the Minnesota Timberwolves. This caused a band-shaped outbreak of zits on my forehead, but I kept on missing layups. I drove around and listened to "It's Alright Ma, I'm Only Bleeding," over and over again. That didn't help either. In my study halls, I whiled away hours trying to freehand copy a picture of the famous drawing of Keats on his deathbed that I'd found in a library book. I just played worse. My nadir came in a game against Augusta when I played just a minute or so with my whole family in the stands.

A couple of games later, the season ended. No thanks to me, for the third year in a row, my team was undefeated.

*

In the spring of that year things took a turn for the better when, to my surprise, I made Bangor's varsity baseball team. Despite it being my favorite sport, I had actually been thinking about giving baseball up. I was a slow singles-hitting first baseman who couldn't keep from flinching at curveballs or getting dizzy when I tried to catch a pop fly. I also liked to pitch, but I was even worse at that. I didn't throw hard, or have a breaking ball, or even stay around the strike zone all that much. I knew that I would never play in a significant game.

But the coaches liked me and I liked them, and they must have innately sensed that I was happy just being around the game. So, I played once in a while, but mainly I acted as a human signifier on offense—I stood on the second step of the dugout alongside the coaches, unless there was a play on, a bunt or a steal or whatever, in which case I went and sat down. Meanwhile, the coaches gave signs like crazy, and none of them meant anything unless I was sitting down.

The old joke about the neighborhood kids who ask the mother of Johnny, the limbless boy, if Johnny can play second base* may come to mind. If there was ever a job for a manager, it was the job of the living signal.

But you know what? I didn't mind. In fact, I liked it.

When we won the 1994 state championship in baseball, I felt that I had truly contributed. The entire season had run, almost literally, through my body. I was baseball incarnate.

Maybe that was how Ronald Petrie felt about still keeping the statistics and lugging the equipment, even now, two years after his graduation—like he was part of something bigger than himself.

That wasn't true, though, no matter what he thought. Because Ronald was never part of the team. He was a fat boy with a mustache who carried stuff. We didn't hang out with him and we didn't respect him. A few, like Peter Lynch, even took an active pleasure in torturing him, in reminding Ronald of his essential smallness and weakness, in reinforcing his inconsequentiality.

I think now that we're lucky Ronald didn't show up one day with

*That is, for Johnny to act as the base.

a hunting rifle and fill us all with lead. I'm not sure it wouldn't have
been justified. He was better than that, though, and he proved it
that summer with a simple, eloquent statement of farewell, then
moved on with his life.

*

Our American Legion baseball team was unfortunately not coached
by the staff of the high school club, a group of old salts that didn't
bother with the bullshit motivational speaking, and just told us to
hustle and hit the cutoffs and keep the grab-ass to a minimum.
Instead, the club was run by Herm Putterman, the athletic director
of our high school and a world-class twerp.

There were many qualities about Coach Putterman that did not
endear him to me, most particularly his constant, false cheer. "Let's
have a little shake, guys!" he'd bark at random moments, and so
we'd all have to hop up and start yelling feverishly for whoever was
up at bat to get a hit. Putterman was a short guy, always bouncing
around; he was like a living dashboard toy. His mere presence in
one's field of vision was annoying, like a muscle tic you couldn't rub
away.

His ever-present children, who, though surely born innocent,
had been raised from infancy to believe that the highest possible
achievement in their lives would be to someday play for the Bangor
High football team,* provided further distraction. About ten and
twelve respectively, the little bastards were forever underfoot, toss-
ing footballs, asking knock-knock jokes, taunting Twinkie, and
monitoring everything we said like a couple of KGB moles.

The Putterman kids, primates that they were, naturally attached
themselves to Peter Lynch. This was Lynch's last summer before college. Perhaps aware of his diminished prospects of influence beyond

---

*This, of course, is the biggest reason Coach Putterman was a twerp. He loved high
school football too much. While students were reading fifteen-year-old abridged
versions of *Romeo and Juliet* that were so battered and worn-down they looked like they
had been stored in Jerry Falwell's ass, Coach Putterman kept banging the drum for new
football gear, and generally getting it. I guess that was his job, but in the immortal
words of Cool Hand Luke, "Calling it your job don't make it right, Boss."

the halls of Bangor High School, he groomed the two boys as his latest, and last minions.

As always, Lynch strutted around the field and the dugout like a goateed peacock, but now Coach Putterman's children trailed behind him. And, as always, Ronald Petrie was our manager.

I don't know what Petrie thought of the situation, if he was jealous. I do recall him gamely attempting to placate the Putterman boys even as they took the attention of his idol, Lynch. I remember Ronald throwing the football with the kids, talking with them—in the process no doubt further gilding their belief in the greatness of Bangor High sports—even wrestling with them. In other words, I never saw him provoke the Putterman boys. I think that he thought they liked him.

Then, on team photo day, at Lynch's whim, they drove him insane.

I remember that the photographer had arranged us in two rows in right field. Ronald stood with us, on the end, stuffed into his blue Bangor Travelers jersey and pinstriped uniform pants, gut bulging, the very definition of unathletic. It was a fine summer day, blue skies, the sound of thudding tennis balls on the asphalt courts hidden behind the bleachers.

In the grass a few feet behind the photographer, the young Puttermans capered around.

"Okay, big grins now!" *Click,* went the camera.

I think one of the Putterman boys flipped Ronald off. Or was he making a jerkoff gesture at Ronald? Was his brother strutting around with his cheeks puffed out, imitating Ronald? I won't claim to remember exactly what it was they were doing. In my own place in the back row I had at least half a mind on taking a nap or going swimming or maybe hitting on the cute girl who worked at Kentucky Fried Chicken and whom I was, briefly, profoundly, in love with.* But rest assured, the Putterman boys were fucking

---

*Nothing much ever came of that, I'm afraid, but she did sneak me an extra crispy chicken breast once. That was neat.

with him, shining some sort of light down on the very large ant that was, in their minds, Ronald Petrie.

"Just a few more now!" said the photographer.

Still, they were only children. They didn't know any better.

The puppetmaster was Peter Lynch, and it was Lynch who lit the fuse. It was Lynch who then whispered something to Ronald. *What* did he whisper? I don't know. I never knew. What did it all mean to Ronald? Maybe it was no specific thing. What nerve did it touch? Whatever it was, it was, finally, too much. Ronald Petrie could take no more.

And this is where my full attention was gained, and the moment is so clear to me now, I can see it in glorious high definition:

Ronald violently burst from the back row, and began to stomp off across the tall grass of the right field. Without turning around, he raised his arm. Then, he raised his middle finger.

"Fuck all y'all!" Ronald added.

Fuck all y'all!

Truly, the image is so dazzling that, like a freeze frame of a massive explosion, it seems to suck the light out of everything around it.

In the stunned silence that followed we watched him stride from the field, the sun falling on his hunched shoulders, highlighting the gloss of his black hair. Ronald crunched across the gravel, climbed into his car, and drove away.

"Did Petrie just tell us all to go fuck ourselves?" someone asked.

Yes. Yes, that was exactly what he had done, and to this day, it remains one of the coolest things I've ever witnessed. Ronald Petrie was heavy, and ugly, and socially crippled—but he had stood up and announced his opposition, claimed his individuality at last, and very smartly and rightly, told us to go fuck ourselves.

Bravo!

*

When I was a senior I finally dated someone I liked, a girl named Mila with blue-black hair, a sweet sense of humor, and a sexy, grown-up confidence. She read books. Her little brother was a cello prodigy.

was expected to do: we went undefeated and won the state championship.

I was able to retire my personal tally of wins and losses at something like 80–0 through four years of high school basketball at three different levels.

In the spring I played baseball again, and stood most of the season on the second step in the corner of the dugout again, and while we didn't go undefeated, we won that state championship, too.

And that was the end of my competitive sports career.

Instead of playing American Legion, as I had the previous summer, I took a groundskeeper's position at the baseball field. I mowed the outfield grass and dragged the infield for minimum wage and all the candy I could pinch from the concession stand. My lasting memory of this time is of sitting on my tractor by the right field fence and reading a bottomless paperback of *Gone With The Wind* through triple-header days, killing time until the game ended and I could drive out to drag the infield again, then park back by the fence and read some more until the next game ended. While my old teammates carried on a few yards away, I was a thousand miles and a hundred years away. On my off days, I was with my new girlfriend.

If I was ever cool, those two or three months were it. I had a job. My girlfriend, a junior, was lovely and strange and calm, one of the most decent people I've ever known. I went to a few parties, drank a few beers. I didn't go to some other parties. I did exactly what I wanted. One afternoon my friend Mark and I went to the mall and had our ears pierced. We ran into Coach Stennett. He grimaced obviously at our new studs, and then wished us the best. What else could he have said, really? In a few weeks we were heading off to college, far beyond the boundaries of Coach Stennett's line.

Few things could have been further from my mind than Ronald Petrie. In fact, I can't remember who it was that told me that Ronald had been killed in a car accident.

*

The man whom the *Bangor Daily News* described as Ronald's best friend was the driver of the car, while Ronald sat in the passenger

Her dad maintained an elaborate system of toy trains in her famil
basement. She gave me a midnight blue candle with stars imbedde
in the wax. Mila was actually cool, and she made me feel coc
While we only stayed together for a couple of months—a period
time encompassing most memorably a Violent Femmes concert i
Portland, and one glorious interlude on my parents' living roo
floor—in the course of things, without really noticing it, I lost inte
est in high school basketball. I stopped running in the mornin
before school and playing rec games in the gym after school.

I was furious when Mila dumped me for some guy who playe
hockey for a school one town over and had a face that looked lik
it had been mixed up in a bowl before he had put it on, but she'
taught me a valuable lesson about myself. The latent homoeroticisn
that hung so heavy in the locker room air—as when a guy lik
Lynch paraded around in nothing but his jockstrap and babblec
endlessly about pussy while all the other guys, also wearing nothing
but their jockstraps, looked on with huge grins on their faces and
a nervous tingling in their testicles—had started to choke. I didn'
just want to have sex with women,* I wanted to be in the company
of women, and not have to worry about winning games all the time.
It wasn't that I no longer liked sports. I just didn't have a stake anymore. Like the managers perhaps, I still dreamed of getting in the
games, it was only that the final scores that had suddenly ceased to
matter.

*

Then I made the varsity basketball team anyway and, in a perfect
irony, I promptly contracted mononucleosis. I only missed a couple of weeks of practice and one game, but whatever vague hope I'd
had of playing a significant role evaporated. My season total was
eight points scored. Not that '94–'95 Bangor High boys' varsity basketball team really needed my help. Our starting five consisted of
four division-one athletes and my friend Matt, who went on to play
pro baseball. We did exactly what the state's largest public school

*Although I did—very much.

seat. The two of them had been out drinking. Ronald's friend was home on leave from the navy. Later that night, sometime after leaving a club, the car somehow went shooting off the road, crashed through treetops, snapped guy-wires, and landed upside down in someone's yard. One article mentioned that a mailbox ended up in the backseat. Ronald was decapitated. His friend lived.

A trial followed a little over a year later and Ronald's friend was acquitted of charges of manslaughter and drunken driving. It was a tragedy, not a crime.

The obituary I have says that Ronald died at age twenty-one. It also says that he was a manager at McDonald's and a paper carrier. I didn't know that. Even now, I find it hard to visualize him in any context outside of the gym or the baseball field, but it's necessary.

Our teenage years are nothing if not a process of reduction, the time when we either sand away our quirks or learn well to conceal them. Consider how you recollect your high school classmates: there's the punk guy, the pregnant girl, the fat guy, the vampire chick, the famous dude's kid, the deaf girl, the one who died in some stupid way.

So with that in mind, I would like to offer the following points for the record:

Ronald Petrie may have been a loser, but he was more than a manager of sports teams, more than his heinous mustache. In one of his employments, for instance, he held a position of responsibility. He worked two jobs; he was highly motivated. Ronald loved his high school. He believed it stood for something and he volunteered for it. Ronald spent his last night on earth celebrating with a friend. To a guy like Peter Lynch—to a guy like me—the very idea would have seemed impossible: Ronald had a friend. He had a whole life we didn't know about it. People loved him. And I don't know for sure, but I choose to believe that one night, in the parking lot behind the high school, he made love to a girl and pleased her, and pleased himself.

*

At the end of August I moved to New York, into an 8 x 11 dorm room that had once been a laundry closet. Right away, I hooked up my stereo system, popped in a U2 CD, and stuck up my poster of Munch's *The Scream*. One of my new neighbors, a city guy, came in to introduce himself. We shook hands. He glanced at the poster. Then, he grimaced at my stereo. "U2 fan, huh?"

I hedged a bit. "Sort of," I said.

"Hey," he said and laughed. "Nice belt."

How to Kill a Boy
That Nobody Likes

WILL CLARKE

When I was a kid growing up in Louisiana, I had the kind of buck-toothed, mouth-breathing face that people wanted to smack—hard and with eye-bulging spite. I was hyper and clumsy and unable to keep my mouth shut. When adults tried to engage me, I ignored them. I lived in my own world, and if you didn't have superpowers or at least a bionic limb, you weren't getting my attention. I really couldn't be bothered, particularly if it required doing something like learning to read or telling time or taking a bath. With other kids this might have come off as cute and dreamy. But I was a defiant and ugly child, so it just came off as annoying and weird.

I was the boy that nobody liked—"The Will-tard." Didn't matter if it was kids or teachers, I elicited everyone's wrath. The actual manifest of attacks on my person is long and tedious. So I will spare you the full blow-by-blow. But I will give you just a little taste of what it was like to be The Will-tard. Here's my short list—these are people I would actually sucker punch if I saw them on the street today:

1) Mrs. Colson, my sweaty music teacher. Her hairy legs were matted under her panty hose and she liked to bust my knuckles with rhythm sticks—you know the green and red ribbed wooden sticks that kids go "tee-tee-ta-ta-tee-tee-ta" with. Well, she went "whacka-crack-crack-crack" with them on my closed fists and

sometimes my butt for something as minor as hitting the wrong note on my recorder. I was a terrible musician, and thus was hit constantly with the red and green sticks. Once in first grade, she slipped and whacked my thumbnail, hitting it so hard that it cracked. My little first-grader thumbnail turned black and fell off.

2) Mrs. Boucheron, my wig-wearing, perfume-soaked language arts teacher. She liked to hit the tender insides of my wrists with a splintered and chalky ruler. She would hit you twice if you pulled away. It was hard not to pull away. She wore a sickening sweet perfume that smelled like Raid. One day, I told everyone in class that Mrs. Boucheron was an android sent to kill and torture children. When I got ratted out by a classmate, Mrs. Boucheron broke the splintered ruler on the back of my legs in a fit that knocked off her wig and revealed her bald, android head.

3) Trent Ogilvy and Mr. Cornwall, these two come as matching set. Actually, this student/principal double team occurred because of my obsession with blood. See, in third grade there was nothing I liked better than picking my nose. I picked my nose incessantly and thought my own nosebleeds were fascinating. I liked the way the blood tasted running down the back of my throat. I could see different Rorschach shapes in the bloody paper towels like normal kids might see in clouds: Bunnies, Kittens, Jesus. I would even pick my nose to make it bleed so that I would have something to do. My nosebleed obsession drew the ire of my classmate, Trent Ogilvy, and thus ensued one of the biggest injustices of my young life. Trent threatened to not just kick, but *kill* my gross Will-tard, nosebleeding ass everyday for almost two months in fifth grade. Every recess was spent running from him and his chokeholds. Trent sent notes to me in class telling me he was going to kill me behind the sixth-grader T-shacks, and if not there, the bus stop. But since I was actually more scared of my teachers than Trent, I never told on him. He eventually cornered me alone behind the cafeteria. He came at me with his bottom teeth jutting out. I punched him hard and fast in the breadbas-

ket. It was reflexive really; I was terrible at defending myself. Trent held his stomach and fell to the ground. He looked like a caught fish, wide-eyed and out of water. That's when Mrs. Boucheron found us. Trent caught his breath and began sobbing like the punk-ass little bitch he had accused me of being. I was dragged by my ear to Principal Cornwall, a man who preferred his fat leather belt to the school board–authorized paddle. Cornwall whipped me, and then told me I was lucky he didn't expel me. I hated Mr. Cornwall and I particularly hated his eyes. He had a second pink and slimy eyelid that always slid out from under his real one when he blinked at you. It was disgusting. After that day, I took a peculiar satisfaction in the fact that Mr. Cornwall's eyes were eternally deformed and that nobody, not even his own family, would ever really take pleasure in looking into them.

4) The headbangers at Youree Drive Middle School who wore faded black Dio T-shirts and scrawled "O-Z-Z-Y" across their knuckles with ballpoint pens. These teenage Satanists used to spit loogies on me. One time, I encountered the whole coven of them, smoking in the bathroom between classes. They didn't hit me. They just spit on me. There were too many to fight. So I just bounced from push to wall to shove like a snot-covered pinball. I finally got pushed to the door and ran out. From that point on, I never went back into another middle school bathroom. I just held it until I got home each day. On a brighter note, Coach Talley actually caught the headbangers spitting on me in PE. He threw one of Satan's little helpers up against the lockers and told him to never do that again. The drive-by loogies miraclously stopped after that.

5) My brother's friends who had just gotten their driver's licenses. These junior NRA members would drive to the nearby 7-Eleven to get their cigarettes, Copenhagen and Slurpees. Then they'd swing by our house to see my brother, but most importantly to kick the Will-tard's ass. My mom would always be off somewhere—getting groceries, or at her garden club, or at her Methodist ladies prayer circle—when these juvenile delinquents

descended upon our house in their Camaros and pickups with gun racks made out of deer antlers. I would be in the den, sitting on my beanbag, eating a spoonful of crunchy peanut butter, and playing my beloved Atari. My brother and his friends would drag me to the backyard and take turns "fighting me." I was twelve. They were sixteen. You can guess how well that worked out for me. One of my brother's friends, Chris Walker, cracked my ribs when he jumped on my chest with his knees so that he could spit his Skoal juice into my screaming mouth. It hurt for weeks to even breathe. I probably could have used some medical attention, but I just couldn't bear to tell my parents that I was now such a loser that people were lining up at our front door to beat me up, and that my own brother was basically selling tickets.

I don't give you this list to make you feel sorry for me. I give you this list so that you have a full grasp of where I was on the food chain when I entered high school. And just how ill suited I was to ever run for any sort of popularity contest. Once you reached the level of scorn and disgust that I had, your image was cast in an amber that was impossible to shatter.

You could join the swim team and shed your baby fat and braces. You could emerge a golden-haired, surfer wannabe in OP shorts and checkered Vans. You could save up your yard-mowing money and buy a pair of Vuarnets. You could wear a different Polo shirt every day of the week. You could punk your hair. You could pinch-roll your jeans and refuse to wear socks. You could drive a Monte Carlo with T-tops. You could run for miles and miles with your safety-yellow Walkman in neon blue Nikes, but the shame of your Will-tard past would follow you like an eye-watering fart, keeping everyone at your high school at least three feet away from you at all times.

Delusion was (and still is) a major part of my personality. When I was a little kid, I used to bargain with Jesus every night: the power of flight in return for a life dedicated to fighting crime. Never happened. But that didn't deter my bargaining. By high school, I was begging Him for popularity. So I ran for every school election I could with all the deluded hope and prayer of a weekly Powerball player. I ran for freshman class president, for student council senator, for homeroom representative, for PTSA delegate, for sophomore class vice president, and for junior class secretary. I tried out for Key Club, Interact, and the yearbook staff. And just like most Powerball believers, I never ever won a goddamned thing.

Despite my campaign losses and the ridicule they sometimes brought me, I held fast to my dream of stadium-shaking popularity. I had faith that one day I would be someone you would want to make a fake ID with and then get drunk on schnapps with and then puke all over your mom's new sofa with. I was unwavering in this belief.

Every new election, I would paint elaborate posters, sometimes with glitter, sometimes with streamers, sometimes with Spanish moss and cartoon alligators, promising a better school with *real* changes for every Captain Shreve Gator! I would give out free sour apple and lemon Jolly Ranchers since our school colors were green and gold. I would wear a large homemade campaign button emblazoned with my class photo, a cheeky alligator, and a slogan that proclaimed that, "Clarke Can!"

But Clarke couldn't and Clarke didn't. In fact, I continued to be so astonishingly unpopular my freshman and sophomore years that I spent every single lunch period alone in the study carols of the library because I wasn't welcome to sit in the cafeteria with even the biggest of dorks. However, it was in the library, just days before I would make a bid for Student Council treasurer, that I stumbled upon a book that I was sure could help me: *Subliminal Seduction: Ad Media's Manipulation Of A Not So Innocent America* by Wilson Bryan Key. The cover of this panicky little paperback had a glossy photo with a double shot of vodka on the rocks with a twist. The letters S-E-X were air-brushed into the ice cubes. A red subhead teased: ARE YOU BEING SEXUALLY AROUSED BY THIS PICTURE?

I was utterly titillated, not by the photo but by the idea. And completely bewildered that such a salacious publication would be shelved in our school library—a library so uptight that it didn't even carry a copy of *Slaughterhouse-Five* because it had Vonnegut's crude drawings of titties in it. I flipped straight to the pictures section and found examples of all sorts of orgies and debaucheries occurring in the shadows of advertising photography. These ambiguous images sent my Will-tard hormones surging. And against my will, I popped a woody. In fact, my erection persisted unwanted and painful for the rest of the school day. In between classes, I carried my books just below my waist to hide the unrelenting boner. The next day, I checked out the book from the library, and read it at home to avoid further priapism in the face of an already leery student body.

I read *Subliminal Seduction* cover to cover in one night. And this is what I learned:

1) Sex and death are taboo for most normal, hardworking Americans. This means that decent people try not to think about sex or death. Ever. They do the right and normal thing. They push their feelings deep down inside and sit on them.

2) Human brains instantaneously perceive all information. Our conscious minds filter out all the inappropriate stuff that pertains to sex and death. Our minds tuck this scary stuff neatly away into our subconscious where it belongs with all our other unmentionable thoughts and desires.

3) Most modern ads embed words like *dick, cunt, whore, prick,* and *death* into seemingly innocent product photos of housewives frosting cakes and sweater-clad couples smoking menthol cigarettes. Advertisers do this to work over a consumer's subconscious, forcing the consumer's safely repressed sexual depravity and murderous impulses to be connected to the advertised product. This then compels the unwitting consumer to buy stuff like Tickle deodorant or Ritz crackers.

4) By secretly unleashing people's unconscious urges, advertising contributes to most of societies ills like VD, drug abuse, insanity, unmarried pregnancy, suicide, the dissolution of the nuclear family, and violent crime.

5) A Sprite ad with an ice cube shadow of a dog fucking a woman—even though the image is impossibly vague and only the size of a flea—will force the reader to drink said beverage against his conscious will. But best of all, this principle worked for everything from Canada Dry to Preparation-H. Which meant it could work for a brand as undesirable as The Will-tard.

God had finally answered all my whining and crying. This book had countless examples of how to discreetly hide bad words or images into artwork, and basically mind-control people into doing things that they didn't really want to do. The only way I was ever going to be elected was if subliminal advertising worked. So I believed every word I read and every ice cube I saw. But even though I believed with all my heart, I actually struggled with how it worked. The science just seemed a little soft even to my eleventh-grade brain.

What if I hid the word *pussy* in my campaign posters and then everyone was manipulated into thinking I was a bigger pussy than they already did? What if a word like *cunt* didn't work on girls? Most girls supposedly hated that word. If I used the wrong word then I could potentially lose 50 percent or more of the vote. How did these ad agencies know what bad words would connect with which depraved urge? What if a guy fucking a dog only worked on the depraved urges that lead to buying liquor? The book was terribly unclear on all of this. In fact, the more I started to think about the science behind this book, the murkier and dumber this idea got. But this wasn't the time to set aside magical thinking or delusion. I had been given what might be the Rosetta Stone of mind control and I was going to at least see if it worked.

So I started making posters chock full of subliminal persuasion. I stayed away from words like *cock* and *poontang*. Words like that could have lost me votes due to gender bias. Same goes for bestiality and death wishes—I didn't want to misfire and be responsible for a rash of suicides or VD. So I did the responsible thing and settled on the tried and true, "S-E-X." Just three letters. Easy enough to hide with my crude art skills, and open-ended enough to appeal to everyone's basest desires—male, female, and canine if need be.

Ironically enough, even though I avoided manipulating my classmates' more beastlike and murderous urges, my S-E-X posters would actually kill the boy that nobody liked. It would bury The Will-tard forever. That's because, to everyone's surprise, I was elected Student Council treasurer. And from that impossible post, I ascended into the ambrosial airs of puking on my friends' moms' new sofas.

STUDENT COUNCIL

The Artist Formerly Known as Will-tard

Student Council was the major source of changes at Captain Shreve. Its leaders were: President, Henry Broom; Vice President, Jennifer Moore; Recording Secretary, Freda Spears; Treasurer, Will Clarke; Corresponding Secretary, Allison Lipe; Parliamentarian, Trey Cox. Student Council's sponsor was Mrs. Martha Goza. This year Student Council sponsored our Back To School Dance, Gator Rock Cafe, and the Homecoming Dance, Moonlighting. They also sponsored the Gator Health Run, SADD, Winter Court, and Sadie Hawkins. Student Council brought life to every aspect of Gator life during the 1987-1988 school year.

Confessions of a Loser Friend:

A Mix Tape

Richard Yañez

Side A
1. "Time for Me to Fly" by REO Speedwagon
2. "I Want to Break Free" by Queen
3. "Renegade" by STYX
4. "Unchained" by Van Halen
5. "Surrender (Live at Budokan)" by Cheap Trick
6. "The Spirit of Radio" by Rush
7. "Heavy Metal" by Sammy Hagar

Other than a minor infraction (which I might also confess in this essay), I was always considered a good kid. At home. During school. In church. Each seemed to bring out the best in me. And, I realize now, helped develop my sense of right from wrong, especially as a teen.

This is what I remember about Valley View Junior High: dark-haired girls wearing tight jeans; several Chicano boys named Gilbert/Rene/Mando; green jerseys with white numbers; cholo fights by the cottonwood trees; and a web of irrigation canals. As the '70s blurred into the '80s, the world of junior high weaved itself around me like its own religion.

As one of junior high's most popular boys (a title I actually won in eighth grade), I'm sure it would surprise many to learn that my best friend, David McKinney, was a "Loser." The quotes should serve as the voices of my parents, my teachers, my coaches—any adult figure, in fact. David was aware of this label, I'm sure. With his feathered, dirty-blond hair, and T-shirt-and-jeans swagger, he carried himself like he dared you to not judge him. If it gave him an edge, he welcomed negative attention from adults and teens alike. David made his own set of rules and challenged those set by others.

One of our favorite things to do growing up in El Paso's Lower Valley was to walk along the irrigation canals. The caliche roads were usually empty; even the canals themselves were dry for most of the school year. A perfect space for a teen friendship to grow alongside the mesquite trees, creosote, and canal reeds. Many afternoons, David and I walked in perfect stride, not in a hurry to get anywhere. (Is it strange that I always imagine him with headphones although this is before any of us got Walkmans?)

One day after school when all I had waiting at home were mindless chores or boring TV, David left my side and disappeared down into a canal. Without thinking about the risks, I followed him through some tumbleweeds and mounds of trash till we crawled to a clearing. Before I could ask any of the questions running through my head, he slipped a joint out of his pocket as smooth as it slipped between his lips. The mini cigarette dangled while he pulled out a lighter.

After a long exhale, he stretched out his arm and asked, "Want some?"

I tried not to do anything to suggest that I was nervous and said, "I'm all right."

"No problemo." He gave me that devilish grin that I always welcomed. "More for me."

This might have been the first time I saw a real joint, as opposed to a "doobie" on a record cover. And each time that David smoked in our canal hideout, I found myself holding my breath as long as he did to see what it was like. I don't remember my best friend ever thinking of me as a Loser for not getting high.

As our impending future as freshmen at "The High" approached, it seems clear that adult advice won out over my teen instincts. I was a good kid, after all. I knew right from wrong. Still went to Catholic Mass with my grandparents most Sundays. Your son will be somebody, my teachers guaranteed my parents. I was a winner. Trophies and framed certificates filled my bookshelf to prove it.

My last vivid image of David in junior high is at the movies. His legs propped up on the seat in front of him. Bell bottoms and hitops. Plain white tee on his skinny frame. Hair past his shoulders.

There seemed to be many minutes before the start of the movie. Like the secrets we discovered along the canal, where as much was shared in silence as in our joking, the near-empty theater felt intimate. Side by side, elbows rubbing, we shared a large soda and popcorn. Just as the lights dimmed, he reached into his tube sock and slipped out a joint.

"I got this from some dudes at The High," he said and placed it in my palm. "They only smoke the best."

"Cool, gotta have the good stuff." I made a fist as the movie screen came to life. The joint was rolled fat and tight. While my blood raced at the thought of lighting up, all I ended up doing was rolling it between my fingertips, like I'd been taught to do with a rosary.

After the movies, we got a bite to eat and hung out before my mom picked us up. David never insisted that I smoke pot as much he wanted me to know that we could if I wanted. I hid the joint in my underwear drawer for a day before I gave it back for my best friend to enjoy.

*

If junior high was a daily adventure, high school was a soap opera of emotions. Adolescence is hard enough. Why would anyone put us all together and expect anything productive to happen?

I survived Ysleta High School by having a brother who was old enough to drive and who had a job. When I was a freshman, he was a senior, so I fully enjoyed the fruits of his labor. Not only did I get rides to and from school, and learn the names of varsity cheerleaders, but I also wore his mall-bought clothes and shoes despite his grumbling. The fringe benefits of his income included plenty of record albums and a cool stereo, as well as many frivolous accessories (remember Swatches?).

While I looked up to him, I never called my only brother my best friend. For tolerating me, I figured, he scored points with our folks. Mostly he came to my rescue whenever I strayed too far from those traditional values preached at home (although he was the one who led us into the serious trouble I might be confessing). Despite the many spiritual questions I have now as an adult, I don't think my brother and I will ever shed our Catholic boy skins.

The earliest of countless concerts I was allowed to attend as a teen were with my brother. Watching a live rock band was a fitting initiation to the adrenaline and anxiety I associate with being a high school teen. I am thankful to my brother for letting me tag along and allowing me entrance to a world of hard rock and heavy metal. This was a separate kind of ritual than those the nuns and priests taught us at Father Yermo Elementary.

The more time I spent in high school the further I grew from anyone who might be considered part of the Loser crowd. Occasionally, I did see David and his buddies at lunch hanging out in the rear parking lot. I was jealous that they always looked like they were having the best time. Still, the promise of reaching my "potential" (a popular word adults used around me) kept me a safe distance from the Loser crowd. All the rocker chicks who were drawn to the open doors of David's van made me envy him even more.

Although the typical rite of passage for high school teens growing up in El Paso is to cross into a world of underage drinking and lax laws, I didn't have to venture into the cultural chaos of Juárez, Mexico, to negotiate borders. Within the world of high school, I was able to experience diverse cliques on any given day. I'm impressed that my former self could go from Honors English class to a newspaper staff meeting to basketball practice to a desert bonfire. These social boundaries were as invisible to many of us as the one that rested between two countries only minutes from our campus.

Side B
1. "We're Not Gonna Take It" by Twisted Sister
2. "Cum on Feel the Noize" by Quiet Riot
3. "Round and Round" By RATT
4. "Rock Rock (Till You Drop)" by Def Leppard
5. "Breaking the Law" by Judas Priest
6. "You Shook Me All Night Long" by AC/DC
7. "No One Like You" by Scorpions
8. "Turn Me Loose" by Loverboy

In my last months at The High, I decided that I'd have as much fun as possible. I'd busted my ass to earn good grades, kept out of serious trouble, and stayed active in extracurricular activities, so I figured I deserved to enjoy what was left of high school. I'd earned enough credits on my transcript, as well as with the vice principal, to have at least half of my school days to myself. I'm sure I had duties for my journalism teacher and the main office, but my memories are more of the beer-run-and-late-night-Chico's-Tacos variety.

An experienced concertgoer by this time, I went to as many rock shows as possible. Since my parents were proud of my induction into the National Honor Society and solid SAT scores, they didn't hesitate to give me more than enough money for a concert ticket and a T-shirt. While adults are always quick to identify the bad influences among teenagers, they seem to miss the signs of those of us on the honor roll who might be doing "Loser" things. And since we hardly ever got caught or seriously punished, we continued to pursue the lifestyle celebrated in our favorite rock songs and glorified in MTV's earliest videos.

The County Coliseum, which always wore the smell of a rodeo, was the place where rock lovers worshipped in El Paso. Like the canals in the Lower Valley, I consider the Coliseum a hallowed space for my teen-self. I am not surprised that I began to hide my written reflections in a spiral notebook—the first of many journals—at this period of my life. My teenaged entries were always filled with whatever challenges I was facing at the time: rivalries, libido, jealousies, and heartaches. Hell, all the ingredients for a good rock song.

The best part of going to concerts wasn't necessarily the show. The live music was only the match to set fire to our good time. A group of us from The High would head over to the Coliseum right after last bell, score some beer from one of the many drive-through markets, and find the perfect parking spot outside the "Shit-Smelling Barn," as Twisted Sister's Dee Snider affectionately called our city's oldest arena. I was a lightweight when it came to drinking. Two to three beers max and I was ready to absorb distorted feedback and screaming vocals, indulging my teenaged body's need for excitement.

Back then, it was all about being right up front, on the floor, not sitting down like all the old fuckers. There was a whole strategy to getting as close to the stage as possible. A strange kind of obstacle course of fellow rockers. Elbows. Knees. Sweat. Entering the Coliseum as soon as the doors opened, I'd scope out the crowd and decide on the best route to the wall of speakers. And it was never a straight line as I remembered some geometry teacher saying was the shortest distance between two points.

Cramped in the Coliseum's concrete-slab-of-a-structure, I found a family of peers who lived in the vibrations of each guitar riff and the pulse of each drumbeat. In unison, we moved our bodies to a frenzy. Song after song, we mouthed what we thought were the lyrics while we grinded our bodies. In the melee, I found a mental solace that I didn't completely understand, a different kind of security than the silence of the canals. There were many moments during concerts when I simply let the force of those around me keep me standing. I'd let myself go limp, close my eyes, and rock out to the high decibels that left my ears ringing for days.

I'd be exhausted once they turned the lights back on and we herded out like cattle. By the time I made it to the parking lot, part of our group would already be drinking again. I would have been happy to go to Chico's for a double order of taquitos with extra cheese, but for most of my peers the party was just getting started.

On this one night, when I'd gone to see _____ (bands like Quiet Riot, RATT, Dokken now all seem interchangeable), my flirtation with the laws of Losers and the laws of Society was put to the test. Drinking and driving, my adult-self rationalizes, were products of the freedom and boredom of growing up in the vast Chihuahua Desert.

David's van was always part of the postconcert crowd. With a constellation of empties at his feet, it was hard to tell how long he'd been drinking since he did it with so much ease. While we'd only bumped into each other a few times at parties and bonfires in the sand hills, we were still buds. Our junior high friendship was as memorable as the slogans he'd tattooed on my notebooks. LIVE FREE. UP IN SMOKE. DISCO SUCKS.

Being the self-proclaimed "Party Animal" of The High, David always knew of a good beer bust. These house parties that spilled out into the streets with many uninvited guests were inevitably raided by the cops. After the concert, David seduced everybody with the promise of a beer bust in the Lower Valley. When he threw his arm around my neck and asked if I was on board, I gave him the answer he knew I'd give.

"Sure, why not," I said as our drunk Loser friends and a few hangers-on from the concert piled into his van. "But I'm driving."

"No problemo," he said and placed his keys in my hand with a wet grin.

After a quick stop for some beer, I drove east on the Border Highway toward the Lower Valley, the stereo blasting the noise of whichever band we'd just seen. David pressed the rewind button more than once to everybody's satisfaction. In the immediate back-seats, they were enjoying the cheap brew and rocking out. We all reeked of tobacco and pot smoke, so if anyone lit up in the far back-seats, I wouldn't have been able to tell. Or care, for that matter. This wasn't my show.

Turning down the street that David swore led to a beer bust, I saw flashing lights ahead, but by the time I recognized them as an ambulance coming toward me, it was too late to do anything but swerve. I ended up cutting off the emergency vehicle and getting an earful of sirens to go with yelling from the crowd in the backseats. Before I could tell them to shut the fuck up, a swarm of more flashing lights descended on us. One cop car cut me off in front. Another shot up on the driver's side. Two more blocked me in from behind. It was right out of the movies, only this time I wasn't in a comfortable chair stuffing my mouth with popcorn.

"Stay cool," David said.

"Shut up," I shot back.

"Let me handle it."

"What the hell—"

Yanked out of the driver's seat, I was hauled to a cop car and thrown on the hood. I was forced through the requisite position—legs spread apart, arms to the sides—and patted down. Face to face with the cop, I was interrogated.

"Where are you coming from?"

"A concert. The Coliseum. What did I—"

"Didn't you see the ambulance?"

"Yeah, but everyone was talking and—"

"Is this your vehicle? Are you the registered owner?"

"No, it's not mine. He is."

The cop asked me more questions and shouted accusations at the same time. His tone pierced a whole other part of my head that was still reverberating from the concert. Scared shitless, I did what I always do when I'm nervous: I start talking faster than I can think: "Don't know everyone in the van . . . I'm an Honor Student . . . Don't smoke . . . I need to be home by midnight . . . Don't take me to jail . . . I'm going to college next year."

My spontaneous act of contrition caught the cop by surprise.

Hands on his hips, close to his holster, he turned to another cop, who had David in his grips. The grimace on the cop's face told me that their exchange hadn't gone that smoothly. No confession, for sure. I wasn't surprised to see the same smug look on David's face that I'd seen him give school security guards.

Under the glare of the cop and the bright lights, I hadn't been as cool as my Loser friend. I worried that I'd sold David out somehow. Pledged allegiance to another group. Saved my own ass with my Honor Roll testimony.

The decision to let us go versus being taken to county jail came down to a cop saying, "You can either spill the rest of the beer right here on the street or drink it behind bars." I am glad that the post-concert crowd in the van had the sense to dump out the beer, as well as conceal any pot they carried. Satisfied with their intimidation, the cops broke huddle to find another party to bust up. I never found out what the ambulance was all about, and I didn't really care, to tell you the truth.

As I had promised the cop who heard my confession, I drove straight to David's. I didn't want to be behind the wheel any longer than I had to this night. Since David's parents were out, the post-concert crowd carried the party from the van to every room of the house. While some raided the fridge and pantries, others were busy picking out the seeds from someone's stash. After watching some TV in the living room, I went in search of David. I wanted to know that everything was okay. Tell him that I was leaving and that I'd see him around.

At the rear of the house, I heard a stereo and followed Jim Morrison's voice. When I peeked in David's bedroom, I saw him on his bed, naked from the waist down, a rocker chick next to him. She was in her bra and panties. Her toking up and blowing smoke into his mouth was the last image I took in before I retreated.

Out the front door, I stepped into the night and took off walking. Not in any mood to enjoy the isolated canal roads, I walked the lit streets that were the straightest route home.

*

Although I did party way more than study my last year of high school, I graduated in the top twenty of my class and earned a university scholarship. My love for concert-driven rock continued through my twenties, but I attended fewer shows every year. While I am nostalgic about the raw power of rock and the sensory rush of being right in front of the stage, I've grown an appreciation for songwriting more than showmanship. (And I don't miss the Tinnitus.)

As promised, the confession that I was arrested along with my brother for shoplifting the summer before turning thirteen seems minor to the one I am admitting to myself as I write this essay. I feel like I let David down, as well as my other Loser Friends. I feel shitty for not staying in touch over the years. While I know that after graduation David had a son with a girl from The High, and moved out of town, I must admit that I didn't look back once I entered college. Even when I returned to El Paso after studying out of state for a while, I didn't try to catch up with any old friends. I'd moved on, as they say, although I still lived in the same neighborhood.

I don't remember exactly when, but I did talk to David one last time when I was visiting a former high school girlfriend in Austin. As it turned out, she'd bumped into David and told him I'd be coming through town. A siren went off in my head when she told me he'd be calling me at her house. When I heard his voice, it seemed that he was drunk or almost there. His slurring of certain words actually made me relax as he asked what I been up to in El Paso. I offered a few short answers and mostly listened.

I learned that he was in trade school. While they weren't together, the mother of his son was also in Austin. He really wanted to be a good father.

After more questions than answers, he asked if I wanted to meet up for a beer or something. I was tempted. The seduction of the past made me thirsty. Still, far from the landscape of the Lower Valley, outside the cloudy confines of the Coliseum, I could see that there was more at stake now. At least for me. I couldn't afford to be a Loser Friend, not even for one more night.

Whether or not he asked, I still regret the inevitable question:

"You too good for me now?" Of course, I denied anything he might've heard or put together, but I do confess that I thought I might be better than who I was back then. If part of the allure of being a teen is breaking the rules, one advantage of being an adult is that you live by your own choices. This is what I hope for David, whom I haven't seen or heard from in as many years as we were old in high school.

IN GOD
WE TRUST

Incredible Hulk Saving Souls

DOUG CRANDELL

In 1981 I walked into the basement of the Friends Church in Wabash, Indiana, for the first time. A buddy from school had invited me; we were in the eighth grade. The basement was cold and smelled like bleach; the spaghetti supper brewing in the kitchen off the main rec room area tried to cover it up, but the bleach wouldn't have it. At the time, I was infatuated with Olivia Newton-John, or at least a poster of her dressed in "Let's Get Physical" garb. I'd recently discovered the agility of my mind, how I could conjure up all manner of situations that would bring her into my life, and into my twin bed. My imagination was regarded with the utmost esteem by my nascent manhood. Oh, how he loved my imaginative, day-dreaming mind.

My mother had dropped me off at Friends. Raised in coal miner churches in Vigo County, she believed in God, and kept a small white Bible stashed in the cupboard, but we never went to church as a family, something she'd always urged my dad to consider. But he was too busy, he'd say, or, and this was true, overtime at the ceiling tile factory on Sundays paid double time. "What do you want Doris, food for the kids or my soul saved?" It was a smart-alecky remark, one my dad delivered with a grin, the full confidence of an excellent alibi building him up from the inside.

More teenagers gathered around the oval carpet. Two peer leaders who seemed shy and embarrassed placed folding chairs in a circle around the room. The partition hiding the kitchen was rolled up and I helped set out paper plates and plastic forks. The full smell of garlic bread toasting took over and the furnace kicked on, the hot air blowing full force down on our heads. I'd asked my mother to "feather" my hair, and she had, spraying it hard with Aqua Net, which produced true wings at the side of my head, as though a little model chariot were indeed taking flight, golden and winged, plastered against my skull at the front, jutting out at the tips over my ears.

With full plates of spaghetti we sat down with the youth pastor and his wife to start a rap session. The topic was drugs and God. I sat with my friend, shyly trying to eat with some manners, making certain none of the watery sauce splashed onto the white Izod I'd bought at a thrift store. Under it, I wore another polo-type shirt, and I made certain both collars were up, as if I had been in an accident and they were part of the rehab, a stylish neck brace. This was the style then, and I practiced it with pride. With my winged hair and two collars turned up, I looked like a contraption built aerodynamically to sustain an arduous and tricky takeoff.

The youth pastor, a bodybuilder with just a hint of Lou Ferrigno going, didn't eat until the session was over. He sat with his legs spread and thumbed through a workbook, the muscles in his thighs not permitting him a more graceful and polite pose. On the cover was a photo of drug needles, an assortment of colored pills, and psychedelic images blurred below and above the title: Just Say No to Drugs! For a moment, he looked stuck on an intro, as he opened the book, then closed it again. He repeated the process several times before finally cocking his large head and clearing his throat.

"How many of you teenagers here tonight feel pressured by your . . ." He pried the book apart to a page marked with a red tassel, and searched the text. "By your peers?"

My friend nudged me as he shoveled a big wad of rolled-up spaghetti, the diluted sauce dripping rapidly from his plastic fork and pattering onto the paper plate, into his brace-face mouth. I ignored him and chewed on the soft garlic bread. A young girl with severe acne spoke up. "I've not been really approached, I mean, not at all, but I know kids who have." She smiled and looked around, and since she was a regular at the youth group, I couldn't help thinking she might've been a plant, put up by the pastor and his wife to get the rap session going.

One by one, starting from her right, each kid shrugged his or her shoulders when the youth pastor tried to get them to spill their guts. My friend nudged me again with his bony elbow and this time the guy saw it. He tuned right in and said, "Doug, you got something to share?" I felt put on the spot. I'd confided in my friend that I'd been offered pot at a basketball game, in the parking lot afterward, and now he was forcing me to confess. The friend also knew about Olivia, and fearing he'd give his slobbery mouth a break from the spaghetti and tattle about her to the youth group, I stopped eating. I'd left the parking lot that night without drinking a drop of alcohol, without ever thinking about using drugs, but I didn't want to tell a group of strange kids some stupid detail about how I'd said no.

But the muscleman–youth pastor was intimidating and before I knew it I was letting it fly, talking nervously about how I'd turned down the dope, said no like a good Christian teenager. When I was through the pastor was impressed. "That's excellent, Doug," he said, as if coaching a sports team. "Let's all give Doug a big hand. I mean, let's really let him hear how much we love him for the choice he made." I wanted to fly away with my stiffly feathered hair. "Come on!" he yelled, like a real fired-up coach, clapping his strong, thick hands with thunderous effect, the echo in the church basement returning to our ears with double intensity. The palms of his hands reddened with each clap, and I thought of spikes in the center of his meaty paws, not like Jesus' skinny, petite palms.

I was thoroughly embarrassed, and felt like throwing the runny plate of food in my friend's face, but instead I only stood up when the pastor asked me to come forward. He said loud and clear, his voice a deep baritone, "I present this pledge to Doug as a challenge." He held in his hand a piece of paper that looked like some type of fake diploma.

"Do you accept the challenge, Doug, to stay drug free, to not give in to temptation and partake in any type of substance abuse that would harm God's temple?" I was confused. I assumed someone had spray-painted graffiti on the church walls or TP'd the trees out front during Halloween. It was the first time I'd heard the term used for a person's body. The pastor's bulging bicep stretched his shortsleeve dress shirt, and I watched it, thinking the material might rip up to his wedge-like neck. He held the paper out to me and I took it. I bowed my head to see a line where my signature was to go. He drew out an ink pen from his pocket and clicked it. The Hulk offered me the pen; his back turned just slightly, also presenting me with a place to sign. "What do you say Doug? Are you with us? Are you with God, son?" I wrote my name on the paper, using his rock-hard shoulder as a desk. Another loud round of applause echoed in the basement, and with that the youth group session was formally over. We mingled around afterward, eating peanut butter cookies as a dessert, and I was about to go out front to check on my ride when the youth pastor approached me once again.

"Your buddy says you've not been saved, Doug. Is that true?" A double whammy. I wanted to punch my friend hard in the arm, but he'd already taken a few cookies for the road, as his older brother came down from another part of the church to drive him home. I was stuck.

The bodybuilder for God escorted me to a little room just off the rec area. It was a classroom used for pre-schoolers, the ABCs in a colorful banner across the top of the room, blocks stacked on nearly every desk and mini-Bibles in a tiny bookshelf. I could smell chalk and the scent of Handi-Wipes.

He asked me to get on my knees while he did the same. He was stiff as he finally managed to kneel completely down. I thought his skin might begin to turn green, and his pants and shirt would split into shreds, and in an instant he'd be clad in the tattered remains of his pastor garb. Don't make him mad, I thought. If those glasses come off and I don't agree with him, it's a full-blown Hulk deal going down. He took my hand in his and prayed for me. "Doug, do you accept the Lord Jesus Christ as your eternal Savior?" His hand was hot and as solid as a brick.

"Yes," I said, peeking at him with my head bowed. His face looked calm. No green; clothes completely intact. Images of Olivia in all stages of undress peppered my mind, in my junior high locker room after hours, she and I meeting through some type of American-Australian exchange student program, a concert in Indy canceled because of blizzard, the big O showing up on my doorstep with her golden bangs damp with tender snowflakes. I was afraid the Hulk knew about my dirty Olivia thoughts.

"And do you commit your life in his name, to worship no God before Him?"

"Yes." If I'd said no, would he have hurled me into the children's desks, pumping his massive arms and chest in my direction, everything moving at ultra slow motion as he bared his pearly whites?

"Amen."

"Amen."

He rose and smiled at me, his massive frame like a short boulder. He switched off the light and it was over. I'd thought there'd be some kind of light shining down on me, or a change in the way I felt inside, that the burning hot desire to bed Olivia would cease to gnaw at my mind, but as my tennis shoes squeaked in the hallway, I followed him back to the kitchen with no more of an enlightened sense than when I'd arrived. We walked together back through the church halls, a creepy hum as the backdrop, the harsh light from overhead pasty and flickering. As we turned the corner, I saw my dad talking with the pastor's wife. He looked utterly out of place, hadn't even taken off his cap, a cardinal sin, a show of disrespect. I didn't get much time with my dad. He was either working the farm or the factory and it was unnerving to have him picking me up on the night of my supposed transfiguration.

I was given a few cookies and a booklet I was to fill out for the next session. Out in the truck, my dad's cigarette smoke still hung inside the cab. It smelled wonderful, like a familiar home, comforting and predictable. I wanted biceps like his, to wear my clothes with manly disregard, sleeves rolled up for real work. He revved the engine and asked me how the group went in a voice that implied he knew what had gone down. It seemed as though he could see right into me. I imagined my body, this newly found temple, owned by God, to be see-through under his sideways glances, like the cells we gawked at under the microscope in science class.

"Fine," I said, my hands sweaty. I felt nervous, as if what I'd done, knelt down next to the Hulk youth pastor, was a sin in itself. I knew how my dad felt about religion and church.

"It was okay," I said, trying to move my antidrug pledge away from the center of the bench seat without him noticing. I'd heard him lightly mock "born-agains" at the factory, saying, "Those sons-a-bitches steal more overtime than us heathens. They got a fellow born-again in the front office that doctors the overtime sheets." He'd smirk and finish with, "Their kinda sin pays better than ours."

"What's that you got there?" he asked, speaking from one side of his mouth, a newly lit cigarette dangling from the other. He looked cooler than anyone I knew. I coveted his Salems and longed to wear loose work boots, blue jeans worn and frayed in all the right places.

"Nothing. Just a pledge." I didn't want to get caught in a lie with him, and I hoped he'd leave it at that, but he reached for the paper, and read it under the passing streetlights on our way through the outskirts of town, heading toward our failing farm.

He handed it back to me, as he rolled down the window to let the smoke out. He bent to tap ashes into the cuff of his jeans.

"That's good, son," he commented, handing the pledge back to me. "Something like that can help keep you focused." He steered the truck off the main road and turned onto the potholed one-laner that led to the farm. It was dark outside the truck; only the lights of different farms twinkled in the distance. I wanted to tell him more, ask questions about why he didn't believe, reveal myself, but when the truck stopped in front of the house it was over. "I got to pull a double shift tonight, son. You get your sleep." He reached over my lap to open my door and I was tempted to hug him as hard as I could. I stepped out of the truck and he yanked the door shut. I watched as he backed up and drove quickly out of sight. The

Putting Out:

How You (and All Your Friends)

Came to Know Jesus

MICHELLE RICHMOND

Chances are you knew me in high school. I was the evangelist in tight jeans and high-tops, the girl whose enthusiasm for God was matched only by her allegiance to ill-advised fashion fads and her devotion to extended foreplay. I did Madonna (the "Like a Virgin" phase). I did sweater dresses. I did everything short of intercourse, and in the intervals I tried to convert you.

Don't blame me. Blame Hillside Baptist Church. More specifically, blame Keith, the youth minister who insisted that my Christian duty was to be a "righteous fox." Okay, I took him too seriously. Okay, I should have known you wouldn't accompany me to the pizza social (Come for the pizza! Stay for the revival!) no matter how often or how earnestly I went down on you.

And go down I did. Do you remember that time at R.S.'s party? Her mother was out of town. The liquor cabinet was well-stocked. You were way gone on Carter's pot. I was way gone on Seagram's and 7. At fourteen, I possessed a literal mind. When you asked for a blow job, I blew. But you must not have known any better, because you raised no objections. I blew, you cooed, and later I asked the Lord for forgiveness.

I spent most of my teenage years asking for forgiveness. This was allowed. I was Baptist, and the Baptists have that loophole: once

crunch of the tires on the gravel road sounded like a mur
prayer, one I didn't think he would ever hear going that fast
from me.

The house was extra still as I crept toward my room; onl
gaudy teapot clock on the kitchen wall ticked like a shabby b
Once inside my tiny hideout, a pantry converted to create a one
sleeper, I plucked a tack from the corkboard and pinned my
pledge next to the winter IU basketball schedule. I stood back
looked at it there, gently rising in the warm air now blowing d
from the heating registers. I'd gotten a certificate for pledging
to drink and smoke, but nothing tangible for the gift of my ete
soul. It was puzzling.

I walked to the mirror and checked on the large pimple in
center of my unibrow. I squeezed and felt a shooting pain, stop
and dabbed it with tissue. In the mirror, I caught the image
Olivia looking at my back, her legs seductively clad in leg warm
ever so mildly parted, the smooth material of her dancing gear c
ering every inch of pale skin. On the dresser I picked up my Jan
sum deodorant and rolled the cold ball under my armpits, givi
myself chills. I put on some REO Speedwagon and dimmed t
lights. Olivia and I held hands and talked about God. She found n
new, born-again soul immensely sexy. That night, in the co
countryside of northwest Indiana, Ms. Newton-John saw the fa
of God many, many times.

saved, always saved—Elvis being the prime example. Unlike the Catholics, the Baptists don't offer a whole lot of incentive for the doing of good deeds.

There was the time in the back of Roland Trombado's car. He was drunk. He was drunk driving. When I raised objections, double-jointed Scotia Stone said, "You. Are. *Such*. A Loser." I took solace in your zipper. It was stubborn, but I was industrious. That time I used my hands. Adjectives, I'm pretty good with. With a *hand* job, it's hard to go wrong. Plus, you get to talk during.

I said, "I can't believe I'm doing this."

I said, "I hope this won't make you think less of God."

You said, "Hallelujah."

You were Jewish. That's what enticed me to join you in Roland's backseat in the first place, drunk driving or no. Of the Jews my mother had said, "Well-intentioned, but misguided."

Meaning: you were going to hell. Meaning: I had my work cut out.

Then there was that time at the Admiral Semmes Hotel, two boys, three girls. Being the odd one out, I had to improvise. I dug my foot into the crevice of your boxer-clad ass while you were dry-humping Linda McDougal. Even I thought that was weird, but you moaned in a way that let me know you enjoyed it. Afterward I felt so dirty, I was tempted to go to confession. But Baptists don't confess; they project. Very quickly, I decided that the foot-in-the-ass thing was your idea. How did you *get* so depraved?

At the beginning of senior year, the youth minister gave me a paperback Bible with the instruction that I must carry it to school. Under no circumstances was it to be hidden away in my backpack or stuffed into my locker. Hide it under a bushel? Oh, no! The whole purpose of the Bible was that it be visible at all times, thus verifying my righteous foxiness.

On the inside back cover, I wrote the names of everyone I was praying for. Your name was included, of course. Along with the guy from R.S.'s party, the fellow from the backseat, the boy at the Admiral Semmes, and at least a dozen others who had managed to garner my favors. I included all of you, every last one.

Which one of you absconded with my Bible during American History and added a name to that long list of the hell-bent? *Mike Hunt.*

Well. That's when I took my Bible into the second-floor girls' room at Murphy High School—a bathroom so filthy that even the grunge set avoided it—and cried. Because it was true. Secretly, I'd already shot that particular prayer into the sky about a million times. I prayed that my desires would be quenched, that the fire in my loins would miraculously be put out, so I could stop putting out. Lust was making me crazy.

Prayer can only take you so far. Once, years before, it had taken me to the fellowship hall of Hillside Baptist Church. Technically, that was the beginning of my double career.

I was thirteen, wearing a denim miniskirt held together with two flimsy zippers on a sweltering Wednesday night. The prayer meeting was in session. Ashley Bender, whom I'd met on a youth trip to Gatlinburg, Tennessee, was in town for the summer. He slid into the pew beside me, fingered the zipper pull on the side of my skirt. Sweat gathered on the pew between my thighs. While a deacon somberly announced the week's ill and infirm, Ashley leaned over and whispered into my ear, "Want to show me around the church?"

We slipped out while the choir was singing "Come As You Are."

"This way," I said, leading him down a flight of shoddily carpeted stairs. I heard his footsteps close behind me, felt his moist breath on the top of my head. The fellowship hall was dark. Its sunk-in odors recalled hundreds of Sunday afternoon dinners—roast beef, yeast rolls, desserts involving custard and Jello.

"Nice facilities you've got here," Ashley said.

He was nineteen and from Quebec, which made it okay that he had a girl's name. When he said, "I've got wiry strength," flexed a scrawny bicep, and recited the Lord's Prayer in French, I was impressed. So impressed I let him feel me up, right there beside the giant coffee urn.

At that moment, I stood on the cusp of slutdom. I could have chosen the prayer meeting, but instead I chose Ashley—because he had chosen me, which meant something. All that talk of Jesus knocking on the doors of sinners' hearts had left me with one unsettling thought: the Lord, though kind, was not discriminating. He chose *everyone*. Ashley, on the other hand, had looked around the vast hall of God-fearing girls and seen me—not Arlene with her perfect lips or Cindy with her perfect hair or Elise with her father's perfect bank account, but me.

Upstairs, the organ droned, the people prayed, choir robes swayed under fluorescent lights. Downstairs, the spirit moved us. Standing with my back to the wall, Ashley's hand up my skirt, the air conditioner sputtering, I remembered a pledge I'd recently made to let the Lord use me however he saw fit.

Then Ashley shuddered, made a weird sound, and came all over my bare stomach.

I loved the slick heat of it, loved the way he completely lost control, the way, for those few minutes beside the coffee urn, he had been completely at my mercy. I felt powerful, but guilty.

Moments later, while he was wiping up with a paper towel, I saw my opportunity to make good on my promise to God.

"Do you know the Lord as your personal savior?" I asked.

"No," he said, "but I'd be willing to consider. On one condition."

"Yes?"

"Meet me here again. Same time next week."

"Okay," I said. It was then that I knew I'd found my calling.

All that, and still, it took a war to pop my cherry.

Oh yes—blow jobs I gave out like candy, hand jobs could be had for a song—but when it came to the big V, I was saving it for my husband.

1992: I am nineteen and living in an old, rambling house in Northport, Alabama, with my boyfriend and two other guys. My boyfriend and I have the top floor to ourselves, with its smell of old wallpaper and dusty upholstery and decades of baked-in heat. His National Guard unit has just been called to go to Saudi Arabia.

Ah. An answered prayer.

Because who can say no to a soldier headed off to war? It is the ultimate loophole for the virgin-'til-marriage set.

His bags are packed to go. His boots have been polished. The barber has ruined his beautiful hair. No telling what might happen to him. Really! It's a war! It's possible I may never see him again.

Oh, of course it isn't very romantic. First times never are. But there is something undeniably sweet about the dirty sheets and rickety bed, the hot Alabama wind blowing through the open window, the branches of the big oak tree tapping against the side of the house.

He's just twenty-one, with small, boyish teeth and baby-smooth skin; no matter, he seems like a grown-up man to me. I clumsily attempt to roll the condom on, so excited my hands shake.

"Here, let me do that," he says kindly.

I'm nineteen and quite aware that I'm very late to the party. Oh, but the party is just fine. It was worth waiting for, really.

I don't even try to convert him. This time, I know, there really is no point. Because I've gone and fallen in love with an atheist. An atheist! The word sounds exotic, profane.

Flies buzz above the bed. Downstairs, our roommates are watching the prelude to the war play out on CNN. My boyfriend's army-green duffel bag sits in the corner of the room, stuffed and zippered and ready to go. The foreplay takes about two seconds. And then we're into it, finally, six long years after my first kiss. I am feeling, I can't deny it, like the foxiest of righteous foxes. And I'm realizing a wonderful thing: blow jobs and hands jobs and the rest have always made me feel dirty, but sex just makes me feel sexy.

"Jesus," he says. And I know just what he means.

No Worries

DEAN BAKOPOULOS

For most of my teen years, I was in love with a guy named Mack. The fact is that we were all a little in love with Mack. Not in an intimate way, mind you—though we did once watch him shoot a bottle rocket out of his ass, which is, in no small way, an act of intimacy. Still, we loved him. By we, I mean my high school friends—me and Mack, plus the Big Ragu, Big Al, Freebs, Noone, B., Norm, Petey, Brain, Gordo, and Tough Pig—a motley crew of eleven guys who spent much of our teenage lives doing the usual teenage things: stealing beer, smoking cigarettes, getting into trouble, obsessing over sex, and, in general, having the time of our lives.

Mack was our unofficial leader. Although at times, one of us might aspire to the level of alpha, it was Mack who was the most charismatic, the most maddening, the most unpredictable, and the one whose attention, I see now, we all craved in some way. I first fell in love with Mack when he threw a knife at me, the nine-inch blade missing my ear by centimeters. We were walking in an open field behind the high school, and he thought it might be funny if he whizzed the knife by my head. I didn't find it funny at all. I got extremely scared and then extremely pissed off. Mack shrugged it off. He said, "You got to be ready, my man."

Ready? For what? Why did I, a teenager in Detroit's bland suburbs, have any reason to be ready for a knife whirling by my head? Why?

The reason, of course, was that there was no reason. There was no reason for many of the things Mack did: Why did he prefer to walk down the middle of the street instead of Livonia's ample side-walks? Why did he drink NyQuil during the school day and then try and force himself to stay awake in class? Why did he climb onto the roof of a movie theater after we'd seen a matinee of *Navy Seals* at the dollar show? Why did he prefer to get Coney dogs at the Coney Island in Detroit's most dangerous neighborhood, after dark, while wearing a cowboy hat? Why did he drive a giant white van named Sal, a beast of a vehicle with a die-cast metal bumpers that he used to plow over shit like street signs and port-a-johns?

If Mack and I still spoke, or e-mailed, or communicated with each other in any way, I might ask him what made him the way he was—reckless, spontaneous, sometimes ridiculous. But Mack and I don't talk anymore, and so I am left to wonder why I thought, and still think, that he was so fucking cool.

*

I was born cautious. As a toddler, I rarely left my mother's side. I wouldn't play with other kids and I wouldn't talk to adults. I liked being alone or with my mother or grandparents. Everybody else I regarded with a great deal of suspicion, if not terror. By the time I was a teenager, I was more outgoing—I had friends, girlfriends, was elected to student council and homecoming court. I captained a var-sity team and in general thought the social world of high school was fairly easy to navigate. I rarely got punched. I was one of *those* kids—good grades, popular, a good complexion, an older sister who helped me pick out my clothes and shaped my musical tastes. Still, my teen years were filled with terror. I was afraid of everything. I suffered from migraines and stomach cramps. I often had insom-nia. For a month or two, I grappled with a panic disorder that made me certain that I would vomit in the middle of an important event or large crowd. Later, I had a stretch of panic attacks that made me think I had to take a leak every ten minutes. I made up some excuse about a bruised kidney and the teachers let me slip in and out of the room, but in reality, I was just plain weird, one of the tensest balls of tension you could ever imagine.

I come from a long line of chronic and heroic worriers. My

maternal grandfather, who'd escaped labor camps and battlefields, worried about the daily grind of life in Detroit until an ulcer burned a hole in his guts. His wife, my grandmother, is still obsessive to the point of psychosis, checking and rechecking the stove burners a dozen times a day, taking out the trash every thirty minutes, mistrustful of every unlocked door or an any dormant electrical appliance. Their daughter, my mother, filled my head with worry when I was still quite young: We never flew anywhere, because our plane was certain to drop from the sky. Outdoor activities were simply stages for bear attacks and killer bees. We ran for the basement at every darkened sky, every thunder rumble. The highways were full of drunks, the woods full of perverts, the lakes full of bacteria, and our Halloween candy ripe with cyanide and razor blades.

By the time I was a teenager, fear was a daily part of my life. I worried from sunrise to sundown, and then lay in bed worrying some more.

When I met Mack, I was thirteen, anxious as all hell, and terrified of doing something dangerous that would break my neck or leave me disfigured. It wasn't the consequences of the trouble that had me worried; rather, I didn't want to get hurt or sick or die, because my mother would be so saddened. Like a lot of young men with single mothers, I was protective of my mother. She worked so hard, sacrificed so much for me, that I was terrified of doing something to jeopardize all of that. Her warnings sounded in my ears every time something was about to get really fun. In many ways, this served me well. I got through my teen years without major injury, drug overdose, alcohol poisoning, or fathering a child. I had a knack for going home about five minutes before the police would show up. Still, I was so risk-averse that every day became an exercise of will. I had to force myself through every terrifying day, certain that danger or disaster would consume me if I made one false or stupid move.

*

Mack was the soul of our gang. Mack even gave our gang a name, the Regulators, which he stole from the western *Young Guns,* the ultimate buddy movie and one we watched over and over and a movie I can still quote from at will. At Mack's leading, we began to wear flannel shirts and cowboy hats and work boots. We took an oath and signed a pledge to abide by the Regulator code of conduct. We hung around the mall dressed as cowboys, waging war with the mall cops, throwing eggs at them, knocking down planters, and, in general, being a brand of asshole very common in suburban America.

I found it all thrilling: the first time I chucked an egg at a security guard, I felt so, well, *alive*! All the worst-case scenarios ran through my head: The mall cop would draw a weapon and shoot me in the chest. The security truck would run me over as it chased me across the acres of asphalt. I would fall off the roof of the parking ramp as I made my getaway. My mother's worries echoed in my head, but I ignored them. I was a big bad Regulator.

I think it was Mack who gave our gang our first mission: stealing a bench. I admit, it was not the most important mission that anyone could have, and it lacked any real purpose or sense, but it was a mission. We were going to go to Oliver Wendell Holmes middle school, on the last day of classes, to unbolt a bench from the brick wall and take it to the woods. We planned to sit on it all summer, I guess. This was the bench where my friends sat every day. (I was the sole attendee of Catholic School, so the bench was not as sacred to me, but heck, free bench.)

We gathered after the last day of school, Mack holding a socket set and some tools. Big Al had made us all fake beards to wear as disguises, and Ragu and I had drawn a map of the crime scene, including the best escape route to the woods, which were not really woods, only a sparsely treed drainage area that passed for wilderness in metro Detroit. We spoke in Spanish, the handful of phrases we knew, as if that would further disguise our identities.

Six thirteen-year-olds walking through an empty school wearing fake beards and carrying a toolbox should arouse some suspicion. But remarkably, we went unnoticed at first. My ticker bombed away at two hundred beats a minute, my guts felt like an angry sea of bile, and my hands shook.

I was the designated worrier. The Catholic school–attending, guilt-ridden, straight-A good boy, and everyone knew it. While my friends went to work on the bench, I stood back, watching out for janitors or a principal, the self-appointed and voluntary lookout. When the bench came off the wall, I ran like hell. I was the first one out the door, the rest of my friends struggling to hold on to the newly released public school seating.

In the parking lot, I grabbed hold of the bench and joined my friends as we darted into the street and stopped the traffic on busy Newburg Road. How amazing we must have looked in our fake beards and cowboy hats, sprinting into the afternoon congestion and heat, carrying our booty on our backs like a bunch of crazed pirates. How liberated and free we must have appeared to the mid-management sales rep, stuck sweating in his Buick, a necktie knotted too tight around his expanding, fleshy neck! Oh, how my feet seemed to lift from the pavement as we yelled "Regulators!" and tore ass to the woods at the end of the drab subdivision, two Livonia Public School maintenance vehicles now in hot pursuit.

Think of the dangers we faced: twisted ankles, drunken drivers, gun-crazed janitors, asthma attacks, perverts in the woods! Who knew what we were risking to bring that bench home? Who knew what Mack would lead us to do next?

In the end, we dropped the bench in the woods and fled in different directions, adrenaline unlike any I'd ever felt coursing through my veins. It was thrilling. When I went home for dinner that night, I felt so secretive and full of danger, like a mob man sitting down to some baked ziti minutes after giving some goon an execution order.

High school became a series of meaningless yet thrilling adventures for me, many of which I watched from the sidelines. I left the Catholic school system and enrolled in public school, partly because I found Mack and my other friends so thrilling. And Mack didn't disappoint. He came up with one adventure after another.

We set up a place we'd call Camp Moc-Moc, a small fire pit in a tiny stretch of woods behind the high school where we'd go to smoke and drink and act like renegade cowboys in a suburb as boring as a dustball. One night Mack and Big Al cooked a chicken over the fire, like a couple of real cowboys might do, but I was too afraid of salmonella to eat any of it. Another time, when Big Al had a bad back, Mack tied him to a tree and beat him with a stick in lieu of chiropractics. I went home before this went down, certain Al would fall to his death and not wanting to be a witness. And another time, my friends, at Mack's suggestion, spent the night at Camp Moc-Moc despite heavy snow and the low windchills. A little buzzed on whiskey, they huddled by the fire. I was too afraid of frostbite and pneumonia, and by midnight, I was home.

Once, again at Mack's suggestion, we saved our piss in two-liter bottles of pop and dumped them all over, and inside, the car of a senior who was dating a girl we all had a crush on. Another time, we drove around in the big white van, following a carload of seniors, including the girl whom Mack had loved and who had recently broken up with him for an older guy. When they pulled into Taco Bell, we came out swinging a logging chain and baseball bats. Another time, we smoke-bombed a fast-food joint where the toughest guys in school were gathered. We craved any adventure, recklessness, the thrill of a chase, a fight, a battle, and Mack was always willing to lead us into something new. Through everything, the stolen lawn ornaments, the endless wars with mall cops, the watermelons busted on our enemies' doors, I was the first one to run away from the scene, the quickest to flee, nimble and light-footed, despite the heaviness of worry and fear in my heart.

When Mack bought a new Mustang with a five-liter engine, he took me and Al and Noone out for a ride. We were cruising down the Jeffries Freeway, and Mack was darting in and out of lanes, pushing 120 miles per hour. In my mind, I pictured my mother and grandparents wailing, praying the Rosary over my casket. I pictured the beautiful family of five whose minivan we would decimate.

"Mack," I said, "Slow down."

He gunned the engine.

"Slow the fuck down!" I yelled.

Big Al and Noone couldn't stop laughing, scared shitless as I was, but perhaps with a greater capacity for cheap thrills.

"Slow down now, you fucker!" I yelled.

Finally Mack took his foot off the gas.

"Hey man," he said. "No worries."

"Fucker," I said.

"The kids love it," Mack said, borrowing a line that his father used to say.

"Asshole," I said.

"No worries," he said again, coasting the car up the exit ramp for Telegraph Road. "It's fine."

*

My strangest and most intense experience with Mack came when we were seventeen, the summer before our senior year of high school. We were all suburban kids, squarely middle-class with a few rough edges thrown in for good measure. I was probably the poorest of all of my friends and I envied their intact families and larger homes, their summer vacations and family outings. So when Mack's family invited me, along with Big Al and Tough Pig, to a summer vacation at a Christian camp in the Adirondack Mountains, I was so excited I couldn't stand it. I literally had to beg my mother for weeks in order to get permission to go along on the trip. In addition to the perilous mountain roads, she worried aloud about drowning, bear attacks, mosquito-inflicted viruses, cliff falls, lightning strikes, water-skiing accidents, and other mishaps that were sure to befall me.

It was a beautiful little spot in the mountains, and having come from a family that never spent any time in the woods, I was intoxicated by the whitewater rivers and giant trees. We'd gone up there in order to water ski and swim and maybe meet some of the isolated mountain town Christian girls who, we believed, in our heart of hearts, were willing to be corrupted by some young roughnecks from the Motor City.

The only requirements that Mack's family had for us was that we attend meals (a way to make sure we weren't on our way to Manhattan, I suppose) and that we attend the morning worship services. I listened to the preacher's sermons the best I could, but mostly focused on all the beautiful, Waspy-looking women in sundresses. They all looked rich, with their perfect hair, expensive sandals, and painted toes. They were blond and brilliant, and crossed their thin legs in a way that I found dignified, ladylike, and sexy. I was seventeen, from immigrant stock. I was easy to impress.

But by the second sermon, something was shaking in my heart. And on the final day of the week, the preacher—Pastor Fred—came out to wild applause. I learned from the rather bellicose introduction that Pastor Fred also hosted a nationwide, syndicated show for teenagers that aired on Christian radio networks. He was sort of famous. I pretended I knew all of that. I looked around at the crowd.

Pastor Fred leaned out into the audience, like he was about to stage-dive into a mosh pit. He seemed to look at me when he yelled—and really, he was yelling—"Do you want to get well?"

He was quoting John 5:5; I know this because he said it over and over again.

"Why," he said, "would Jesus—in John chapter five, verse five— why would Jesus ask a man, who has been paralyzed and in pain for thirty-eight years, this question: *Do you want to get well?*"

He said it exactly like that, the same way, a second time:

"Why," he said, "Would Jesus—in John chapter five, verse five—why would Jesus ask a man, who has been paralyzed and in pain for thirty-eight years, this question: *Do you want to get well?*"

The auditorium—which had been buzzing with the shifting sounds of restless teenagers, the murmurs, giggles, and fidgets— went flat and silent. The woman ahead of me had tears all down her face. Other people stifled sobs or wept openly.

Fred was short and bald and fairly thin. He had a high-pitched, frantic voice. He did not have an ounce of commanding personality, but I could not stop listening to him. He said God had spoken to him years ago.

God said, Fred, why are you ignoring me?

Fred, God said, why are you so scared of change?

God said, Fred, do you want to get well?

Fred then went into a story of how he used to be obese and smoke cigarettes and drink too much. How everything in his life had always been filled with self-destruction and anger. And relationships? Forget about it. He had more failed relationships than Elizabeth Taylor and Zsa Zsa Gabor combined!

He paused here and allowed the crowd to breathe and laugh. We took a collective breath, then laughed, then held our breath again.

Do I remember what happened next? I should, because here would be a pivotal moment in my life. I was about to be born again, to be converted, to see God and his seraphim and cherubim and the heavens open and Jesus on a throne. People were shouting and sobbing, and many of them were on their knees, arms stretching up toward Heaven. I saw what was going on, and then I realized, I was right there with them, on my knees, arms outstretched ready to meet my Lord.

Fred called out, "Do you want to get well?"

And I shouted, "Yes!"

"Whoever wants to come forward," Fred said, his shouting becoming more and more muted until what was left was a passionate whisper. "To come down here and make a personal commitment to Jesus Christ, to say Jesus Christ is my Lord and Savior, please come down now. If you're tired of a life without Jesus, if you're frustrated by emptiness and sadness and strife and a life without Jesus the Savior, come be embraced by the Father. Do you want to get well?"

I stood up and looked around. When I saw Mack stand up, too, and when I saw him head down the steps to the altar, I turned and made my way to the aisle. I went forward, following Mack to the bottom of the auditorium where people were weeping and singing and handing over their hearts.

Afterward, Mack and I filed into a small room with punch and cookies and stood around for a while with all of the new converts. We were standing around blank-faced, red-eyed, and sheepish, as if we just got busted for pissing in public or something. Fred came in and gave us each some pamphlets, and shook our hands and gave us free pocket New Testaments. I slipped mine in my back pocket.

*

When we got back from camp, I did the usual things. I went back to my job as a lifeguard, made out with my girlfriend, and paid a laid-off gym teacher to buy me beer. I drank pretty much every night. It was summer. Sometimes, after my mother had gone to sleep, I'd have a beer or two in my basement and once I got a buzz going, I'd read the Bible.

It was an absurd summer. On one hand, I was doing everything a teenage boy should have been doing—working a crappy job, scheming to get beer, making out with a cheerleader, asserting my aloofness by moving my bedroom into the basement. On the other hand, I was already up to Lamentations in my Old Testament.

Then, I started to have dreams. In one dream, Jesus appeared. I was sitting on the edge of a dock exactly like the one at the Christian camp in upstate New York. Jesus looked at me and put his hand on my shoulder; he stared out over the lake for a long time, and then turned back to me and said, "So, what do you want to do now?"

Mack called me a few nights later from New Mexico, where he was doing mission work on an Indian reservation with Pastor Fred and a team of youth. He was living in a trailer, studying the Bible, and going around casting out Satan from the lives of troubled teenagers. I had desperately wanted to go on the trip, but I had my summer job, and, besides, working-class immigrants' kids don't go on things like mission trips to Indian reservations. It's just not done.

When Mack called me that night, I was in the basement drinking beer and reading the Psalms. Mack said, "Get ready. When I come back this fall, we have some serious work to do."

*

When school started, Mack and I spent hours alone, talking about our newfound faith, praying, studying the Bible. We began to "witness" to our friends; we quit drinking beer and smoking cigarettes. A few of our friends became born again too. I preached to my family, urging my mother and sister to give their lives over to Jesus. I remember overhearing my sister, who was home from college for the weekend, saying to my mother: "Either he's a prophet or he's gone crazy."

I felt like a prophet. With Mack, even something that sounds as square as being a born again Christian became an adventure. We made big plans. We felt the Lord was calling us to travel the world together and preach the Gospel. It was like we were on a secret, divine mission. We considered dropping out of school and making a pilgrimage to Jerusalem.

I stopped going to church with my mother and grandparents, our rundown Ukrainian Catholic Church in a dying Detroit neighborhood, and I began attending a vast and sparkling suburban evangelical church with Mack's family. They'd pick me up every Sunday, and afterward, they would take me out to a restaurant nicer than any of the restaurants my mother and I would go to. They said I was like another son, and I could always consider myself welcome. I remember thinking how amazing it was that Mack's parents got along so well, that they seemed genuinely happy to be together. It freaked me way out. Mack's mom would call me "Just Dean" because, every time I would walk into their house, I would say, "It's just Dean." Mack's father was always willing to offer me fatherly advice; he considered my teenage problems to be very real problems and he didn't mind talking to me about them. Mack's older sister was quite simply the most beautiful woman in Livonia; I'd have followed her anywhere. Mack's older brother seemed to me cooler than any older brother anyone could have. And, after our conversion, Mack and I considered ourselves to be as tight as brothers. It was like being invited, suddenly, into a beautiful family: blond, thin, well intentioned and striking. They never yelled or threw shit at one another. They were kinder than almost any family I have encountered since; they were generous and welcoming and tolerant.

One weekend, Mack and I and our newly converted friend, Jen, all drove down to Wheaton College in Illinois to check out the campus. It's a very conservative Christian establishment, Protestant and expensive, and I knew, within seconds of stepping onto campus, that I didn't belong there. I can't tell you why: it just seemed too squeaky-clean, too orderly, too civil and well lit for me. As much as I thought that this was the kind of life I craved, somewhere in the Billy Graham museum I realized that I wasn't living a life that made any sense to me. People like me didn't get to go to places like Wheaton. But Mack and Jen ended up applying and enrolling there; I went to Michigan and I got older and everything changed.

My time as a born-again evangelical ended as suddenly as it began; it's not that I no longer believe in God. I do. I even consider myself a Christian, in a broad sense of the word. I just left the conservative, evangelical scene, a scene that creeps me out to this day, probably because I had been a part of it and know how much of your brain needs to be turned off to fully partake of this kind of religion.

My fall took place my first week on campus; while Mack and Jen went to chapel every morning at Wheaton, I wandered around Ann Arbor every evening, looking for something to do and a place to fit in. And, despite what fundamentalists might say about secular college campuses, it's not like I was won over by some lefty professor or sexy atheist who made me change my religious views. Instead, my fall from faith happened when I attended a meeting of the Intervarsity Christian Fellowship, and stood in the crowd of preppy, well-scrubbed college students who waved their hands and arms and swayed zombie-like to a flat soulless style of song that everyone called contemporary praise music.

Our God is an Awesome God, they sang.

Lord, I lift your name on high.

I felt cornered. I held on to the stupid song sheet they'd given us, and realized I was a fraud. Standing there, scared shitless by the certainty of everybody's faith, the striking blandness and boredom of everybody in the room, I missed Mack. I missed the excitement of living your life scared out of your mind and hurling yourself into one extreme after another. This wasn't faith; this was summer camp. Summer camp with a glee club and no beer or cigarettes.

I decided I wanted to get drunk and left the room just as everybody was about to join hands and pray about sexual sins. I paid a hall mate with a fake ID to buy a few bottles of wine. I showed up at the dorm room of a friend I had made in my English class, a Jewish girl from Connecticut who seemed as exotic as the Galapagos Islands to me. God, and her daddy's deep pockets, had blessed her with a single room—and I said, "I'm looking to fall from grace tonight."

She and I were just friends, and she had teased me about being a born-again Christian, so when I blurted out my desire to fall from grace, she smiled and knew what I was talking about. I was young and already wanted to become a writer, and I said ridiculous, dramatic things about once a day, usually to women I thought I loved.

But she was poetic and moody and loved melodrama and she told me to come into her room.

She said she was about to take a shower but I could wait in her room. This was the longest eleven minutes of my life. What fantasies ran through my head!

She came back with her long black wet hair, her skin scrubbed clean and shining like the sun. We put on some music and opened the wine. Neither of us had had any dinner, and we got so drunk that we passed out before we got much past the kissing phase. She turned off the light, curled up on the futon with me, and started to snore.

I woke up at dawn, thinking of Mack. I wondered if he would be disappointed in me, if he would think I had failed in some way by getting drunk and quitting the born-again scene. The truth was, it just wasn't that much fun without him. Nothing was. A few years later, he too would leave the born again world and head off to India. We were moving in opposite directions, literally and figuratively, but we stayed in touch. Just recently, I found a few postcards that he'd written to me when I was in those first few months of college. On one of them, he'd closed with the words *don't worry.*

*

In one of the great buddy stories of all time, "The Body" by Stephen King (which later became the film *Stand by Me*), the narrator says: "I never had any friends later on like the ones I had when I was 12—Jesus, did you?"

No, of course not.

And you know, when I was fourteen or fifteen or sixteen, you could have asked me if I was willing to die for my friends and I would have told you, without hesitation, that yes, I would. I imagined us to be an unbreakable army. I thought of our recklessness and occasional rage as a mission, with some vague yet noble goal. Now that I am older, and a husband and a father, I can say that I would die for my family and I know how deep some bonds can be. I also know now that I probably wouldn't really have died for my friends back then. And I certainly know that I wouldn't die for them today. I have other responsibilities and concerns. We all do.

But I'm still in touch with all of them, to some extent, and am always happy when I hear from them or see one of them. We joke about a Regulators reunion, though it never seems to happen. Some of the guys I only talk to rarely, via e-mail; others I have dinner with when I am on the road doing readings and happen to be in their city. A few of them are still in the Detroit area, and we visit when we can. I still consider all of them to be the best friends I've ever had.

Mack, oddly enough, is the only one I don't keep in touch with anymore. After college, we still saw him every now and then. He came out to stay with my wife and me in Wisconsin, shortly after we were married; he remodeled our bathroom as a wedding present. We listened to his stories about traveling across the world, into the remote regions of South Asia. I was still enthralled by him, and he was still exceedingly fun to have around. He also charmed my wife and my friends who had the chance to meet him. He brought my wife a Santa suit as a birthday present, a costume he'd taken from the attic of a convicted pedophile, a guy for whom he'd been house-sitting while the guy served his prison term. He handed it to my wife, explained its origins, and said, "I figured he probably shouldn't have this anymore, you know?" We laughed our heads off; the whole thing seemed so absurd, so *Mack*. He still dripped with charisma, though he never seemed to understand it.

When Big Al got married, Mack was supposed to stand up in the wedding with the rest of us, but he was in one of his reclusive phases, had recently married a woman he'd met online, and he didn't show. We were all so mad at him for not showing up. I think we got drunk and called him a half a million times. I think if it had been me, or somebody else, who hadn't showed up for the wedding, we wouldn't have been half as mad. But Mack was the leader, and everybody, all the old gang, was there, except Mack, and we wanted him to be there and to raise a glass with us.

The last I heard, he was in New Orleans. When Hurricane Katrina battered that city within an inch of its life, I pictured Mack staying there. I couldn't imagine him evacuating; I couldn't imagine him running away from anything. I could almost picture him on the rooftop of some flooded neighborhood, shouting down the storm. I've heard snippets of information, filtered through family and friends, that he is okay. He made it through the storm in one way or another. Still, in the weeks after the hurricane, after numbing my mind with hour after hour of horrible footage on the evening news, I had this daydream, this vision. In the vision, Mack pulled up in front of my house driving an old truck, which was piled precariously with all the possessions he could carry. He was soaked, as if from rain, though in the dream, in my neighborhood, the sun is shining. He climbed atop the mound of furniture, clothes, bicycles, and other cargo, which shook and buckled under his weight, and stood there, grinning. The passenger door opened with a heavy groan, and from the truck came Mack's wife, a woman whom I've never met, but in my dream, she was beautiful and tall, her bare legs bronzed and long. Her dress and hair blew in the wind and she smiled and waved. Mack navigated to the top of the junk pile and stood on one foot.

"Mack!" I yelled. "Careful."

He leapt down from his hurricane-battered heap, falling twenty feet to the sidewalk, landing on his feet.

"No worries," he said. "No worries."

MORE LOSERS
IN LOVE

Someone, Somewhere Else

Emily Franklin

It's the summer of 1988 and I've left sophomore year—and my undating self—back in Boston while attempting to learn French as a three-month native. So far, I've a cursory knowledge of French art, picked up some cooking tips, and can now have a decent conversation without thinking in English (read: *"Comme dessert, que me suggereriez-vous pour effacer le goût du plat de resistance de ma bouche?"* or "What could you recommend to get the taste of the main course out of my mouth?").

Most importantly (though this was certainly not part of the course description offered to my parents in the brochure), beautiful boys abound. I've plucked Ron—who works for the summer as the gardener—as my crush. I camp out for hours on the terrace where I'm afforded a view of shirtless Ron, his long hair tied in a ponytail, his full lips twisted into a grin as he jokes with his buddies. Pretending not to watch him, I mouth vocab words to myself while writing in my journal (example: "he just pruned the rhododendrons—he is so amazing"). I was excellent at pining, and writing about pining, and thinking about longing.

Ron the Gardener (my mother's moniker after the boys from away got to be too many or too similar in her mind) was mythical—foreign in a foreign land, older, his good looks outmatched only by his biting wit, his kind demeanor. And I got him.

In the daylight of my prestigious prep school, I would have pined for Ron the Gardener the entire academic year—watched from afar as he kicked through the autumn leaves with his left-of-center popular friends, or had a snowball fight with some girl he later wound up kissing on the quad. In short: I would have set my sights on him but would have had no hopes of any reciprocity. Not that I was from the underworld of high school's lowest ranks. I wasn't top tier, probably not even middle—more an afterthought. Or a nonthought. Maybe there were girls people dated, rotated through like sweaters and seasons, and girls they didn't. It's easier sometimes when thinking back to my teenage years to define myself by what I wasn't rather than what I was—I wasn't a stoner, wasn't a nerd, wasn't a shiny popular girl floating between the top-dated senior boys, wasn't an athlete; I wasn't a lot of things. Trying to pinpoint what—or whom—I actually *was* is tougher.

Some kids, it seemed to me, had the luxury of existing right in the moment. I was present, but not fully accounted for—I'd be in American Lit wondering if I'd ever be published, or in sex ed wondering where on the *who guys would sleep with if they could* ranking I'd fall. I spent many weekends away from campus, exploring other places, keeping up with people from far away. So maybe it wasn't just that I wasn't thought of as a potential girlfriend, but also that I wasn't giving off that vibe of being around—of committing to the crucial teenage present. On campus, I was a writer, a good student when interested and a great student when fully engaged, I sang in the octet, I had friends.

But I never had a boyfriend.

Correction: I never had a boyfriend on campus.

I could again define myself by the groups of which I wasn't a part: I wasn't in the tight-knit group of dateables—the most popular kids who went out with one another and overlapped boyfriends and girlfriends so much that by the time they'd graduated they'd pretty much all been together at some point. I wasn't one of the sweetly pretty girls who got swooped up by older classmen for a year or two and then dumped after the first fall college visit. And I did not find my home among the girls who never showed up at the dance because they knew no one would ask them onto the floor. I had a good shot at being asked to dance, at being spoken to, and becoming friends with boys—popular ones, even—but I didn't make that next cutoff. In the tryouts for the role of girlfriend, I wound up excelling instead at being "friend girl."

This is not necessarily loserly—in fact it shaped my romantic future in a way I'm happy with now—but at the time, continually being relegated to "the one I can really talk to" didn't feel anything other than loserly. Why wasn't I "the one you can really make out with"?

So for all those cycles of fall leaves through flirtatious snowball fights to sweaty springs spent lounging on the grass, I was never an "and." As in Emily *and* ___.

And yet there was Ron the Gardener. With his pruning shears and worn-through T-shirts that heralded bands who peaked before we were both born, he and I struck up an easy friendship that segued into a gut-jolting first kiss in broad daylight by the tool shed.

Ron was not the first. Before Ron there was Alex the summer before—New York slick and so cute I couldn't describe him properly in my journal so I just wrote his name. And after AJ, Rob the surfer with his ocean-blond hair and bare feet at dinner. After the *I'm trapped in a body that doesn't quite feel like mine* experience of eighth grade, freshman year hit me full on with what would be my only on-campus high school "go out." AJ was the "it" boy of that year, and after I made him laugh and he poured his fourteen-year-old mind out to me, he announced, "You're the only girl I've ever been able to talk to—like, about the Beatles or my parents, or anything."

It was quite a declaration and one that only reinforced my feeling that while I was pretty enough, my draw had less to do with my outside and more to do on my inside. While mothers, pediatricians, child psychologists, and philosophers alike will tell you this is a good thing—being not so dependent on what my exterior had to offer—at the time, it half-sucked. I wanted to be that pretty girl who would have her pick of guys. Like Tonia M. or Ellen D.—life seemed easy and simple for them, as though unlike me, they never had to waste hours falling asleep at night wondering when—or if—they might be liked back. Like Xander, who captured my attention with his preppy puppy looks and place as the most shy of the popular set and accounted for many journal entries.

My high school romantic roster reads like a vacancy sign. After three weeks of "going out" with AJ, our kisses stopped the conversations and in back of the science building he spelled it out, "Would it be okay if I got together with someone else right away?" When I asked who and why, he did me the sharp courtesy of explaining. "Alle. She's like you, kind of, but I don't tell her as much when we talk, and she wants to kiss more."

Less talk, more rock.

What I didn't know then, was that the same boys—AJ, Xander, and so on—would become readily available during the summer or during vacations. In short, anywhere off of my picturesque boarding school campus. Within the confines of the brick buildings and leafy quads I had permanent friend status with the boys, but as soon as classes ended and I hauled it to England, or summer camp, or France, or Martha's Vineyard, Canada for Columbus Day, I was all set. Was the *don't think about dating me* label slicked so early on my forehead at high school that it became indelible? Or was it partially me? Did I shy away from potential rejection from the boys I befriended in the hallways and block off any chance of going out with them as a matter of self-protection from heartache?

There was Ron the Gardener. Rob the Surfer. Alex from New York. Steve from Canada. Ian from England. Piles of letters accumulated, hours of expensive long-distance phone calls erupted on my parents' bills and which I had to pay for with chores and tears ("I know we talked for fifty minutes . . . But . . . he likes me . . . and . . . I like him!"). These guys were cool. They were the ones I'd have wanted during the academic year—and the ones I couldn't get.

Back on campus, they began to sound mythical. When I think of it now, even I scoff at myself, at the little campus mailbox-checking for the fifth time that day and saying things such as, "Yeah, I met a guy . . . he's gorgeous and likes me . . . but he lives in Canada. He's in a band." Sure.

*   *   *

"So, let me get this straight," Jen says looking at the photograph of Ron. I developed the picture myself in the photo room, its black and whites mottled with my fingers, the rhododendron bush gauzy, having been left not quite long enough in the development solution. "You don't go out with anyone here. Ever. And then you get *him*?" Jen points to Ron. To his hair. To his mouth. To his sleep sexy eyes and tanned shirtless self. I nod. "Awesome." Jen will later, years later after we've left high school and solidified a friendship based on other things, admit that one of the reasons she became friends with me was that photo. "I figured, if she can land a guy like that, she's the kind of girl I want to be friends with. It was like you were already dating the people we'd want later on."

Maybe that was it. Maybe I never had the typical high school boyfriend—one who took me to dances and wrote me Valentines, and slipped notes into my mailbox—because I was only partly living there and partly elsewhere. The immediacy of teenage living never seemed enough to me—what else was there after classes, exams, high-drama friendships, this current life? Part of me longed to have my hand held as I walked to class, and the lack of it gnawed at my stomach as I watched countless girls with the right shoes (worn-in bluchers), the right hair (blond at the front from beach walks with a ponytail), the right figure (not too this, not too that) snag the guy and bask in the glow of coupledom.

And then—after summer romances, vacation connections—I finally got my steady boyfriend. Only, at high school—and probably boarding school to a greater extreme—anyone who goes to a different school appears to be a figment of your romantic imagination.

"So you have a . . . boyfriend?" K. says to me after Thanksgiving vacation. K.'s one of the campus steadies—she and D. have been together for nearly two years.

"Yeah," I say, the smile ballooning my face. I have a boyfriend! Dave and I met through a mutual friend. I'd returned home from visiting him for the first time to find a coupon in my bag "for a hug and kiss—good until the end of time." What else did I need? Proof.

"But he doesn't go here?" She raises her eyebrows as if to question how this would be possible.

"Right—he's at college." I say the words and feel their glamour. "His name's Dave."

"Dave. Hmmm." K. thinks about this for a second as though I've scanned the room for a quick-thinking word—mailbox? Sneaker? No, she'll never buy that. How about Dave? "He's at college? Nearby?" K. wants to know this to calculate how often Boyfriend and I will be seeing each other. If he goes to Harvard, or BU, somewhere in Massachusetts, we can almost bypass the label of "long-distance."

"At Penn, actually." I explain more than I need to, probably to justify in my own mind the validity of this—my first serious boyfriend. "He's there, I'm here, but we'll get together on weekends—or vacations. He's a freshman." The two-year age difference didn't mean much—his lack of proximity did.

"I guess you could write letters." K. considers this and tucks her perfectly lemon-streaked hair behind her ears before finding her place among the snack bar crowd. "Then at least you get mail."

This was a perk—having nearly daily envelopes delivered to my on-campus mailbox. Packages, notes, letters describing college life—all of this was good. I could counteract the longing I felt counting campus couples by rereading Dave's latest list of things he missed about me. Looking back, I wonder if he, too, was defining me not so much by what I was in his life, but what he missed of me while I wasn't there.

Probably there were people who thought I made them up—these off-campus boys. The ones who wrote letters and sent photographs of the two of us by European monuments or feet in the sand in some faux arty shot on the beach. But my friends knew, and I knew. And when the time came for the prom and my first serious relationship with Dave from Penn had ended with my first serious dumping (on the phone, in a friend's basement, the night after the

SATs), my best friend and I eschewed boys and went to the prom together. My mother got us both beautiful corsages—long-stemmed roses wrapped in green silk ribbons. (Side note: the boy who'd asked me to the prom and then reneged, and to whom I said a very kindly no and then yes, to our mutual embarrassment, would later be roommates with my future husband at college and lead me to the love of my life.) With or without a prom date, with or without a boyfriend present, I began to suspect that what I liked the best about my loserly status among the datables at high school was the distance it allowed me.

Knowing I wasn't an option for the boys around me opened doors to friendships with them that later proved invaluable. I don't want to make it seem as though not being the girl people wanted to date felt good. It didn't. What I did feel, though, was something I think gets at the heart of being fourteen, fifteen, sixteen, seventeen: the feeling that around the corner, somewhere else, there's the place where you *are* that person you want to be. That fantasy we carry with us in our backpacks of getting the hell out of high school and home and away from the same friends and crushes is the one that suggests we might stumble onto the mythical us during a summer, a vacation, a trip to visit faraway friends. When I went to Toronto to see people I'd met the summer after junior year, I had all the confidence of a girl who knows that if she likes a guy he just might like her back. I had learned from past experiences. And when I visited Jen at college in New York while I was still stranded back in high school as a senior, I found it easy to get together with the shiny blond boy who I figured wouldn't have looked twice at me had he gone to my school. There was something about getting out of the sameness of those high school days, of first bells to last, lunch periods, hallway chitchat and exam stress, that made it possible for me to put myself out there with a crush and have it reciprocated.

Of course, there was the inevitable vacuum suckage back to the reality of each fall, winter, spring; each weekend filled with dances where I was a safe choice, guys I became friends with who—at least in my mind—never considered anything other than talking and the odd platonic backrub. But I had those other boys—the boys of summer, of holidays, of other countries or schools down the street—anything but my own.

Looking back is bittersweet; there are many opportunities I missed to try my hand at everyday romance, that everyday confidence needed to tell someone you see on a daily basis that you like them. *In that way.* But there are letters, postcards, photos, journal entries: proof I had all those teenage feelings, experienced those kisses, the hand-holding, the longing, the clean purity of missing someone you've not fully gotten the chance to know.

Boner

BRAD LAND

for Lauren F

1

We lived, then, in the upper northwest of South Carolina, in the outcrop of a town called Kershaw, in what some might call a hamlet, or a village, even, a gathering of huts named Heath Springs, and there our father served as pastor to Salem Methodist; the church was made of large stones in varying hues of grayness; once a man who dressed like Jesus (flowing robes, sandals) came there, and I thought he was Jesus, and probably he was, and then later, while he worked in his office, my father put my two brothers and I to play in an empty Sunday school room, and after a while he announced, through the intercom system, a box speaker on the wall above our heads, that the voice in the room was that of God, speaking to us, and that he, the voice in the dark, the booming growl, God, knew what we were doing, and that he was watching, all the time. We (Brett, a year younger than me, and Matthew, almost four younger) ran shrieking across the gravel drive between church and parsonage.

Our father served, also, as pastor to another church nearby, in accordance with Wesleyan circuit theory, but even farther into the trees and fallen leaves, named Hanging Rock; there was a very large rock, a boulder, grained, striped lichen, near the small white plank church with Indian graves in back, and there, at the rock, upon the rock, near the rock, above the rock, before the rock, a hanging once took place, or the rock had a hanging, or drooping, (a sagging, if you will) quality to its visage. Both of these seem quite possible. But I am no geologist.

2

In second grade, one of my teachers was injured badly when pine logs, like telephone poles, jumped loose from a rig she followed; she avoided (we the class were told) only with skillful driving and a fondness for safety belts, a certain, most tumultuous death by crushing or impalement. My brother Brett and I pissed from the porch of the deacon onto colorful geraniums valued highly by the deacon's wife (later, we apologized). A club I joined, formed in the closet at school by a girl named Ruth and another named Lorna, was disbanded after I told the teacher about the club. She asked what it was, and I told her that Lorna's idea, a great one, was that the club be called the Playboy Club, and at club meetings (held in the glue closet at school, during art hour) she and Ruth and I (maybe, after a few meetings, others could join) would look at an issue from her collection of *Playboy* magazines (stolen from her older brother after he moved) and take note of bare, pendulous breasts and rabbit ears. The women in the magazines had very large nipples. Ruth asked me at the last meeting to take my penis out and show it to them and I did and Lorna flicked it with one finger, like she was snapping an insect from a bare arm, and laughed when it wobbled. Ruth also swiped at my penis, backhanded, and laughed when it wobbled as well. Ruth said you have a boner but I wasn't sure what she meant. Lorna said, yeah, a boner. The teacher asked me what we did at the club and I told her we looked at *Playboy* magazines, because that's what we did, and then she took us, me, Ruth and Lorna, the first and only members of said club, into the hall outside of the classroom, and lined us back straight along the wall, asked if we knew what sort of magazines those were, and we all said, yes, they're *Playboy* magazines, the women have their shirts off in them, they wear bunny ears and fuzzy puff tails on their butts. The teacher told us we couldn't do the Playboy Club anymore because the *Playboy* magazines were for older people who could look at things like nipples.

3

A year after we moved to another outcrop in South Carolina named Knightsville, called so for the many people who lived there with the last name Knight. There were many of these Knights. I knew some of them: Trey, Randy, Gladys, Loyless, their various cousins and offspring. This section adjoined a town called Summerville, named so when rich people from Charleston once escaped there during summer because of the mosquito droves in the port city full of churches and dead slaves. The church our father served in Knightsville was newer, slightly larger than Salem in Heath Springs, or Hanging Rock in Hanging Rock, but built of red brick, as was the parsonage, to the east of the church. In the acre of backyard, there was a stationary replica of Noah's arc, although it was much smaller, and mostly just looked like a sailboat, although someone had hammered a plaque to the bow that read Noah's arc. Some animals, I thought, could fit inside, but not many. And the flood never came, even though we waited.

4

I started high school. Ninth and tenth grade went to one school (population close to two thousand) and eleventh and twelfth grade went to another (population, also, near two thousand). A path connected the two schools, concrete meandered like a runner vine through a stand of woods between them. A fat man named Dan patrolled this path in a golfcart and as a raptor. Often kids adjusted the governor on the engine (a lever regulating speed) when Wayne left the cart untended. This caused Wayne to accelerate very fast, often uncontrollably, when next he went on rounds, and sometimes, even, the cart toppled over when the tires caught a deep rut or when the whole thing went fast down a slope. The path was watched over in this manner because kids groped each other in the trees and smoked grass. On days that were very cold or wet, or both cold and wet, two yellow buses ran between the schools, because some kids had classes at both, the smart ones traveling up, to be with older kids, the not so smart ones traveling down, to be with us, the younger ones, the lesser.

5

In fall, on gamedays, the school held pep rallies in the gymnasium. The junior varsity football team was very important. The coach of the varsity team was approaching a number of wins unrivaled by any coach, in any sport, on any level. I saw him once, but never close up. These rallies often included violence, semi riots of various factions, metal kids or hopeful criminals, and always, various fluids were thrown about, flung into hair and onto faces: shaving cream, baby powder, spray from fire extinguishers, can soda shaken then sprayed in clouds bursting over someone's thumb. I left soaked always, hair and face white, shirt damp. Everyone seemed to think these rallies were very important, and valuable, almost sacred. But I never felt part of it, not really, because a great deal of these people were very big, often with facial hair and droves of sexual conquests. I was hairless, mostly, and tiny, but recently I was quite proud of my armpit hair beginning to come in. I was also beginning to need deodorant and antiperspirant. Often girls looked at my rail thin arms, held theirs up next to them and noted how much more hair they had on their forearms than I did.

6

I wanted to lose my virginity very badly, but no one would help. Later, when we moved to another town, a girl named Margaret told me if I turned seventeen and my chastity was still intact, she'd do me, just because it wasn't right to be seventeen and not have sex. I was very happy to know this. Once, she gave me a handjob and I went almost as soon as she touched me. I wilted, one might say; shuddered convulsively, and when I turned seventeen I reminded her of the promise, but she didn't come through. She gave me more handjobs at various times. They were good ones, too. She broke, though, long before the rest of us were left quivering, slobbering over our broken heads. My debt to her is great.

7

But before the handjobs, in the season of the football pep rallies, in the year of the gymnasium, I pledged myself to one Constance Woolworth, the tenth grade class president, the lean, flax, pale beauty, the genius. The smell of her hair shuffling, or her shoulders, or the absence of her empty desk and when she sat to fill it again, all of this gave me a confused, jumbled head (I felt sometimes like crying and sometimes like cheering and sometimes both at once and more things) and also a boner. She sat one seat ahead of me, in Geography, in a classroom on the upper level of the gymnasium. My prayers then were that the teacher not think of me, not call me to the front, to the blackboard with the boner in my pants to label the capitols of northern African countries. My prayers were also for breasts, Constance Woolworth, and some marijuana. I often thought of a brave deed in her presence, but for a long time, there were none.

8

I was not patient, nor steadfast; but November came, and I knew the names and capitols of South America and Europe, I carried a cassette tape in my knapsack because I liked having it there going around with me, and by then I'd smoked grass until I couldn't see, I'd put my hands on some large tits, the rain fell cold for weeks, my bones hurt, and the act, the beautiful deed for Constance Woolworth came, anyway, even with my lack of faith, and sure belief it would never come at all; the hero, God, Indiana Jones, Bill Murray, descended upon me in Geography class, and I was them.

9

I understand now, even after many deep snows and slight apocalypses, everything I'd ever done, all of it up until then, was because of Constance Woolworth, all of it because on a Thursday in Geography class in middle November she turned around to face me, put her arms on my desk and leaned closer to me than any woman has since. I thought of sirens, of Jennifer Connelly staying the night in a department store, of unicorns. I thought, I'd leave everyone, I'd run with you, wherever you should name. I thought, I'd build you a house with a waterfall and many animals. I thought, I'd do any vile deed you might ask of me.

She told me about the doom, impending, if music for the rally could not be found. The music Constance Woolworth needed was not just music but big music, music for grand entrance, music for a parade of giants. It was the tiny part of a big thing she'd remembered only half an hour before, during the fifteen minute break between second and third period. It was the bell ringing that made her remember. And now, thirty minutes left before Geography ended and the rally began, she was stuck, with no ideas, and with no help. The only people she could think of with headphones, tapes and whatnot, were punks, and death metal kids, or rich kids listening to Jimmy Buffet, and none of them could help her, whatever they had wouldn't be right, too singular, no grace there. She needed something democratic. She fretted the rally would fail, would be ridiculous. Her politburo, the vice president, the treasurer, was hiding. Her life, all she knew, fell around her. And there, finally, finally, I could help Constance Woolworth, I could be important and glowing before her. I gave her the tape. She looked it over.

I said, play that first song. I said, it will work. I said, it is the one you need.

She said, it will work, will it?

I said, the capitol of Columbia is Bogota.

She said, the capitol of Peru is Lima.

I said, yours is easy.

She said, yours is too.

10

In the gymnasium (a hollow, rectangular building) for the rally, bleachers were staired to one long side, ceiling high, and kids who sat at the top could touch the steel beam rafters. This gave the place the feel of an amphitheater. Kids sat by class: ninth grade, if facing the opposite, blank wall, at the east, and tenth grade, on the west, and in the middle of all of it, an unmarked line where two classes met at the shoulders. This was a most volatile zone, and up high in the bleachers, near the roof and in opposite corners, was also quite prone to stampede. After the teachers got everyone inside and worked to spasm, the football players filed into the dark gym, ridiculous, bloated from dumbbells, thirty five pound plates stacked three deep at the ends of straight bars for bench or shoulder press, four deep on squat bars, but they were beautiful, too, because they'd be that way, chiseled from stone, terrifying, leviathan, only for a breath; soon their bodies would collapse, swell to fat, and then some would be dead, and some would work for the meek who

feared them most. Spotlights bore down upon them. I thought of
Saxons, Goths, Angles, Jutes, all that.

11

Constance Woolworth, in a booth high above everyone else on the
far wall and watching, pressed play on the tape I'd given her (*Never-
mind*), on the thing that held all things before us together. In two
years the man who sang on the tape (Cobain) would be dead by
shotgun, and I'd weep for him. And the song did work. The punk
kids in the high bleachers kicked each other into a pit, the whole
mass, then, swirling, copulatory, everyone in the stands, every sort
of kid possible, a manic, dazzling mess. My cassette tape, the soon
dead man, screeching, filled the place, and I was carved there part of
it, my name spelled out, my deed before Constance Woolworth bigger than any I'd conjured in daydream. I imagined her smiling at me
through the glass, because I saved her, in beautiful way. A large wave
of lime soda and shaving cream rained down on me and I didn't
flinch, not once. I stood crossarmed, bodies pentacostal around me,
and looked at the glass across the gym where I thought for a few
moments Constance Woolworth dreamed of me.

12

Afterward I was soaked, happy, stoned, sure I'd help a goodness in
the world, but I knew, too, Constance Woolworth would not love
me because of the tape and the deed, would not love me because I'd
helped save the world when no one else could. I knew she'd turn
around and smile at me only a few more times, and that after the
semester would change, when the class split and Geography became
Civics, I'd never see her again, and I haven't, although once, many
years later, I heard someone say her name and my heart beat fast and
I looked for her, frantically, as one might for a light in the dark. But

these things do not matter. They are writ before time. She was something different than I was. The lot I came from might clean her house or tend her mother's begonias, but we'd never sleep next to her, never wake to watch her calm and breathing, we'd never see her heart, her radiant, sun red heart.

Dancing in the Dark

Johanna Edwards

I did not go to my high school prom. For a long time, I insisted this was by choice.

Whenever anyone mentioned the dreaded P-word during senior year, I just shrugged my shoulders and tried to look indifferent, as if all the talk about dresses and limos and who was going to fuck who at the hotel afterward was such a bore. "You guys are wasting your time. Prom is *so* overrated," I'd say, making a sour face. "No way I'm going. Wild horses couldn't drag me there."

"Come on, Jo, how can you miss this? It's the most important dance of the year . . . probably our lives!" my friends would counter.

"My point exactly. It's a *dance.* We've been to enough lame dances at this school. Why spend hundreds—possibly thousands—of dollars to go to another one?"

I used the same line on my parents. I figured it was best to have a position, to pretend like I was taking some sort of angsty teenage stand against "the establishment." I couldn't tell anyone the real reason. The real reason, the *fat* reason, was too depressing.

You see, I'd spent all of my teenage years as a fat girl. I'd had a fat first kiss, a fat homecoming dance, a fat junior high graduation, a fat Sweet 16. I didn't want a fat prom, too. I wanted a *perfect* prom, a *thin* prom. I wanted to miraculously lose sixty pounds overnight so I could strut into the dance in some sexy, strapless number, with a hot guy on my arm. It was my final hurrah, my last chance to morph from ugly duckling to swan before I left high school. My last chance to prove I was a winner. And I'd blown it.

If I did go to Prom, I'd have to stuff my size-18 body into one of the sequined nightmares that pass for plus-sized evening gowns. Oh, I'd seen the "extended sizes" prom dresses available at our local department store—all five of them—and the idea of wearing one of those eyesores appealed to me about as much as the thought of turning up naked. It was easier just to opt out altogether.

Plus, there was the not-so-small matter of a date: I didn't have one, couldn't get one, saw no point in even trying. I knew it was a fruitless undertaking. I'd found my place on the social ladder some time ago: I was a fat chick and no teenage boy in his right mind was willing to be seen at the prom with a fat chick.

To be fair about it, there were a *few* contenders. Like the pockmarked geek from first period, a *Star Trek* loving, hygiene-shunning loner who talked to himself and was widely regarded as the classmate most likely to become a serial killer. He seemed game. In fact, he'd spent the first part of senior year making his bizarre attraction to me known.

In between picking his acne scars in public and stalking the girls' soccer team, he found time to pursue me. He blew kisses in my direction, and sent creepy love notes complimenting my "bewitching eyes" and my "full hips." Several times he cornered me in the hallway between classes. "You look great today, Johanna," he'd say glancing up and down my body with his creepy, borderline psychotic stare. Once or twice he suggested we get together outside of school, and was undaunted when I politely turned down his requests.

"Sorry, I'm gonna have to pass. I've just got a lot going on right now." And for the rest of my life.

When prom rolled around I avoided the *Star Trek* lover like the plague until he finally lost interest and asked out a freshman.

A slightly better option was my gay best friend, Demond. "Since neither one of us has a boyfriend, why don't we go together?" Demond had asked.

"That could be fun."

"Fun? Trust me, girl, it will be *legendary*. We'll have the *best* time!" It sounded like a plan, until I found out Demond's idea of "legendary" included the two of us wearing color-coordinated dresses.

"I don't know . . ." I hedged. "Won't people make fun of us?" This was my biggest fear. I'd been picked on quite a bit over the years and I was keen to avoid anything that drew too much attention to me.

"So what?" he challenged. "You shouldn't care what these people think. After this year, you won't see any of them ever again."

I appreciated his gusto, but I wasn't sure I was ready to face that kind of torment. A few weeks later Demond abruptly left school, thereby taking the decision out of my hands.

So I was back to square one: dateless and depressed. I made a last-ditch effort to improve my situation: the old starvation diet. Even though I knew it was a losing battle, I held on to the hope that I could drop enough weight to actually land a prom date. I drank foul-tasting herbal teas and skipped meals. Hunger pangs be damned; I was a woman on a mission.

I blew off breakfast, ate nothing but a small bag of pretzels for lunch, drank Diet Coke by the gallon, and had a low-fat yogurt as an after-school snack. The only tricky spot was dinner, which I normally ate with my mom and sister. But I soon found a way around that, too. "I think I'll have dinner in my bedroom from now on," I told my mother, picking up my plate and carrying it upstairs. "This way, I can do homework while I eat." I'm sure she found this odd, but she didn't question me.

Once in the safety of my room, I would carry my dinner into the adjoining bathroom where I would proceed to mash up whatever food my mom had prepared—chicken, casserole, pasta, carrots—and flush it down the toilet. I had constant headaches and my hair began falling out in clumps, but I stuck to my guns. Slowly, but surely, the pounds started to come off. But slightly slimmer body or not, there was still no prom date on the horizon.

And then it happened. *He* happened. Out of nowhere, Tim

Granger emerged. He transferred into my history class midsemester and we hit it off right away.

Tim was an attractive jock with a well-toned body and a boyish smile. Guys like him rarely acknowledged my presence, but Tim was different. He was bright and easygoing, and we became fast friends, sharing history notes and swapping life stories.

Tim was the kind of guy I'd always dreamed about finding. Meeting him felt surreal, almost too good to be true. He was on the fringes of the popular crowd—a bona fide "cool kid" who went to all the right parties, sat at the in crowd's table during lunch, but never really gelled with their vapid, empty lifestyle. He cared about his schoolwork, kept up with politics, and was more interested in books than bongs.

Tim loved classic movies—a passion none of his jock buddies seemed to share. He flipped out when he discovered one of my favorite films was Alfred Hitchcock's *Rear Window.*

"I can't believe you like it, too!" he exclaimed, giving me a high-five. He held onto my hand for a minute, his fingers curling around mine. It felt weird, electrifying, when he touched me. "This is so cool, Jo! None of my other friends have even heard of *Rear Window.*"

Before long he was lending me his copies of *The Sting* and *Casablanca* and I was turning him on to *Vertigo* and *North by Northwest.* From there we moved on to music. I made him mix tapes of U2 and Luscious Jackson and Tim dubbed me copies of rare Green Day bootlegs and R.E.M. b-sides.

I secretly hoped Tim would stop lending me movies, and instead invite me over to watch one. But despite how close we became, or how well we got along, he never gave me his phone number, never made any effort to get together outside of class. The end of the year was fast approaching and I knew if I didn't make a move soon graduation would be here and I'd lose my chance. When I heard there was a classic film festival coming up I saw my opportunity. My plan was perfect. I could casually mention the film festival, suggest we catch a friendly afternoon movie, and then move in for the kill.

Friends first had always been my motto. If I could win Tim over with my personality, maybe he'd get past my less-than-perfect physique. I just had to get up the nerve to ask him out . . .

Then, as we were leaving class one day, Tim said, "Hey, Johanna, I was wondering something." He paused. "I hope this isn't awkward."

Awkward? My heart started racing. Maybe he'd heard about the film festival? Maybe he was going to bring it up himself!

"Hey, have you lost weight?" he asked suddenly.

Oh. So *that's* what he meant by awkward. I nodded. "Yeah, a little." I was pleased, but embarrassed. I didn't like anyone talking about my weight, even if they were giving me a compliment.

"You look good," he said.

"Thanks."

We stood there for a moment and then he asked, "Well, I wanted to talk to you about Prom."

Holy shit! My face must have gone white. I was too stunned to speak. I mumbled some sort of response although, to this day, I still don't know what it was.

Tim looked at his watch. "I've actually gotta get to practice right now. Here, let me give you my number and you can call me tonight. Sound okay?"

I nodded.

He took my hand, which was sweating quite profusely at this point, and wrote his number across my palm. It tickled where he touched me and, like the proverbial dork, I vowed to never wash my hand again.

The rest of the day went by in a blur. I couldn't get my mind off Tim, and couldn't stop counting the hours until I'd make The Call. I couldn't concentrate on homework, couldn't watch TV, couldn't call my friends. I skipped dinner that night, although this time it was due to anxiety, not diet.

I paced around the house, burning up nervous energy. Could this really be happening? All these years I'd hoped and prayed for a boyfriend, period—I hadn't even been cocky enough to ask for the *perfect* boyfriend. I'd just wanted *someone.* And my standards were pretty low. Given my track record, I didn't think I could afford to be picky. As long as he had a good personality and decent body odor and social skills, I was willing to give a guy a chance.

But Tim was perfect. He was everything I wanted, and then some.

And now he was maybe, *possibly*, going to be mine.

I just had to call him first, which proved more difficult than expected.

Timing was everything. Since Tim had sports practice right after school, I figured he wouldn't be home until five o'clock, at the earliest. He'd need time to shower, change, and eat dinner. Plus he'd have to do his homework, and he'd probably want to watch a little TV and call a few friends before settling down for the night. To be on the safe side I decided to wait until nine o'clock to call. That way he wouldn't feel rushed. He could just settle down and relax as he talked to me on the phone. Who knows, maybe we would even have one of those great conversations where you wind up chatting well into the night.

I sat by the phone, ticking down the minutes. But when the clock struck nine, I got cold feet. If I called him right at nine on the dot, it would seem like I'd been waiting here all night. No, I had to be more inconspicuous, less eager. I couldn't call Tim at *exactly* 9:00; I needed some perfect, casual time, something that said *I just got the urge to call you, completely out of the blue.* I settled on 9:13 p.m. But when 9:13 p.m. rolled around my sister was on the phone, which meant I had to wait. Finally, at 9:41 p.m., I was ready to proceed with The Call.

With shaking hands, I dialed Tim's number.

Someone picked up on the second ring. "Hello."

"Hi, is Tim there?"

"Yeah, this is him."

I swallowed hard, and tried to regain my composure. I was eighteen years old, for God's sake. You would think I'd never spoken to a guy on the phone before. I was acting like a lovesick twelve-year-old girl. "Hi, this is Johanna."

"Huh?" This should have been my first clue that things were not going to turn out well.

"Johanna Edwards. From school."

"Oh." He cleared his throat. "Hey." He sounded subdued, disinterested.

"You asked me to call you tonight," I reminded him. "You wanted to talk about Prom." I felt a little chill as I said those words. Here it was, the big moment!

"Right." There was a moment of silence. "I'm really busy right now. Can I talk to you tomorrow?"

"Um, okay."

"How about before homeroom? You have Mr. Cox, right?"

I felt my mood brighten. He knew what homeroom I was in. That had to be a good sign.

"Yeah, that's the one."

"I thought I saw you go in there the other day. My friend is in that homeroom, too, and I sometimes walk up there with her."

I didn't know what to say. "Oh, that's nice."

"I'll meet you there right after the first bell. Sound good?"

"Sure."

I hung up the phone feeling crestfallen, confused. All those wasted hours and I wasn't even going to find out tonight. And why had he asked me to call him, if he was just planning on waiting until we got to school the next day? By the following morning, I was on pins and needles.

True to his word, Tim was waiting for me outside Mr. Cox's homeroom when the first bell rang.

"Hey, Jo!" he called as I approached. He seemed a lot more cheerful now. Maybe he'd been having a bad night when I called.

I sidled up to him. "How are you?"

"Great! It's such a beautiful day outside. It finally feels like spring."

His enthusiasm was contagious. "Yeah, the weather's gorgeous." I decided to cut right to the chase. "So, what did you want to ask me?"

"Okay, so about Prom . . . I don't have a date yet and I was wondering something." Tim cleared his throat. He looked nervous.

Here it is, I thought. He's going to do it!

"You know your friend Sherry? Do you think she'd want to go to Prom with me?"

I felt as though I'd been punched in the gut. My friend Sherry? He was interested in my fucking friend Sherry? I stood there for a moment, too stunned to answer. "No, she has a boyfriend," I finally managed. "Sorry."

"Oh." Tim looked disappointed. "Hey, what about your friend with the dark brown hair and the really nice legs? That girl I always see you talking to outside of French class. What's her name? Erica?"

"Yeah, it's Erica," I said. "But I don't really know her that well. We just talk sometimes after class."

He considered this. "Do you know if she has a date?"

Oh my God, I thought. He had never spoken to Erica before. He barely even knew her name. But he would rather go with a total stranger than ask me. Anyone is better than me.

"Um, I don't know. We don't talk about that kind of stuff." Truthfully, I knew Erica was single, but I didn't want to let on.

"Could you give her my number?" Tim persisted. "I'd love to ask her. She's so cute."

I nodded. "Yeah, I could do that."

"Thanks, Johanna, you're the best!" He gave me a high-five and a big grin. Then he turned and walked off down the hall.

I stood there, feeling sick. On some level, I had known it all along. Guys like Tim didn't ask out girls like me. They asked out skinny girls, popular girls. Girls like Erica and Sherry.

True to my word, I passed on Tim's number and Erica, for her part, was thrilled. "We're going to the Prom together!" she gushed a few days later.

"That's terrific," I lied, feigning excitement. Then I spent the rest of the year avoiding Tim. I didn't talk to him as much in class, didn't lend him movies, didn't make him mix tapes. It was my own form of mini-revenge. And I thought he would care. I thought he would ask me why I was giving him the cold shoulder. But he didn't. Enamored by his new relationship with Erica, he barely seemed to notice.

And when Prom night rolled around a few weeks later, I sat at home in my pajamas, watching *Friends* reruns and eating Chinese takeout while Tim and Erica and pretty much everyone else I knew danced the night away.

"You're so weird. Why didn't you go to Prom?" my sister asked, when she caught sight of me.

"Prom is *so* overrated," I said, going into autopilot. "It's a *dance*. I've been to enough lame dances at that school. Why spend hundreds—possibly thousands—of dollars to go to another one?" I popped a piece of sweet-and-sour chicken into my mouth and turned up the volume on the TV. "No way was I going to that lame-ass Prom. Wild horses couldn't drag me there."

ABOUT THE CONTRIBUTORS

DEAN BAKOPOULOS's first novel, *Please Don't Come Back from the Moon,* was a New York Times Notable Book in 2005. His second novel, *Harmony,* will be published by Harcourt in fall 2007. He is the recipient of a National Endowment for the Arts fellowship and lives in Mineral Point, Wisconsin.

JULIANNA BAGGOTT is the author of four novels, including *Girl Talk* and *Which Brings Me to You* (co-written with Steve Almond) as well as a series of novels for younger readers, *The Anybodies,* under the pen name N. E. Bode. Her third book of poems, *Compulsions of Silkworms and Bees,* is being published this spring. She teaches at Florida State University's Creative Writing Program.

KELLY BRAFFET is the author of the novels *Last Seen Leaving* and *Josie and Jack.* She holds an M.F.A. from Columbia University. She currently lives in Brooklyn with two and a half black cats, a great deal of clutter, and her husband, the novelist Owen King.

WILL CLARKE's first novel, *Lord Vishnu's Love Handles,* was originally self-published, and attracted a cult following via the Internet. The self-published novel was eventually taught at George Washington University and the film rights were optioned by Paramount Pictures. In 2005, *Lord Vishnu's Love Handles* hit the mainstream when it was published by Simon & Schuster in hardback. Clarke's second novel, *The Worthy: A Ghost's Story,* was a BookSense Notable Book and optioned by Sony/Columbia Pictures. Will splits his time between Dallas and Los Angeles. For fun, he likes to write self-aggrandizing bios about himself in third person.

K. L. COOK is the author of a novel, *The Girl From Charnelle,* and a collection of linked stories, *Last Call,* which won the inaugural *Prairie Schooner*

Book Prize in fiction. His stories and essays have been published in many journals and magazines, including *Threepenny Review, Poets & Writers, Harvard Review,* and *Shenandoah.* He teaches at Prescott College in Arizona and Spalding University's M.F.A. in Writing Program in Samtucky. His Web site is www.klcook.net.

ELIZABETH CRANE is the author of two collections of short stories: *When the Messenger Is Hot* and *All This Heavenly Glory.* Her work has also been featured in publications including *Washington Square, New York Stories, Sycamore Review, Book, Florida Review, Eclipse, Bridge, Sonora Review, Chicago Reader, Sleepwalk, Believer, McSweeney's Future Dictionary of America, Banana King,* and *All Hands On: The 2ndhand Reader.* She received the Chicago Public Library 21st Century Award, granted by the Chicago Public Library Foundation, in October 2003. A New York City native, she now lives in Chicago with her husband and teaches writing at Northwestern's School of Continuing Studies and the University of Chicago. Her next book is *You Must be This Happy to Enter.*

DOUG CRANDELL is the author of *Pig Boy's Wicked Bird* and *The All-American Industrial Motel.* His stories and essays have appeared in *Atlanta Magazine, Glimmer Train, Indianapolis Monthly, Smithsonian,* and the *SUN* and have been published in the anthologies *Mother Knows: 24 Tales of Motherhood* and *Stories from the Blue Moon Cafe III: An Anthology of Southern Writers.*

QUINN DALTON is the author of a novel, *High Strung,* and a story collection, *Bulletproof Girl.* Her stories have appeared in literary magazines such as *Indiana Review, The Samyon Review,* and *One Story,* and collections such as Glimmer Train's *Where Love is Found: 24 Tales of Connection,* Hourglass Books' *Peculiar Pilgrims,* and *New Stories from the South: The Year's Best.* She lives in Greensboro, North Carolina with her husband and two daughters.

SEAN DOOLITTLE is the author of four crime novels: *Dirt, Burn, Rain Dogs,* and his latest, *The Cleanup.* His books have been praised by Dennis Lehane, George Pelecanos, and the *Wall Street Journal.* Short fiction has appeared in a variety of publications, including *The Best American Mystery Stories* (Otto Penzler and James Ellroy, editors). Doolittle lives in Omaha, Nebraska, with his wife and kids.

JOHANNA EDWARDS's novel *The Next Big Thing* landed on both the Barnes & Noble bestseller list and the Nielsen BookScan bestseller list its first week out.

Johanna graduated with honors from the University of Memphis in December 2001. For her day job, she produces WYPL's nationally syndicated radio and TV program *Book Talk*. Her most recent novel is *Your Big Break*.

EMILY FRANKLIN is the author of two novels, *The Girls' Almanac* and *Liner Notes*, as well as a critically acclaimed seven book fiction series *The Principles of Love*. She edited the anthology *It's a Wonderful Lie: 26 Truths about Life in Your Twenties* and the forthcoming *Eight Nights: Chanukah Essays*. She is co-editor of *Before* and *After*, a two-part fiction collection about pregnancy and parenting. Her work has appeared in the *Boston Globe* and the *Mississippi Review* as well as in *Don't You Forget About Me: Contemporary Writers on the Films of John Hughes*. She lives near Boston with her husband and their young children.

LISA GABRIELE is a novelist and journalist, and her work has appeared in the *New York Times Magazine, Washington Post, Vice, Salon,* and *Glamour,* among other publications, and she's a frequent contributor to Nerve.com. Her first novel, *Tempting Faith DiNapoli,* was published by Simon & Schuster, Doubleday Canada, and Virago. Her second novel will be published in the fall of 2007, tentatively titled *More Than the Moon*. Her essays and short stories have appeared in *The Best American Non-Required Reading 2003, Sex and Sensibility,* and *28 True Romances from the Lives of Single Women,* among others. She's also directed and produced documentaries for CBC-TV, History Channel, and the Life Network. She writes the CBC radio program, *The Current*. She lives in Toronto.

TOD GOLDBERG is the author of the novels *Living Dead Girl,* a finalist for the Los Angeles Times Book Prize, and *Fake Liar Cheat,* and, most recently, of the short story collection *Simplify,* winner of the Other Voices Short Story Collection Prize. His column Goldberg: PI appears regularly in *Jewcy* (Jewcy.com) and his journalism and essays are featured regularly in the *Los Angeles Times, Las Vegas CityLife* and *Palm Springs Life Magazine,* as well as the recently released anthology *Don't You Forget About Me: Contemporary Writers on the Films of John Hughes*. Tod Goldberg lives in La Quinta, California, with his wife, Wendy, and teaches creative writing at the UCLA Extension Writers' Program.

DAVID HAYNES is an associate professor of English at Southern Methodist University and directs the university's creative writing program. For the past decade he has also been on the faculty of the M.F.A. Program for Writers at Warren Wilson College. He is the author of six novels for adults and five books for younger readers. Several of his short stories have been read and recorded for the National Public Radio series *Selected Shorts.* He was selected by *Granta* magazine as one of the best of the young American novelists. His most recent novel is *The Full Matilda.*

OWEN KING is the author of *We're All in This Together.* He holds an M.F.A. from Columbia University and his fiction and nonfiction have appeared in *Book, Bellingham Review, Boston Globe,* and other publications. He has been nominated for a National Magazine Award and is a recipient of the John Gardner Award for Short Fiction. He currently resides in Brooklyn with his cats, his action figures, and, inexplicably, a beautiful woman.

ERIKA KROUSE has published short stories in the *New Yorker, Atlantic Monthly, Ploughshares, Story, Glimmer Train, Shenandoah,* and *Glamour.* Her short story collection *Come Up and See Me Sometime* was a New York Times Notable Book for the year. Her new novel will appear whenever the publishing gods deem it to be so, and she is currently working on her third book. Erika has never returned to Japan.

BRAD LAND is the author of a memoir, *Goat,* and a forthcoming novel. His writing has appeared in *Gentleman's Quarterly, Third Coast, Quarter After Eight, Ecotone,* and *Rivendell.*

ZELDA LOCKHART is author of *Fifth Born.* The novel was a Barnes & Noble Discovery selection and recently won a finalist award for debut fiction from the Zora Neale Hurston/Richard Wright Legacy Foundation. She is also the author of *The Evolution,* a serial novella, currently appearing in the archives of USAToday.com's Open Book series. Lockhart has just finished a second novel, *Cold Running Creek.* A graduate of Norfolk State University and Old Dominion University, Zelda currently resides in Hillsborough, North Carolina, with her two children.

JOHN MCNALLY is the author of two novels, *America's Report Card* and *The Book of Ralph,* and one story collection, *Troublemakers.* He's received numerous awards for his writing, including a Chesterfield screenwriting fellowship, sponsored by Paramount Pictures, and the Jenny McKean Moore fellowship from George Washington University. He is the Ollen R. Nalley Associate Professor of English at Wake Forest University in North Carolina, where he lives with his wife, Amy, and their many pets. He will be Visiting Writer at Columbia College Chicago in the spring of 2007.

MAUD NEWTON is best known for her Web site, MaudNewton.com, where she writes about books, politics, her crazy parents, and whatever she's stewing about on any given day. She has contributed to the *American Prospect, Maisonneuve, New York Times Book Review, Boston Globe, Washington Post Book World, Newsday, Mr. Beller's Neighborhood, Swink, Eyeshot,* and other publications. She lives in Brooklyn and is at work on a novel set in Miami, her hometown.

AIMEE NEZHUKUMATATHIL is the author of two poetry collections: *Miracle Fruit* and *Corpse Flower.* Her poems and essays have appeared in such magazines as *Tin House, Quarterly West, Prairie Schooner,* and *Virginia Quarterly Review.* She is associate professor of English at SUNY-Fredonia where she was awarded the Chancellor's Award for Scholarship and Creative Endeavors. She lives in western New York with her husband, fiction writer Dustin Parsons, and their dachshund, Villanelle.

JAMES P. OTHMER is the author of the acclaimed first novel *The Futurist.* His short story of the same name was a finalist for the National Magazine Award in Fiction. A graduate of the Creative Writing Program at New York University, his stories and humorous essays have appeared in *Virginia Quarterly Review, Nylon, The Chattahoochee Review, The Madison Review,* and *The New York Times.* He is currently writing a novel about reverse outsourcing, falsified vasectomies, mommies who do witchcraft, and an American ultra-filtration membrane salesman in China.

MICHELLE RICHMOND is the author of the novels *The Year of Fog* and *Dream of the Blue Room,* and the story collection *The Girl in the Fall-Away Dress,* which won the Associated Writing Programs Award. Her stories and essays have appeared in *Glimmer Train, Playboy, Salon,* and many other publications. She lives in San Francisco, where she teaches creative writing and publishes the online literary journal *Fiction Attic.*

TIMOTHY SCHAFFERT is the author of three novels, *The Phantom Limbs of the Rollow Sisters, The Singing and Dancing Daughters of God,* which was a Barnes & Noble Discover Great New Writers pick for spring of 2006, and *Devils in the Sugar Shop.* He organizes a literary festival in Omaha, Nebraska, and is a contributing editor of the literary journal *Prairie Schooner.*

RICHARD YAÑEZ, an El Paso native, is the author of *El Paso del Norte: Stories on the Border,* a finalist for the Texas Institute of Letters first book award. His work is anthologized in *Our Working Lives: Short Stories of People and Work, U.S. Latino Literature Today,* and *Hecho en Tejas: An Anthology of Texas-Mexican Literature.* He is a founding member of Con Tinta, a coalition of Chicano/Latino writer-activists. Presently, he is an associate editor for Momotombo Press and an assistant professor at El Paso Community College. He is married to the Chicana poet Carolina Monsivais. They live in Santa Teresa, New Mexico.

PERMISSIONS

ACKNOWLEDGMENTS

Many thanks to my editor, Wylie O'Sullivan, for her keen eye; to my agent, Jenny Bent, for her support of this project; and to my wife, Amy Knox Brown, whose advice is always wise and sound. Special thanks to the authors in this book, who didn't flinch when I asked them to write about their days as losers, and who agreed, with great dignity, to make themselves vulnerable.